Unsettling

Unsettling

Jews, Whiteness, and Incest in American Popular Culture

ELI BROMBERG

Rutgers University Press
New Brunswick, Camden, and Newark, New Jersey, and London

Library of Congress Control Number: 2020004941

A British Cataloging-in-Publication record for this book is available from the British Library.

A version of chapter 2 was previously published as "Incest, Exogamy, and Jewishness on *Roseanne*," in *Shofar: An Interdisciplinary Journal of Jewish Studies*, vol. 35, no. 1, 2016, pp. 1–28; copyright Purdue University Press.

"Chain." Copyright © 1978 by Audre Lorde, from *The Collected Poems of Audre Lorde* by Audre Lorde. Used by permission of W. W. Norton & Company, Inc.

Excerpt(s) from *The Color of Water* by James McBride, copyright © 1996 by James McBride. Used by permission of Riverhead, an imprint of Penguin Publishing Group, a division of Penguin Random House LLC. All rights reserved. Non-exclusive UK and Commonwealth excluding Canada permission provided by Bloomsbury Publishing Plc.

Excerpts and images from the Henry Roth Collection, AJHS Archives P-694, and the Henry Roth Papers, AJHS Archives P-702, American Jewish Historical Society, NY, used by permission of the Henry Roth Literary Trust. Images used courtesy of the American Jewish Historical Society.

∞ The paper used in this publication meets the requirements of the American National Standard for Information Sciences—Permanence of Paper for Printed Library Materials, ANSI Z39.48-1992.

www.rutgersuniversitypress.org

Manufactured in the United States of America

For Leroy Lewis

Contents

Unsettling

Introduction

In November 2014, less than a year after Dylan Farrow wrote an op-ed in the *New York Times* restating her decades-old assertion that her father, Woody Allen, had sexually abused her as a child, Eric Andre asked Seth Rogen an unexpected question on his cable talk show:

> ANDRE: You think Woody Allen should get Chinese castrated so he stops jerking off his ex-kids?
>
> ROGEN: I don't know. ("Seth Rogen Part 2")

There is a lot to unpack in Andre's question. But first I want to draw attention to what happens *after* Andre makes this convoluted, provocative, disturbing inquiry, and Rogen proffers his noncommittal answer. Andre, whose avant-garde talk-show parodies the conventions of the genre, incorporates the question into a piece of physical comedy. The segment begins with the odd reveal that Rogen's talk-show-guest easy chair and Andre's talk-show-host desk are both rotating slowly on separate but adjacent circular platforms. After Andre asks Rogen about Allen, Andre's platform accelerates, and the centrifugal force sends Andre flailing. As he attempts to resituate himself on the interview chair, the desk is destroyed and the interview derailed. The interview, literally, spins out of control.

Andre and Rogen enact a visual approximation of the consequences for speaking frankly about Allen's alleged and admitted sexual behavior with his "ex-kids" (a phrase that provocatively signifies both Dylan Farrow as well as Soon-Yi Previn, Allen's former partner Mia Farrow's adoptive daughter and Allen's current wife). As layered as Andre's question is, it functions largely as a setup for this staged, elaborate pratfall. Andre's joke intimates not merely that asking about Allen's sexual behavior can derail a conversation, but that choosing to ask a recognizable Jewish celebrity about it functions as a self-defeating act.

This book contends that closely examining how Jews and non-Jews discuss high profile stories involving Jews and incest reveals important aspects of how whiteness operates and disguises itself. It argues that acknowledging the historical import of the Jewish incest stereotype allows us to see the hidden logic undergirding how conversations about incest involving white and nonwhite figures proceed, even when (especially when) the Jewishness of these persons goes unmentioned. I contend that Jewish community protective politics set the terms for how discussions about Jewish sexual transgressions play out in the public sphere. I define Jewish community protective politics as a phenomenon in which collective mainstream societal anxiety about white Jewish male vulnerability to antisemitism results in various actors (Jewish and non-Jewish alike) privileging white Jewish male interests above those of other figures involved in these allegations. These politics manifest themselves as a societally condoned impulse to avoid alleging or affirming that Jewish men have transgressed in ways that align with historically antisemitic stereotypes regarding Jewish men. Reading Andre's joke as being about Jewish community protective politics reveals that the dangers of publicly discussing the specifics of Allen's incestuous behavior are such that even posing a question about them can be a (self-)destructive act. That both Andre and Rogen are Jewish is important, but secondary to the unarticulated notion that discussing Allen's behavior in detail might *read* as antisemitic regardless of the identities of the discussants. Jewish community protective politics set the terms for what non-Jews *and* Jews can discuss when it comes to Jewish men alleged to commit transgressions associated with antisemitic stereotypes, and the viability of this power dynamic emerges from white Jewishness's proximity to, or mainstream incorporation into, whiteness. Ironically, and tragically, this community protective impulse expressly fails the women and children—other more vulnerable members of Jewish communities—victimized by male Jewish predators.

This phenomenon plays out not just in celebrity spheres, but in various societal contexts regarding white Jewish male transgressions involving incest. It has probably generated the most attention in iterations involving observably, religiously Jewish community contexts. Amy Neustein's *Tempest in the Temple*, for example, collects scholarship on how various forces enable abusers in different Jewish communities, focusing (as its title suggests) on how these dynamics function in places of worship, and communities built upon religious tradition. Regarding Orthodox Jewish communities, Joyanna Silberg and Stephanie Dallam suggest the threat of antisemitism influences community members to defend Jewish men accused of pedophilia, even when Jewish children and Jewish women do the accusing: "The historic effects of being a persecuted outsider living within a closely knit family unit, combined with interpretations of religious precepts, have aided the forces of denial in the Jewish community" (93). This project considers this premise, but investigates how very similar forces operate in secular but still meaningfully and observably Jewish contexts, and how race and ethnoracial markers operate in these spaces. For example, we can observe Jewish community protective politics operating in how Jewish second-wave feminists framed their Jewishness and recast Freud's Jewishness as whiteness in their important activist and scholarly criticisms of Freud during the 1970s. These politics also emerge in how critics and scholars have come to talk about the first run of the television show *Roseanne*, which possessed more Jewish content than widely acknowledged, due to subsumed anxieties about Roseanne Barr's allegations that her father incestuously abused her. We also see these protective politics operating in literature and publishing, in the revision choices made by Henry Roth's editors in advance of the publication of the second volume of his *Mercy of a Rude Stream* (*MORS*) novel, which minimized and erased Roth's confessions of rape and racism in order to protect the literary icon's image.

While I more comprehensively frame the history of the Jewish incest stereotype in chapter 1, drawing attention to how Freud navigated it in his early writings, here I want to detail its two distinct aspects—vertical and lateral. The lateral Jewish incest stereotype involves both Jewish and non-Jewish antisemitic anxiety about Jewish endogamous tradition (Jews marrying other Jews), and apprehension that this phenomenon equates to incestuous practice. The lateral Jewish incest stereotype dates back to at least the nineteenth century, where Sander Gilman has suggested it functioned as an antisemitic response to Jewish endogamy practices (that is, Christians encountered Jewish cultural proscriptions in which Jews only married other Jews and willfully misconceived of this practice as incestuous) (*Love + Marriage* 137). Gilman contextualizes this by noting how the lateral incest stereotype was just one aspect of how sexual antisemitism cast Jews as sexually nonnormative.[1] The vertical Jewish incest stereotype sits in that all-important gap marked by Freud's move from the seduction theory to the Oedipal complex (which he first considers in 1899's "The Interpretation of Dreams"). While the Oedipal complex suggests that children negotiated their sexual development via their fantasies of the parent of the opposite sex, the seduction theory intimated, albeit imperfectly, that adult hysteria (in women in particular) stemmed from childhood sexual trauma initiated by adults ("Aetiology"). But while Freud played a key role theorizing and recasting how agency functioned for parents' and children's negotiation of sexual dynamics in nuclear families (from what fathers might do to daughters to what sons felt for mothers), the notion of the sexually predatory Jewish man was not merely an incestuous stereotype. It was also pedophilic.

In this regard, the vertical incest stereotype links inevitably with one of the most virulent, resilient, and consequential antisemitic ideas of the last several centuries: the blood libel. Historically, accusations of blood libel "often led to criminal investigations, interrogations under torture, executions or judicial murder, popular riots, and even wholesale expulsions" (Kieval). Despite scholarly and popular discussions about the blood libel more commonly referencing cannibalism than sexual predation, the blood libel actually sublimates sexual antisemitism and pedophilia anxieties about Jewish adults into a stereotypical framework that accommodates a more fantastical, and thus easily discussed and dismissed transgressive behavior (cannibalism).[2] If teaching the history of the blood libel means teaching the history of how antisemites libelously insisted that Jews eat Christian babies, we can relatively easily dismiss the notion that Jews ever ate Christian babies. But drawing attention to how sexual antisemitism may have underscored the blood libel would force more uncomfortable reckoning with the fact that, historically and contemporarily, more men sexually assault children than practice cannibalism. And because Jews are human beings, and some percentage of human beings are sexual predators, we know that some Jews are sexual predators. The Jewish incest stereotype, then, draws upon historical confusion and anxiety about lateral endogamy as well as centuries of blood libel that suggested Jewish men served as sexual threats to children.

Returning to Andre's talk show, consider that Andre never so much as utters the word "Jewish" in questioning Rogen. This unspoken element is revealing, given Allen's status as a Jewish icon and the other ways that Andre makes the joke about race. Andre's mention of castration calls to mind lynching's horrific history as a form of domestic terror wielded against Black men, under the guise of punishment for supposed sexual offenders. White Jewish men have been less common targets of such vigilante justice. "Chinese" castration is specified less for the specific type of sterilization and deformation it denotes than for its racist signification of the Asian members of Allen's current (and former) family. For Andre to ask a white comic about Chinese castration signals to the viewer that Andre, a Black comic, is inquiring about Allen and race simultaneously. Consider also that Andre acts as a comic provocateur; his interviews are often designed to offend and push boundaries. Andre's choice not to make any mention of Allen's Jewishness here, to choose not to emphasize the questionable act of asking a recognizable Jewish comic to pass judgment on another recognizable Jewish comic, signals a limit to how far Andre can go—or is willing to go—in navigating these taboos.[3]

And so, a second question from this sketch underscores this project: why does Andre, comic provocateur extraordinaire, shy away from *that* observation? Why does identifying incest within Jewish family constructs committed by (or alleged of) Jewish men register as deeply taboo, even unspeakable? Why does the Jewish incest stereotype have such a strong hold on how we discuss the Allen narrative, despite the fact that very few people would list "incest" among the salient antisemitic stereotypes about Jews?

To be clear, the fundamental question at the heart of this project is not Andre's; it is not *if* Allen did the things he is alleged to have done. Rather, it is why is it so difficult to frankly discuss whether Allen, or other prominent Jewish men, *might* have engaged in predatory incestuous behavior? My thesis is that the stereotype of Jews and incest has not really gone away, and that, in fact, the tension between white Jewish privilege and sexual antisemitism has yielded a curious by-product: sexual antisemitism, inclusive of the Jewish incest stereotype and Jewish pedophilia stereotype, is so fundamentally antithetical to the notion that white Jews are, in fact, white, that it is virtually unspeakable in mainstream society. And yet, this phenomenon requires explication, as it bears enormous import regarding contemporary conversations about sexual assault, patriarchy, racism, and white supremacy.

On that note, consider that while Rogen and Allen are largely celebrated as Jewish comedians, Andre is also a Jewish comedian who discusses his Jewishness in interviews and performances.[4] Unlike Rogen, though, Andre is Black. Andre's Blackness and Jewishness remind us that Rogen and Allen are not merely Jewish comedians—they are white Jewish comedians.[5] Furthermore, all of these comedians are men, as Andre's humor also targets the (a)moral suppositions we might associate with a male gendered subjectivity. But I walk through the important racial distinctions among Jews here to point out that Jewish community protective politics may better be considered as explicitly *white* Jewish community protective politics.

Jewish Community Protective Politics and Their Adherent Arguments

This notion of (white) Jewish community protective politics sits at the heart of my argument about these incest narratives. I define Jewish community protective politics as a phenomenon in which Jewish community anxiety about white Jewish male vulnerability to antisemitism results in white Jewish male interests being privileged above anyone else within the broadly defined Jewish community.[6] In essence, Jewish community protective politics idealize notions of Jewish masculinity by doing one of two things: asserting the innocence of accused white Jewish men, or de-Judaizing accused white Jewish men so that they will not reflect poorly on the Jewish community (think of this as secular excommunication). The first approach, of asserting white Jewish male innocence, occurs not only in the face of considerable evidence, but even alongside defiant pseudo-confessions of the accused. A concomitant effect of this assertion of white Jewish male innocence is the silencing of voices that assert otherwise, including victimized Jewish women, girls, and boys, as well as, importantly, non-Jewish and/or nonwhite family members that illustrate the arbitrary borders involved in imagining an exclusively Jewish American community. This book identifies the mechanisms of these phenomena, while also specifying who conducts these acts of silencing or excommunication. It is unsurprising that white Jewish men accused of sexual transgression might actively work to question the credibility of their accusers. But the excommunication phenomenon operates in sometimes surprising ways; the manner in which Sigmund Freud "becomes" white in second-wave feminist literature criticizing him speaks to how ostensibly progressive feminist Jewish women protected white Jewish masculinity by depicting Freud not as a recognizably secular Jewish intellectual but as a universal "white" icon.

In its investigation of the cultural logics of Jewish community protective politics, this book makes six central arguments:

First, incest narratives require more careful consideration in terms of how these narratives construct whiteness out of the components of the specific subgroups that make up "white people," especially given histories in which some white groups were more vulnerable than others. This intervention is particularly relevant to incest studies, where scholars have made crucial observations and analyses regarding how whiteness and nonwhiteness operate in fictional, historical, and legal contexts. But understanding how popular consumable narratives pathologize nonwhite figures and families requires a more intricate understanding of how these stories simultaneously protect previously pathologized groups from the very same othering that is presently visited upon nonwhite (and also poor white) families.

Jewish family incest narratives present a vital context for considering racial formation because exogamous Jewish families in the late twentieth and early twenty-first centuries provide subjects that can be read, recognizably, as both "white" and "other."[7] However, the narratives also reveal that white Jewish otherness is almost always overshadowed when juxtaposed against Black, Asian, or other inarguably nonwhite figures. This involves considering the history of incest in a specifically American context, reflecting the legal and historical realities of how incest and rape were condoned when instigated by white men under the institution of slavery.[8] Understanding Jewish incest stereotype is crucial to contemporary incest studies because some white male predators operate with a privilege that weaponizes a history of actual social class vulnerability. Though theoretical and speculative, we might consider whether the various imagined "ethnic characteristics" that form whiteness possess transitive proprieties. Put differently: if mainstream whiteness incorporates white Jewishness, does that incorporation also mean that particular aspects of white Jewish history convenient to whiteness reconstitute in a fashion flattering to *all* white people? Does that mean that all white people (and white men in particular) can consider the history of white Jewish ancestors' vulnerability to sexual antisemitism as evidence of white ancestral vulnerability to false accusation?

Second, the Jewish incest stereotype, however muted it may seem at present, can neither be scrubbed from the historical record nor be expected to fully disappear in any contemporary or future moment. Its resilience may be observable, counterintuitively, in its seemingly "muted" quality. The stereotype may have become simultaneously universalized and normalized (the Jews' Oedipal complex is now *everyone's* Oedipal complex) and made unmentionable in its unnormalized qualities (i.e., pedophilia). Quite often, colleagues, friends, and acquaintances have expressed surprise to hear that Jews and incest were/are stereotypically linked. These comments may have been completely genuine. Alternatively, the polite response, given the extent of the taboo of associating Jews with incest, may be to feign ignorance that the stereotype even exists. However, not only was the Jewish incest stereotype prominent enough in the nineteenth century to be arguably determinative of how Sigmund Freud addressed incest in his scholarship, it finds expression in the invocations of other stereotypes involving Jews and Jewish sexuality.[9] As I have indicated, the blood libel can be—and should be—understood as having important sexual overtones: Jewish adults (and most threateningly, men—or genderqueer men) preying upon non-Jewish children. The historical blood libel stereotype's connection with contemporary stereotypes of Jewish pedophilia requires critical attention, especially as we witness how contemporary white supremacist politics link pedophilia and antisemitism in their convoluted conspiracy theories. Slander premised upon Jewish pedophilia, which sits adjacent to Jewish incest stereotype, operates prominently in the "alt-right" movement. Conspiracy theories like QAnon and Pizzagate imagine pedophilic enterprises being financed by "globalist" entities and liberal Jewish donors, like George Soros.[10] The fact that stereotypes associating Jews with pedophilia have become so normalized in the increasingly vocal, dangerous, and assertive elements of the reactionary white nationalist movement makes it all the more vital to consider how the dangers of antisemitism can be disingenuously weaponized to protect Jewish men who do commit sexual abuses.

Third, white Jewish authors made choices indicating an awareness of the Jewish incest stereotype as they crafted their narratives, even if they did not explicitly draw attention to its existence. In fact, the choice to avoid explicit invocation of the stereotype's existence reveals something of the strategy for navigating it. Furthermore, in each of my chapters, we can see these authors negotiating the incest stereotype in a fashion that actively displaced stereotypes involving incest or hypersexuality onto other groups, particularly Black men/families, Asian women, and white working-class families. This displacement reveals itself in narratives built around secular excommunications, as well as in those marked by refutations *and* defiant assertions of white Jewish male perpetrated incest. Notably, the excommunicative model (the notion that the Jewishness of a male perpetrator of incest or sexual violence could be obscured, unspoken, or recast as "white") occurs in both of the examples of female-authored narratives in this book, with the Jewish second-wave feminist authors discussing Freud and Barr's sitcom text's engagement with her father. Equally noteworthy, the refutation of allegations in the male-authored narratives often functions directly alongside defiant (if thinly veiled) admissions or pseudo-admissions of incestuous behavior.

Fourth, these high-profile Jewish incest narratives reveal how during the 1990s, white Jewish men tended to be treated sympathetically by most mainstream media coverage when the specter of sexual antisemitism reared its head.[11] This may seem underwhelming: white men, in general, receive sympathetic treatment by mainstream media outlets, and very little scholarship regarding Jews and whiteness suggests white Jews were not white by the 1990s. However, this phenomenon possesses underexplored significance regarding how these 1990s narratives reveal the working mechanisms of white Jewishness. The fact that white male Jews functioned as white in mainstream media reporting about sexual taboos involving incest and pedophilia—precisely the circumstances when they might have been most vulnerable to othering—is a remarkable measure of just how potent the privileges of this whiteness had become. Furthermore, this privilege pronounces itself via a rhetorical sleight of hand: white Jews operate from a subjective whiteness even as their actions reflect an awareness of the history of sexual antisemitism, which ostensibly renders them the vulnerable objects of sexual antisemitism and false allegations. By subjective whiteness, I refer to the way in which figures like Barr, Allen, and Roth assert a *white* Jewish identity in varied but unmistakable ways, as it involves people and communities of color: conjuring autobiographical whiteness as a salient identity in comedic art (Barr), blatantly erasing the presence of communities of color in their films (Allen), or trading in racist stereotype to dehumanize and mark nonwhite figures as distinctly other (Roth). This aspect of white Jewish identity is most salient and troubling in these incest narratives: white Jewish artists play an important role in shaping contemporaneous mainstream notions of whiteness, but part of that articulated white Jewish identity acclimates and advances the false notion that white Jews have never possessed historic advantages associated with whiteness.

On this note, I want to briefly address my own use of the phrases "white Jewishness" and "white Jew." I am indebted to rigorous and complex scholarship regarding how racial formation has operated for Jews in the United States, and the numerous texts that deal with the way white Jews have "become" white over the course of the twentieth century have been invaluable to my understanding of American Jewish history.[12] Today, white Jews benefit more comprehensively from white privilege than they did prior to the GI Bill, or certainly in 1924, when nativist forces curtailed Jewish (among other groups') immigration via the Johnson-Reed Act. But referring to white Jews from the 1910s and 1920s as just "Jews" fails to allow for a comprehensive examination of racial formation during that period. Even when nativist and antisemitic forces did their best to craft and implement laws that excluded white Jews from whiteness, particularly in an American context, white Jews were more societally privileged than contemporaneous Jews of color. My choice of terminology seeks to avoid erasing nonwhite Jews, operating under the assumption that white Jews can be understood, across historical eras, as being institutionally and individually vulnerable to antisemitism in myriad ways, but also institutionally and individually privileged relative to how Jews of color experienced racism (and, importantly, in positions of power relative to the Jews of color within their communities or excluded from their communities).

My goal is not to minimize the severe and consequential racialization of white Jews over the course of the nineteenth and twentieth centuries. Rather, I hope to acknowledge historical Jewish racial diversity even as so much scholarship excavating the histories of American Jews of color remains to be done. I also do not imply that "white Jewish" means the same thing, regarding privilege and power dynamics, in 1924 as it does in 1991 or 2018.[13] But the terminology permits focusing on how various white Jewish subjectivities conceived of race in ways that imagined white Jewishness as compatible with white supremacy in troubling but undeniable ways.

Fifth, I argue that Woody Allen and Henry Roth successfully marketed autobiographical protagonists with sexually transgressive reputations to audiences who would viscerally thrill to stories involving heterosexual incestuous transgressions by playing on anxieties about Jewish male sexuality, including homophobia. I do not claim that art is evidence of legal, real-world wrongdoing. However, reading Roth's second novel alongside his biography and viewing Allen's films alongside his biography suggest that their iconic appeal involves their success cultivating images of sympathetic male protagonists who have gotten away with transgressive and specific sexual acts and, notably, specific sexual acts that (ostensibly) prove just how disinclined they are to *other* sexual orientations. These narratives also play to some audience members' surreptitious appetite for stories where a white Jewish man gets away with the sort of transgressive sex act that antisemites have, for centuries, considered as justification for murder and genocide. Roth's and Allen's artwork reveals not only an awareness that sexual antisemitism historically functioned in ways that feminized and queered Jewish men, but that they could exploit in their storytelling some audience members' desires to see white Jewish sexuality as pronouncedly heterosexual and also above the law. While the taboos of Jewish incest and pedophilia are considerable, flouting that proscription was also a way to implicitly broadcast the unmistakable strength of their heterosexual inclination. Allen's and Roth's stories need to be read in the context of historical, societal sexual antisemitism and homophobia that insinuated that Jewish masculinity was not only incestuous and pedophilic, but also homosexual. For these white Jewish men, defiantly admitting or pseudo-confessing to heterosexual incest with women/girls was also a way to articulate an immutable heterosexuality.[14] These texts appealed to audiences who were attuned to histories of sexual antisemitism, but also undoubtedly to those who prefer to imagine white maleness as historically vulnerable; historical context aside, some people thrill to seeing white Jewish men get away with asserting just how straight they are—and some people thrill to seeing a white man do it. White Jewishness may accommodate both vicarious identifications. To these points: Henry Roth's last novel invites readers to see its protagonist as essentially boasting upon having committed statutory rape on his cousin on numerous occasions. And Woody Allen's post-1992 filmography features numerous detailed and layered allusions to aspects of his biography, alongside involved examinations of what it means for his protagonists to get away with heinous crimes, seemingly combining to present a voyeuristic invitation for viewers to consider that perhaps Allen did sexually molest Dylan Farrow, despite his public claims to the contrary. In essence, these artists accentuate the vulnerable historical qualities of Jewish men while also depicting their white Jewish male (autobiographical) protagonists as societally privileged victimizers. In so doing, Roth and Allen craft incest narratives for popular consumption by men who find this sort of representation of white males—unfairly persecuted even when they're guilty, because white men are *supposed* to be able to do what they want—appealing.

This last point relates to my sixth and final central argument: Jewish community protective politics are mobilized for white Jewish men's interests, but they also serve the interests of white men more broadly. While Allen and Roth found champions and support within the Jewish community, their narratives reinforce the privilege and status of white men outside of the Jewish community as well. These stories reveal, upon close readings, how the Jewish attributes of the narratives were tuned to frequencies that alerted Jewish audiences to the perils of antisemitism; however, they also show that the conflation of Jewish with white permitted these authors to simultaneously craft narratives in which *all* white men were vulnerable to false allegations from women and children (and even Jewish women). While the case studies in this book take place decades prior to the apex of what Tarana Burke has coined the Me Too movement, the significance of Jewish community protective politics to how contemporary conversations happen with high-profile Jewish figures alleged of sexual transgressions contemporaneously cannot be understated.

Some Contextualization Regarding the Term "Incest"

Defining "incest" poses a set of problems; it has meant different things at different times in different societies. I employ an inclusive definition: prohibited sexual conduct within traditional family units. This definition reflects my interest in social stigma, and how this anxiety regarding social stigma finds expression. As such, I also explore how cousin marriage functions in subsequent case studies, as these relationships sit on the outer boundaries of proscribed familial sexual relations, a liminal space that generates commentary and questions about why it is, or is not, incestuous. Multiple states prohibit cousin marriage. And yet, many Americans (Jewish or otherwise) can locate cousin marriage without going too far back in their family tree. Even if we do not call it incest, conversations about cousin marriage and relations almost inevitably reveal incest anxiety.

Relating to the definition issue, language itself historically presents problems for addressing even "clear-cut" instances of incestuous transgression (i.e., consanguineous, father-daughter). This insight undergirds a number of invaluable incest studies texts, among them Lynn Sacco's *Unspeakable*, a history of American incest that foregrounds, with its title, the challenges of discussing, let alone historically documenting, a transgression so taboo as to preclude utterance.[15] And yet, incest scholars have also observed how incest became a popular topic in activist, academic, and media engagement starting with second-wave feminisms and culminating in the 1990s.[16] Incest functions as a topic that is both ubiquitous (in some forms) and historically resistant to straightforward discussion.[17] The Jewish component of incest narratives adds another layer of unspeakability, even amid the spike in incest story consumption. Gillian Harkins suggests that we consider incest narratives vis-à-vis their position as object of neoliberal consumption and elucidates how this phenomenon operates for largely female authors and consumers, as incest narratives found mass consumption during the 1990s. My project shows how during the 1990s some male-authored narratives (such as Allen's and Roth's) operate as a countervailing trend to "reclaim" the historically privileged white male incest subjective authority encroached upon by feminist and queer voices. While Harkins and Janice Doane and Devon Hodges correctly note the increased production of consumable incest content through the 1990s, the role played by Jewishness in these narratives remain obstructed by meaningful silence. If the logic of whiteness involves a resistance to sexual stereotype, the intersection of Jewishness and historic incest stereotypes are meaningfully muted in discussions regarding these narratives. In setting up the ways in which my project links incest theory with Jewish studies, I aim to underscore the relevance of historical Jewish sexual antisemitism and stereotype to these more recent narratives.

Jewish Community Protective Politics across "High" and "Low" Culture

This book weaves together a wide range of texts, disciplines, artists, and artistic genres. The subsequent chapters examine how activist literature historicized Freud in the 1970s; the entirety of a television sitcom's inaugural run during the late 1980s and 1990s and the scholarly assessment of that show; cable news and sketch comedy treatment of a celebrity filmmaker, as well as a set of that artist's films; and the revisions that scrubbed a literary icon's long-awaited second novel of explicit racism and sexual violence. What links these stories, these figures, and these seemingly disparate modes of analysis?

This set of texts and readings emerge from a hypothesis: independent of medium, assessments of "high" or "low" culture, or genre, certain cultural logics operate to consistently privilege white Jewish male interests above those of the girls and women that accuse them. Ultimately, what I set out to prove is that even given vastly different expectations regarding how audiences view sitcoms, for example, as opposed to prestige literature, Jewish community protective politics operate remarkably consistently. This consistency is not the product of conspiracy or coordination, and I cannot emphasize this enough. Rather, this is the problematic consequence of an ostensibly defensible cultural logic: the extent to which American Jewish society has succeeded in educating Jews and non-Jews about the vulnerability of white Jewish men to antisemitic libel has resulted in a propensity for individual cases of critics, activists, reviewers, editors, sketch comedians, and comics protecting white Jewish masculinity in their studies, reviews, monographs, and revisions because of an ingrained morally justified sense of the danger of antisemitism. However, this ingrained morally justified impulse displaces consequences onto parties more vulnerable than white Jewish men. Sensitivity to the dangers of antisemitism does not adequately or immediately incorporate sensitivity to other similar society-wide dangers such as racism, misogyny, and homophobia, among other modes of oppression.

Each of my chapters explores how storytellers navigate the tension between white Jewish male vulnerability as a class and the prospect of individual white Jewish men sexually transgressing in incestuous fashion. The different genres of these case studies facilitate considering how artists, activists, critics, academics, and editors all make consequential choices as they wrestle with the anxiety surrounding this class vulnerability and theoretical individual culpability placed in close proximity. The mainstream acceptance of white Jewish male vulnerability as fairly indicating a social class in need of protection is broadly granted largely because it also intimates that white men are a class in need of protection. Jewish community protective politics operate in a variety of ways and are put into motion by any number of agents (Jewish and non-Jewish alike).

But tracing how they operate with larger-than-life figures—in overlapping fields like television, film, comedy, psychology, feminist activism, and literature—reveals just how broadly the phenomenon operates in mainstream popular culture, be it "high" or "low."

Thinking Back to the 1990s and Thinking Back from the 1990s

In weaving the above arguments through the subsequent chapters, I center the reader's focus on the 1990s, but this relatively recent historical era functions also as a departure point for considering these phenomena. Each chapter engages with earlier eras of Jewish history, and so the 1990s serve as an era for investigation, as well as a lens through which we can consider how white Jewish racialization has been actively written, filmed, and televised. The chapter on *Roseanne* examines how a television show set in the 1990s grappled with nostalgia, while the chapters on Woody Allen consider how his films' conceptions of American and Jewish history combine to assert white Jewishness as white while also perpetually sympathetic in its otherness. My examination of Henry Roth's *MORS* most explicitly reveals how the past can be rewritten and revised in a fashion that whitewashes an ideology of misogyny and anti-Black racism; even white-Jewish-accommodating white supremacy. While my first chapter, on second-wave Jewish feminist criticism of Freud, anchors itself in the 1970s, this exception to the 1990s focus frames the subsequent chapter dynamics by revealing how the very discussions about incest and Freud that accompanied the women's movement and helped shape more progressive strategies for engaging patriarchy in subsequent decades actually revealed the limits of how white Jewish male patriarchy might be discussed. This first chapter reveals how the tension between Jewish whiteness and Jewish otherness not only informs how the Jewish feminist activists and scholars of the 1970s told stories about Freud's shortcomings, but can also be found in Freud's own inconsistent, troubling, but understandable anxiety about how to write about incest when everyone would assume he was talking about Jewish incest.

I do not mean to highlight the 1990s as some definitive fulcrum point or era. Some scholars have made arguments to that effect, and while these claims have persuasive elements, my sense is that the era is recent enough (many of the prominent figures of the nineties remain newsmakers and culture producers today), such that we are still seeing the decade, even all these years later, play out.[18] Still, Daniel Itzkovitz makes a strong case for localizing white male Jewish normalization to the 1990s, a phenomenon he contends involves a pair of vested interests: white Jews are made mainstream, with all of the adherent benefits, while Jewish "liminality" (and all its adherent threats) is domesticated by an ostensibly non-Jewish, white power structure. In Itzkovitz's words, "the ascendance of the liminal Jewish man to normative American everyman suggests a profound popular identification with the unsettling and unsettled Jewish man in the postmodern era, and the desire to contain that liminality" (245).

This notion of "unsettling" permeates this book. How "unsettling" can normative white Jews get before they become too unsettling? And what does it mean that the two available options afforded by Jewish community protective politics, secular excommunication and defiant assertions of innocence, are so insufficient for navigating the ways that antisemitism, racism, homophobia, and misogyny operate and oppress? Close reading of Jewish incest narratives may not definitively answer that question, but it can help orient us as to why this is an important, if uncomfortable question to ask, and remind us that in American society, there is almost always another, more vulnerable ethnoracial other beyond the liminality of the white Jewish figure.

A Brief Outline of the Chapters

Chapter 1 sets up the subsequent discussion of the 1990s by considering the role Jewish second-wave feminists played in how Sigmund Freud, a towering historical figure central to any and all twentieth- and twenty-first-century conversations about incest and incest theory, came to become "white" in the popular American imagination. The chapter investigates how Betty Friedan, Shulamith Firestone, Susan Brownmiller, and Florence Rush navigated their and Freud's Jewishness in critiquing various aspects of his theorizations of sexuality and incest. It reveals how even among Jewish feminist scholars and activists, the subconscious impulse toward protecting Jewish men, and father/father figures in particular, from antisemitic stereotypes yielded likely unintended consequences: a displacement of pathology from Jewish men onto Black men and a secular "excommunication" in which Freud's Jewishness evaporates from the critical discussions of his flawed theorizing. The chapter spotlights Florence Rush's groundbreaking *The Best Kept Secret* as the exception to Jewish community protective politics that proves the rule, as it discusses child abuse with a vocabulary that directly engaged incest within Jewish cultural and familial contexts, as well as the author's autobiographical experience as a survivor, even as it too avoids any mentioning of Freud's Jewishness. Chapter 1 also considers Freud's choice to back away from his early incest theorizations in "The Aetiology of Hysteria," which inadvertently implicated the Jewish fathers of several of his clients as incestuous, as an early instance of Jewish community protective politics.

In chapter 2, I argue that the television show *Roseanne* reveals a pair of complex, interlinked, and largely overlooked incest metanarratives. The sitcom's incorporation of these metanarratives reflects Roseanne Barr's anxiety over her family's lateral close endogamies, as well as her experiences of her father, Jerry

Barr, whom she alleged in 1991 of sexually molesting her as a child. I reveal how *Roseanne*'s television father, Al Harris, conjured Jerry Barr in meaningful ways, as Al Harris was depicted as physically abusive and the subject of an extended somber plot arc in which the show's rejection of patriarchy finds expression in its negotiation of a Jewish father figure. Given widespread media coverage of Barr's allegations, I suggest that Jewish community protective politics played a role in how anxiety about the show's depiction of paternal abuse resulted in the historical critical and scholarly record claiming that *Roseanne* had no explicit Jewish content.

Chapters 3 and 4 both deal with Woody Allen. Chapter 3 focuses on how Allen exerted influence on how the media told the story of Allen and his two daughter figures: Dylan Farrow, a white Catholic seven-year-old who alleged sexual molestation, and Soon-Yi Previn, an of-age Korean American pseudo-stepdaughter with whom Allen had a consensual relationship. The chapter considers how race, religion, and racism informed how various figures attempted to tell this story, while paying particular attention to how Allen appealed to Jewish community protective politics to suggest he was the victim of antisemitic persecution by Mia Farrow and Connecticut investigative authorities. I also reveal how media depictions of Previn consistently employed sexualizing and racist attempts at humor that often featured significations of Dylan Farrow, whose sexual abuse allegations were often otherwise too taboo for direct commentary.

In chapter 4, I continue with Allen, but move to a more traditional set of close readings of some of his films. Here, I argue that Allen's post-1991 films engage incest and, in particular, his own incest narrative explicitly, rewarding his knowledgeable viewers with what I refer to as "incest Easter eggs." The chapter contends that Jewish community protective politics can be inferred from the consistency with which scholarly attempts to grapple with Allen's autobiography's relationship to his films consistently depart from a flawed premise that forswears Allen's alleged transgressions with adopted daughter Dylan Farrow as meriting analysis vis-à-vis his films. Ironically, Allen's films actually demand such investigation, as they reveal complex meditations on incest and the notion of getting away with family-destroying crimes (such as incest).

My final chapter, on Henry Roth's *Mercy of a Rude Stream* argues that the autobiographical novel's supposedly scandalous depiction of a sibling incest relationship is secondary to its normalization of the young adult protagonist's routine statutory rape of his first cousin. This chapter functions as a stress test, so to speak, for the theory of Jewish community protective politics: what happens when a Jewish icon essentially confesses to incest? The importance of protecting the image of white Jewish masculinity remains paramount, but other transgressions—in this case, anti-Black racism and rape—are disguised in order to make ostensibly lateral incest read as deliberately provocative and its confession a celebratory marker of growth. By showing the pattern of revisions between *MORS* manuscripts and published text, I contend that Roth's iconic status compelled his publishing house to eliminate evidence of Roth's protagonist being a rapist and racist by raising his cousin's age by two years (from eleven or twelve to thirteen or fourteen years old) and deleting dozens of instances of Roth using racist slurs, accommodating white readers' participation in what Jonathan Arac calls narcissistic mirroring.

Like all authors, my hope is that readers approach this book with an open mind. And yet, this book approaches widely celebrated, iconic Jewish American artists like Woody Allen and Henry Roth with a critical eye. This is not an attempt to write these figures out of their place in Jewish film or literary history but rather a gesture toward contextualizing their place in that history and wrestling with how idealistic notions of white Jewish masculinity, predicated on the notion of its historical vulnerability, can actually help to foment rape culture and toxic masculinity. Buying into Jewish exceptionalism has consequences, but exposing the unintended consequences of that exceptionalism does not mean accepting or perpetrating negative stereotypes. It means acknowledging Jewish men as, fundamentally, human and thus necessarily partly composed of some individuals who might be said to confirm stereotypes, even though those individuals who have committed sexual assault, regardless of their religion, nationality, or ethnoracial identity, actually reflect the human condition and not that of their religious, national, or ethnoracial community.

1

A Victorian Freud

A Rhetorical Analysis of Jewish Second-Wave Feminist Criticism of Freud

This chapter argues that the rhetorical choices Jewish second-wave feminists made in critiquing Sigmund Freud reveal how even in an activist, feminist context, Jewish community protective politics dictated that Freud be depicted as white and not Jewish. Jewish second-wave feminists challenged Freud, but in so doing cast him as a universal and Victorian patriarchal figure, almost never mentioning his Jewishness. These rhetorical choices, which had the effect of de-Judaizing Freud, functioned as a form of secular excommunication. In order to accommodate second-wave feminist critiques of Freud, Jewish community protective politics *whitened* Freud, a rhetorical act that effectively protected the image of Jewish male patriarchy by ensuring that Freud and his flaws were discussed as representative of a universal, white patriarchy. Second-wave feminists criticized Freud for a number of reasons, but I focus on the role his theorization of incest played in this criticism because of the intersection of the Jewish incest stereotype and Freud's ostensible culpability for facilitating men getting away with incestuous transgressions on account of his widely accepted revision of his own incest theorization.

While Freud's incest theorizing is most famous for the Oedipus complex, a flawed theory based on the notion that children universally sexually fantasized about the parent of the opposite sex, Freud initially proposed the "seduction theory," a flawed theory based on the notion that adult trauma could be traced to childhood sexual abuse (inclusive of, albeit not limited to, incest).[1] In essence, anxiety about Freud's status as a Jewish progenitor of misogynistic and patriarchal ideas and, crucially, specific anxiety about his theorization of incest incentivized second-wave Jewish feminists to accentuate his white, or "Victorian," qualities in order to avoid the appearance of holding a Jewish male icon responsible for society's misogynist failings.

While the majority of this study focuses on the 1990s, I begin with the 1970s for three reasons: first, to show how Jewish community protective politics operate in activist circles. Even for feminists dedicated to critiquing misogynistic attitudes among men, negotiating Jewish identity often resulted in ambivalent concessions to Jewish community protective politics. Second, this community protective whitening of Freud, which emerges among otherwise progressive and secular Jews, happens concurrently with a displacement of the incest stereotypes from Jewish men onto Black men and Black families, prefiguring the displacement of stereotype that occurs with Jewish community protective politics in the 1990s. And third, this chapter harks back to how Freud himself negotiated the problem of the Jewish incest stereotype in the 1890s, revealing how Jewish community protective politics function across eras.[2]

That Freud's whiteness would be asserted by his most ardent critics, among them many Jewish women, calls attention to how race (and anti-Blackness in particular) intersected with considerations of sexual antisemitism for Jews across eras and across the political spectrum. By analyzing the ways that Jewishness was invoked, or conspicuously left unspoken, in Jewish authored second-wave feminist texts dealing with incest and child abuse, as well as texts that were specifically critical of Freud, this chapter shows how anxieties about Jewish male vulnerability impacted how Jewish feminists levied their critique of patriarchy, and how authors implicitly protected Jewish men even as they critiqued white men and pathologized Black men. Regardless of intent, these choices had the effect of displacing sexual stereotypes from white Jewish men onto Black men. I do not contend that this was done consciously, but even in an otherwise progressive movement, Jewish community protective politics found Jewish second-wave feminists protecting some patriarchal interests, such as the image of white Jewish masculinity. They accomplished this via whitening (and de-Judaizing) Freud and refraining from any engagement with culturally Jewish components of male patriarchal behavior (even as this framework was used for Black men). This keen, deeply felt awareness of Jewish male vulnerability to sexual antisemitism informed how Freud was discussed and functionally secularly excommunicated in these texts.

In examining Freud criticism, we will see how Jewish community protective impulses were personal and central to second-wave feminist activism and scholarship that rhetorically protected masculine Jewish vulnerability and, in so doing, helped whiten ethnoracial Jewish identity. These veiled community protective politics informed groundbreaking works that levied vital criticisms against white male patriarchy, while avoiding mention of the particular vulnerabilities and exploitative acts of white Jewish patriarchy, even as they unambivalently voiced criticisms of Black patriarchy. I do not suggest that these authors should have differently invoked their Jewishness in levying their critiques, or that the minimal mention of their Jewish subjectivity was in and of itself problematic. I do, however, find these choices meaningful as it relates to the content of their writing, specifically, the corresponding inattention to Freud's Jewishness, especially when juxtaposed with the racist presuppositions observable in how these authors deconstructed Black patriarchy. In comparison to Jewish second-wave feminists, Black feminist authors of this era (such as Toni Morrison, Maya Angelou, and Gayl Jones) addressed incest and criticized Black patriarchy in specifically Black terms. The rhetorical choices that forged these second-wave feminist movements thus muted the association of incest with Jews and ultimately realigned it with the pathologized Black family. And, concomitantly, these rhetorical choices discursively facilitated Jewish women's continued integration into the more empowered construct of "white women."

Second-wave feminism's consequential integration of secular Jewish identity into whiteness essentially protected Jewish men from ethnoracial pathology, establishing the terms for subsequent discussions regarding Jewish white figures and incest and helping displace that pathology onto Black men. For all its insight, this criticism of Freud failed to straightforwardly negotiate his Jewishness, Jewish vulnerability, or problematic incest theorizing in the context of his anxiety regarding the Jewish incest stereotype. While Freud was rightly criticized by second-wave feminists for building a psychoanalytic structure that too often cast daughters' testimonies as fantasy, identifying him as Jewish while accusing him of this moral failure risked branding him as an antisemitic stereotype writ large: a Jewish man responsible for societal failure to deal honestly with the reality of incest.

In building this argument, I contextualize Freud's own Jewish racial identity amid the pervasive geopolitical antisemitism of its era and examine how numerous classic Jewish-authored second-wave feminist texts, with the notable exception of Betty Friedan's *The Feminine Mystique*, consistently cast Freud as a Victorian, while never presenting him as Jewish. Considering how these authors articulated their own subjective Jewish perspectives reveals how that invocation (or lack thereof) conspicuously operated alongside anti-Black cultural logics that accommodated post–civil rights white Jewishness's further incorporation into whiteness. The chapter concludes by contrasting these patterns with how Black feminist authors dealt with incest in their novels, memoirs, and poetry.

When Did Freud Become White?

Asking "When did Freud become white?" is certainly anachronistic. Applying "white" as a racial construct signifying power and privilege extending to and enveloping European Jews during Freud's lifetime threatens to elide the ubiquity of antisemitism during that era. And yet, Freud today is commonly discussed *as* white; he is often invoked in popular American discourse as a figure representative of a sort of hegemonic, supposedly universal, "normative" racial quality. Jewish feminist criticism of Freud during the 1970s went a long way toward cementing Freud's whiteness, as decades after his death, his critics projected a racial identity onto him.[3]

Though it goes unmentioned in many Jewish-authored second-wave feminist texts critical of him, Freud lived in a Europe in which Jews were targets of broad societal discrimination and racial violence for the duration of his lifetime. Freud was born in 1856 in the Austrian Empire, shortly before a wave of pogroms across Russia and Eastern Europe. He died in 1939 in the United Kingdom having escaped the Nazis and the fate of six million Jews systematically murdered during the Holocaust. Freud was secular, but his own religious nonobservance would have been irrelevant to the vast majority of antisemites.[4] The antisemitism Freud encountered in Vienna clearly impacted his social and professional opportunities.

While contemplating Freud's Jewishness is imperative to any comprehensive effort at understanding the historical figure, his textual engagement with race (and racism) reminds us that he also helped shape a medical discourse that impacted how Europeans conceived of racial difference. *Totem and Taboo* (1913), Freud's anthropological attempt to theorize incest, endogamy, and exogamy, relies on Indigenous Australians to consider issues of family and partnering. In setting up a dichotomy of "savages" and "neurotics" in discussing sexual partnering practices, Freud creates distance between European Jews and non-European "savages." An alignment of Jewish identity and normative "whiteness" is formulated through sexually othering nonwhite figures around an issue widely associated with European Jews at the time.[5] As Alys Eve Weinbaum reminds us, "In Austro-German medicine and science, as in the immediate sociopolitical milieu of Freud's Vienna, race invariably called up the constellation Aryan/Jew" (146). While Freud's theorizing began rhetorically recategorizing European Jewishness as European, he did this as a Jewish man whose secularity provided no meaningful reprieve from the weight of systematic state-sponsored antisemitism. And yet, as the following section shows, Freud is almost invariably categorized as Victorian by Jewish second-wave feminists, a reinvention that renders him, within the anachronistic logic, as a flawed but iconic white father figure, as opposed to a Jewish man whose theorizing facilitated men getting away with incest.

A Consistently Victorian Freud

This section details how various Jewish second-wave feminists identified Freud according to racial, ethnic, national, and cultural categorizations. Classic second-wave feminist texts authored by Shulamith Firestone (*The Dialectic of Sex*, 1970), Ellen Frankfort (*Vaginal Politics,* 1972), Phyllis Chesler (*Women and Madness*, 1972), and Susan Brownmiller (*Against Our Will*, 1975) all levy significant criticisms against Freud's patriarchal theorizing, and while each of the aforementioned authors identifies as Jewish (even if not in these texts), none of these texts mention Freud's Jewishness. Instead, they depict Freud as culturally "Victorian," as Viennese, and, ironically, as a sort of religious father figure for secularism. But in contrast to brief but meaningful comments depicting Freud as Jewish in Betty Friedan's *The Feminine Mystique* (1963), these influential texts never identify Freud as Jewish. The subsequent close readings examine how each text represents Freud and consider how Friedan's language reveals an alternative choice that might have rendered Freud vulnerable to ethnoracial pathologizing.

Jewish second-wave feminist authors often characterized Freud as a product of a repressed Victorian society and framed their criticisms of his patriarchal theories on that formative culture. Ellen Frankfort published *Vaginal Politics*, a thorough condemnation of various systemic instances of sexism and misogyny within the health-care industry. Addressing Freud's influence on medicine, Frankfort writes, "Like many older doctors practicing today, Freud was, however, the products [*sic*] of a repressed Victorian upbringing and an authoritarian education" (202). Phyllis Chesler's *Women and Madness* indicts sexism in psychology and the categorization of women as "mad" as a historical tool for oppressing women. Chesler identifies Freud's tone in the "Case of Dora" as "cold, intellectual, detective-like, controlling, sexually Victorian" (80). Chesler never identifies Freud as Jewish, nor does she identify either Anna O. or Dora as Jewish. In *Against Our Will*, a touchstone of rape scholarship and history, Susan Brownmiller labels the psychoanalyst Helene Deutsch a "traitor to her own sex" (350) for her thesis on female masochism; Brownmiller considers both Deutsch and Freud as products of their culture, defined quite narrowly; Deutsch's "attitude was in keeping with the Victorian times in which she and Freud lived" (351). Brownmiller makes no reference to Freud's Jewishness, despite her analysis of Jewish women as victims of rape in Europe during pogroms and the Holocaust. Instead, she marks Freud as "Victorian," subsuming his Jewishness with a shorthand for a broad-brushed mainstream culture that Frankfort describes as "repressed," and Chesler describes as "cold" and "controlling."

References to Freud as a father figure were also commonplace. Brownmiller calls Freud the "father of psychoanalysis" (*Against Our Will*, 305), and Judith

Lewis Herman, in her comprehensive study *Father-Daughter Incest* (1981), describes Freud as "the patriarch of modern psychology" (9). While Herman sets Freud up explicitly as a cultural father figure, she never roots him in any specific historical cultural context; she marks him as neither Jewish nor Victorian.

No text does more to present Freud as Victorian, father figure, and culturally iconic, while still avoiding any mention of his Jewishness, than Shulamith Firestone's *The Dialectic of Sex*. Firestone's influential text outlines socialist terms for feminist revolution and spends a chapter analyzing Freud and Freudianism, labeling the phenomenon a "misguided feminism" (38). Firestone distinguishes between Freud and Freudianism—the contemporaneous mainstream popularity and influence of a watered-down version of psychoanalysis. But despite asserting that she interrogates Freud's "cultural bias" (13), the chapter focuses almost entirely on his American cultural impact. Firestone writes, "If we had to name the one cultural current that most characterizes America in the twentieth century, it might be the work of Freud and the disciplines that grew out of it" (38). Indeed, the chapter mocks American preoccupation with Freud by considering him as a cultural phenomenon wholly extracted from his historical context: "Freudianism has become, with its confessionals and penance, its proselytes and converts, with the millions spent on its upkeep, our modern Church. We attack it only uneasily, for you never know, on the final day of judgement, whether they *might be right*" (38).

Firestone's acerbic writing, throughout her chapter on Freudianism, punctures the image of Freud as godlike figure. But the extent to which she draws our attention to Freud as a religious figure also reinforces the association. Firestone says of Freud, "at the end of each new critique we find a guilt paean to the Great Father who started it all. They can't quite do him in" (39). Numerous constructions identify him as a recognizably Christian figure (references to church, confessionals, and proselytes all contribute to this imagery), revealing a fascinating contrast with the man's historical secular Jewishness. Firestone's diminishment of Freud also enshrines him: his singular impact constitutes the one cultural current characterizing twentieth-century America and simultaneous evidence of his false godhood. Yet Firestone consistently engages Freud's "cultural bias" in limited terms: "Both Freudianism and feminism came as reactions to one of the smuggest periods in Western civilization, the Victorian Era, characterized by its family-centredness, and thus its exaggerated sexual oppression and repression" (41). Throughout, Firestone anchors her assessment of Freud's "cultural" characteristics with familiar nods to "Western civilization," "Victorian Era," and Vienna. His Jewishness never comes up.

And yet, despite her criticism of Freudianism, Firestone's assessments of Freud's failings are, occasionally, sympathetic: "Given [Freud's] own psychic structure and cultural prejudices—he was a petty tyrant of the old school, for whom certain sexual truths may have been expensive—he can hardly have been expected to make such an examination part of his life work" (42). But why should Freud "hardly have been expected" to look inward? Firestone's sympathy may reflect her ambivalence about her own choice (conscious or otherwise) not to examine aspects of cultural tyranny and sexual truths in terms of her ethnoreligious upbringing. But before analyzing how Firestone and other Jewish second-wave feminist authors rhetorically positioned their own Jewishness, we should examine Betty Friedan's *The Feminine Mystique.*

Betty Friedan's Prayer

In 1963, Betty Friedan published *The Feminine Mystique*, an influential, canonical text marking the advent of second-wave feminism. Friedan also holds Freud and Freudian influence to account for contemporaneous American sexism, but unlike the aforementioned authors, Friedan remarks on Freud's Jewishness. Given the importance of Friedan's book, and the chronology (she published her study seven years before Firestone's *Dialectic*), Friedan's invocation of Freud's Jewishness suggests that subsequent texts *removed* it from the narrative.

Friedan's cultural assessment of Freud considers the various components of his national, contemporaneous, and ethnoreligious identities. The fifth chapter, "The Sexual Solipsism of Sigmund Freud," distinguishes Freud from American Freudianism (as Firestone would later do). Friedan writes, "It would be half-wrong to say it started with Sigmund Freud. It did not really start, in America, until the 1940s" (103). Questions of temporality and nationality complicate conversations of Freud and Freud's influence from the outset, and Friedan tracks this discrepancy in her analysis. She also roots her first assessment of Freud's culture in familiar terms, referring to "penis envy" as "a phenomenon he observed in women—that is, in the middle-class women who were his patients in Vienna in the Victorian era" (105). In the same paragraph, Friedan once again refers to Freud's patients as "those Victorian women" and, more vaguely, suggests Freud "was a prisoner of his own culture" (105) and that "his culture denied sex" (106).

Freud's culture, thus far in the text, is readable only as Victorian/Viennese. But while Freud has not yet been described as Jewish, his female patients have been described as "middle-class women" and "Victorian women." This is true, yet Freud's female patients were also, as Weinbaum notes, most commonly Jewish woman whose Jewish identifiable qualities were muted, if not omitted, from Freud's writing (178).[6]

While Friedan never identifies Freud's female patients as being largely Jewish, she does, six pages into her chapter, reference Freud's Jewishness. In stating that Freud saw women as "childlike dolls," Friedan writes: "Freud grew up with this attitude built in by his culture—not only the culture of Victorian Europe, but that Jewish culture in which men said the daily prayer: 'I thank Thee, Lord, that Thou hast not created me a woman,' and women prayed in submission: 'I thank Thee, Lord, that Thou has created me according to Thy will'" (108).

Friedan alludes to a blessing that is referenced extensively in subsequent second-wave feminist texts and throughout the women's movement. Friedan also mentioned the blessing in the keynote speech she delivered for the Women's Strike of 1970, and Vivian Gornick invoked the same prayer a year later (Jacobson, "Roots Too" 259). Elizabeth Martinez recalls Firestone alluding to the quote in the late 1960s in the *Feminist Memoir Project* (118). By the early 1980s, reference to the blessing had taken on a life of its own. Letty Cottin Pogrebin discusses the repeated feminist "invocation" of the blessing as evidence of antisemitism in her 1982 essay "Anti-Semitism in the Women's Movement." Pogrebin quotes Pnina Tobin as saying, "I wish I had a nickel for every time a feminist has quoted that prayer to argue the supreme sexism of the Jewish faith. . . . That prayer has probably been spoken more by anti-Semitic non-Jews than by Jewish worshipers" (70).

Hyperbole aside, Tobin fairly interrogates whether Judaism might be targeted more than other faiths that developed on similarly patriarchal foundations. But even if we are sympathetic to Tobin's assessment, a Jewish-authored text seems to be the launching point of the blessing's second life in feminist criticism infamy, and the prayer itself is actually far less potentially evocative of antisemitism than the Freud family observation that directly follows it. Indeed, the subsequent sentence is unique in Jewish second-wave feminist assessments of Freud's "culture": "Freud's mother was the pretty, docile bride of a man twice her age; his father ruled the family with an autocratic authority traditional in Jewish families when the fathers were seldom able to establish authority in the outside world" (Friedan 109). Subsequent references to Freud's cultural milieu return, exclusively, to allusions to Victorian norms. This ethnographic linking of domestic Jewish patriarchal autocratic behavior to societal antisemitism, though, is absent in subsequent second-wave feminist texts addressing Freud. The blessing anecdote speaks to a criticism of organized religion, yet Friedan's reference to "Jewish families" evinces a far more overt framework for how social science can pathologize minority groups.[7] Friedan's reading suggests that the large-scale psychological costs of societal antisemitism rendered Jewish masculine insecurity so severe as to yield a predictable, "traditional" Jewish male autocracy in the domestic space. In short: Friedan implies Jewish men ran their houses in autocratic fashion *because* of antisemitic persecution.

While Friedan's "autocratic authority" observation is not applied to Jewish men in subsequent Jewish-authored second-wave feminist texts, it is displaced onto Black men. That is, the specificity/spectacle of Jewish male vulnerability yielding a domestic Jewish autocracy vanishes, while strikingly similar hypotheses emerge in Brownmiller's and Firestone's assessments of Black families. Essentially, the model Friedan presents for analyzing Jewish male historical patriarchy is removed from Jewish men and applied to Black men. The erasure of Freud's Jewishness facilitates the erasure of specifically Jewish male instances of patriarchy and misogyny, while instances of Black male patriarchy and misogyny are instead incorporated, racialized, and pathologized.

In considering this phenomenon, we might also investigate how Jewishness emerges elsewhere in these Jewish-authored second-wave feminist texts. How do authors allude to their own Jewish identities or their white identities? How does subsequent scholarship contextualize these authors' battles with identifiably Jewish patriarchy that goes unseen in these earlier texts?

When Do White Feminists Become Jewish?

Throughout the long 1970s, many Jewish second-wave feminists made only minimal mention of their Jewish subjectivity. Having tracked Freud's emergence as Victorian, and thus "white," across specific texts, we might also inquire: how do these particular texts position their authors' own Jewishness? Considering these two questions together illustrates how meaningful choices about the depiction of Jewishness and the occupation of "white" subjectivity consistently worked to fold Jewishness into an expanding, white ethnic collective. The choice to render Freud as a white father figure also mirrored the choice to protect actual Jewish fathers from specific scrutiny by rarely affixing recognizably Jewish characteristics to the representations of patriarchy mobilized in these texts. Yet while Jewish patriarchal specificity evaporates, Jewish feminists framed their critique of Black patriarchy in specific, sustained, pathologizing arguments reminiscent of Friedan's assessment of Freud's autocratic Jewish father.

Numerous scholars have commented upon the considerable involvement of Jews among second-wave feminists, as well as the corresponding purported disengagement with specifically Jewish issues. Paula Hyman suggests that a combination of post–World War II social factors yielded a larger number of young Jewish women in college communities where the feminist movement developed (223). But Hyman distinguishes between Jewish involvement in "mainstream" second-wave feminism and what she terms "a specifically Jewish feminism" (224); she characterizes the work of Firestone, Friedan, and Robin Morgan as not having "dealt specifically with Judaism or with the Jewish community" (223). Sylvia Barack Fishman suggests something similar: "Although a substantial proportion of early feminist writers were Jewish, the milieu they identified with and wrote about was melting-pot America—that amorphous amalgam of ethnicities and religions blended into a secularized white Anglo-Saxon Protestant culture" (6). Matthew Frye Jacobson's read on the era challenges Fishman's construction, contending that the specifically Jewish, Italian, and Irish "accents of white feminism . . . help to explain both the obstacles that arose and the alliances that were forged as white women and women of color reconfigured the personal and the political" (*Roots Too* 248). Second-wave Jewish feminists were not blending into "WASP" culture so much as helping to create a new normative "ethnic" whiteness. Jacobson helps remind us that secular Jewish feminist texts were creative, not simply assimilative, forging new links between secular Jewishness, and eventually even religious Jewishness, and white identity.

The fact that Jewishness emerges rhetorically in 1980s feminist texts also draws attention to its prior absence. Fishman sees this phenomenon as a type of mainstream surfacing of a more Judaism-inflected form of Jewish feminism, breaking away from assimilative pressures. She posits, "In reaction to the pressure that they either repudiate or at least keep silent about their Judaism, even secular Jewish feminists have frequently discovered, explored, and begun to take pride in their Jewishness" (12).[8] For Fishman, then, antisemitism accounts for the turn to more assertive Jewish identification.

We might consider, in addition to Fishman's accounting, another reason that "keeping silent" about Jewishness played a very specific role in whitening Jews: it facilitated, amid criticism of patriarchy, a way to assert Jewish community protective politics. It kept Jewish men out of the spotlight in texts where Jewish feminist authors frequently, assertively, moved Black men into the spotlight.

In the subsequent close readings of Firestone's *The Dialectic of Sex* and Brownmiller's *Against Our Will*, I highlight how the authors invoked their own Jewishness beside their sustained consideration of Black male patriarchy. I do not believe these authors made conscious decisions to displace negative stereotypes associated with Jewish male vulnerability onto Black men. However, independent of intent, the rhetorical consequences of their choices to omit a specific contemplation of Jewish patriarchy from their analyses helped fold white Jewishness into the confines of American ethnic whiteness. Simultaneously, this rhetoric subjected Black masculinity to a racialized critique whose tenor and tone may have been amplified due to the ambivalence of unwittingly othering Black men in the precise ways that Jewish men had been historically othered.

Firestone's Father and the Undissolved "Ties of Blood"

Firestone's *The Dialectic of Sex* (1970) focuses considerable attention on Black male patriarchy and omits any reference to identifiably Jewish patriarchal behavior. Firestone theorizes racism as an extension of sexism, basing this theory upon a metaphorical familial construct for understanding social dynamics between white men and women and Black men and women (where Black people are children). Angela Davis has criticized this theorizing for relying on the "timeworn myth of the Black rapist" (182–183) and embedded notions of Black pathology. Black/white racial constructs dominate Firestone's theorizing of American society, but she mentions Jewishness only once. In a footnoted aside regarding Jewish education in Firestone's community resembling (in a positive fashion) medieval European approaches to educating children, Firestone writes, "In the orthodox Jewish milieu in which I grew up, considered anachronistic by outsiders, many little boys still begin serious study before the age of five, and as a result Talmudic prodigies are common" (75). This is Firestone's lone reference to her Jewish upbringing.

Yet personal experience of Jewish patriarchy may have informed Firestone's feminist politics in significant ways not broached in her book. Susan Faludi's "Death of a Revolutionary," published after Firestone's death in 2012, examines Firestone's family history and her battles with mental illness, juxtaposing these struggles against her early influence within the women's movement. Faludi interviews Firestone's youngest sister, who reveals, "My father threw his rage at Shulie." Another sister recounts a physical fight between Firestone and her father that featured "Sol shouting, 'I'll kill you!,' and Shulamith yelling back, 'I'll kill you first!'" (Faludi). The article provides a devastating portrait of a tyrannically patriarchal household and includes an excerpt from a letter that Firestone wrote to her mother when she and Firestone's father moved to Israel in 1977, in which Firestone wrote, in capital letters, "I DISSOLVE MY TIES OF BLOOD" (Faludi).

Despite its omission in *Dialectic*, Faludi's telling of Firestone's story highlights how centrally Firestone's Orthodox Jewish familial upbringing, and her father in particular, impacted her experience of domestic patriarchy. Firestone's decision to theorize American patriarchal oppression in exclusively white and Black racialized formations makes her omission of a culturally specific Jewish patriarchy (that she herself experienced) conspicuous. I do not mean that Firestone ought to have addressed the Jewish elements of her life experience. Rather, I posit that her own specific experiences may indicate a projection of her specific Jewish domestic experience of what Friedan called "autocratic authority" onto Black men en masse. Indeed, Firestone's theorizing of race and gender, in which Black men's behavior with white and Black women exists as a function or consequence of white male racist oppression, reflects Friedan's assessment of Freud's father's "autocratic" behavior. Both constructs feature a large societal oppressive force (racism/antisemitism) compelling a male minority to exert his power over more vulnerable members of the same minority community

(Black women/Jewish wives and Jewish children). This formulation also maps onto Faludi's presentation of Firestone's Jewish father as autocratic.

Firestone divorces her ethnoreligious experience from her specific familial experience of being a Jewish daughter of an autocratic Jewish father, though. The very social phenomenon that might (albeit, too simplistically) account for her father's behavior (antisemitism/racism) is repackaged, re-raced, and projected onto Black men. Firestone's discussion of Black male sexism manifests as a placeholder for anger and ambivalence about Jewish patriarchy that Firestone cannot articulate.

This very omission is thus deeply protective of Jewishness, Jewish claims to whiteness, and Jewish fathers. Firestone's father called *Dialectic* (which he never read) "the joke book of the century" (Faludi), and yet Jewish fathers are spared any ethnographic analysis as Jewish fathers. While one Jewish father does appear extensively in the text, Firestone never identifies Freud as Jewish, as demonstrated earlier. The overall effect is to rhetorically disappear Jewishness behind a facade of Freud's purported whiteness and displace the problematic behavior of Firestone's father onto Black men. Proving a negative is impossible, and, admittedly, I make a leap in theorizing this space between "omission" and "protection." And yet for a movement so famously aligning the personal with the political, the omission of Jewish fathers depersonalizes these texts. Ascribing these omissions to the protection of Jewish fathers suggests one possibility for how these texts operated politically.

From "I Was a Jewish Girl" to "I Speak as a White Woman"

Susan Brownmiller's *Against Our Will* (1975), a groundbreaking study of rape as a ubiquitous phenomenon, makes more extensive reference to Jewishness than Firestone, but a similar rhetorical pattern emerges: American Jewishness disappears into whiteness, while Black male rape is pathologized. However, Brownmiller employs a transnational approach distinguishing American Jews from European Jews. Angela Davis has commented on Brownmiller's racist construction of Black men as sexual predators of white women, but this sits against a related construction in which non-Jewish European men are sexual predators of Jewish European women. Assessing Brownmiller's language regarding her identity (sometimes marked as Jewish, other times as white) helps us read *Against Our Will* not just as an important, if imperfect, critical history of rape, but as a racially formative document producing Jewish American whiteness.

It is fully 350 pages into her study that Brownmiller first invokes her Jewish identity. As she analyzes the "Red Riding Hood" fairy tale as a parable of rape, she considers its lessons against her own experiences of geopolitics as a child:

"This was the middle of World War II, the German Army had marched through Belgium a second time, and I was a Jewish girl growing up in Brooklyn. I could not help but conclude that the Hun and the Nazi were one in [*sic*] the same and, therefore, I had to be Belgium" (Brownmiller, *Against* 345). Brownmiller reconstructs her childhood subjectivity in national terms. Huns and Nazis are "one [and] the same," yet despite first specifying her ethnoracial identification as "a Jewish girl," she pivots, fascinatingly, to identifying as Belgium. Like Firestone, Brownmiller's invocation of Jewish identity is located in her childhood. The ethnoracial ordering to Brownmiller's anecdote is far more complex, though; the allusions to Nazis and the German Army sit beside an identification as Jewish, which she transfers to Belgium, given its status as a plundered country. The sequence of these identifications initially claims, and then immediately disassociates, Brownmiller's Jewish identity. While "being Belgium" exposed her to the same violent threat, the metaphor creates distance in contemplating that violence. The only purpose of "being Belgium" is the metaphor's capacity to replace the harrowing fact of her distinct Jewish vulnerability.

By themselves, these words reveal something of the painful process of distinguishing her own ethnoracial identity in an American context versus a European genocidal one. But they are even more significant given that Brownmiller writes extensively about Jewish vulnerability to rape in a chapter titled "Riots, Pogroms and Revolutions." Jewish women are discussed, as Jewish women, as victims of extensive sexual violence throughout Eastern Europe. In that chapter, Brownmiller does not remark on her Jewish American subjectivity. Yet in "A Question of Race," a chapter that bore considerable scrutiny for its assessment of Black male rape and its deployment of Emmett Till, Brownmiller frames her positionality thusly: "There is no unemotional way to approach the subject of interracial rape, and no way for me to pretend to an objectivity of my own. I speak as a white woman whose first stirrings of social conscience occurred when I read of certain famous cases, now legend, in which black men had been put to death for coming too close to white women" (*Against* 230). Brownmiller identifies her subjectivity in a very straightforward fashion. Speaking as a "white woman" does not preclude identification as Jewish. But there is something noteworthy about the tenses of her two invocations: "I speak as a white woman" accompanies a contemporaneous assessment of Black male sexual threat. "I was a Jewish girl growing up in Brooklyn" places Jewishness in the past tense, as something formative.

This shift in subjectivity reveals how racially formative language navigates complicated terrains of national and racial categorization and also speaks to power dynamics. Speaking as a white woman asserts greater social currency than speaking as a Jewish woman, evidenced by Brownmiller's earlier preference to identify as Belgium to negotiate her gendered vulnerability in the context of World War II.[9] But Brownmiller's mode of speaking/writing as a white woman functions less, in Davis's reading, as an acknowledgment of privileged subjectivity, than as an assertion of "an unthinking partisanship which borders on racism" (Davis 198).

While Davis correctly critiques Brownmiller's implicit assumptions in speaking as a "white woman," Brownmiller's construction of her own subjective identity, combined with her depictions of Jewish men, illuminate the racially formative aspects of the text. As established earlier, while Freud appears extensively in *Against Our Will*, he is never identified or analyzed as a Jewish figure, though Brownmiller discusses Till and others in regard to their Blackness. Other Jewish American figures emerge in a similar fashion: unidentified with regard to race, religion, ethnicity. Jews are identified as Jews when discussing the rape of European Jewish women, but only in that context. Otherwise, they are represented as white insofar as they are not identified as anything else. Norman Mailer is identified as a buffoon, but not a Jewish one (Brownmiller, *Against* 339).

Having explored the rhetoric within texts that address patriarchy and Freud generally, I want to juxtapose Florence Rush's markedly different approach in her 1977 article "The Freudian Cover-Up" and her 1980 book *The Best Kept Secret: Sexual Abuse of Children.* Rush's texts exposed how patriarchy provided the opportunity for the sexual exploitation of children, especially within familial settings. Judith Herman cites Rush extensively in her own work, and Susan Brownmiller was also close friends with Rush and alludes to her work on incest in *Against Our Will*, though it had not yet been published.[10] Brownmiller wrote the foreword to *The Best Kept Secret.* Rush and her scholarship never achieved the same broad influence and cultural impact as Firestone, Brownmiller, and Herman, but her work was vital. She presented on incest at the New York Radical Feminist Conference on Rape in 1971, wrote about incest and Freud for the feminist publication *Chrysalis: A Magazine of Women's Culture* in 1977, and published her monograph in 1980. Writing a journal article presents different challenges than writing an entire book on a subject. Yet the choices Rush makes in presenting material in 1980, versus 1977, help illustrate how the racialization of incest depended, at foundational levels, on how Freud was depicted and how authors depicted themselves.

Florence Rush, "Dr. Greenberg," and "Uncle Willie"

Chrysalis's first issue appeared in 1977. Its cover, a mosaic of racially and generationally diverse women's faces, visually indicates the editors' more inclusive aspirations relative to *Ms.* magazine's 1972 iconic debut image of "Wonder Woman for President." Rush's article, boldly titled "The Freudian Cover-Up," takes direct aim at her eponymous subject: "When Freud claimed that children who reported sexual abuse by adults had imagined or fantasized the experience, he was quite wrong. Children know the difference between reality and fantasy, often with more accuracy than adults, and sexual advances are in fact made to children in the course of everyday life" (31). Rush's article, to my knowledge, is the first to address the issue of Freud's abandonment of the "seduction theory" from a feminist critical perspective. Relying heavily on Freud's correspondences with Wilhelm Fliess, which had been translated and published in 1954, Rush argues that Freud abandoned evidence of female patients testifying that their fathers sexually abused them as children. Freud's arrival at the Oedipus complex and male childhood fantasy for the mother as his predominant incest theory is portrayed as a deliberate move away from his earlier patriarchy-challenging discovery: that some men, even respected and wealthy ones, took advantage of their power in society and family to sexually exploit their daughters.

Rush's readings of the Freud/Fliess letters are enormously compelling and textually supported quite effectively. But despite Rush's profound influence within the women's movement and generally positive reviews, Catharine MacKinnon described her book as "groundbreaking and largely overlooked" in a *New York Times* feature on "summer reading" for presidential candidates in 1988 (MacKinnon et al.).[11] Rush was the first second-wave feminist author to attempt a book-length theorizing of child sexual predation and incest in conjunction with sustained focus on Freud; examining her book alongside her article reveals the high stakes of Rush's choices in recasting scholarly and activist conversations about incest.

Rush's 1977 essay's cultural depiction of Freud is entirely consistent with Firestone and Brownmiller. She states that Freud "informed a society still deep in Victorian prudery that very little children had strong erotic drives" ("Freudian Cover-Up" 31). Rush references Freud's "Victorian world" (35) and Freud's patients as "middle-class Victorian women" (38). She suggests that Freud's "cover-up" required "only that forbidden sex be practiced with tact and discretion so that surface Victorian respectability was in no way disturbed" (45). Consistent with other Jewish second-wave feminists, Rush emphasizes "Victorian respectability" while making no mention of "Jewish respectability." But Rush is the first Jewish second-wave feminist to argue that cultural mores specific to Freud's time, place, and identity informed his decision on whether to "name the offender" in the case of incest. The Freudian cover-up, in Rush's view, centers upon this failure to name fathers as implicated by their daughters.

These daughters, cast by Rush as "middle-class Victorian women," were also predominantly Jewish women. Rush characterizes these women in the same universalizing terms used later by Judith Herman, who calls them "women from prosperous, conventional families" (*Father-Daughter* 9). Yet, as Weinbaum has established, Freud's female patients were almost all Jewish, and antisemitism in Freud's Vienna was pervasive such that he "had difficulty securing an academic position" (146). I return to Weinbaum shortly to demonstrate how the community protective politics of Jewish-authored second-wave feminist texts simplify the complexity of Freud's Jewish milieu, but I want to emphasize that de-Judaizing Freud also featured the de-Judaizing of Freud's patients. Jewish daughters became Victorian daughters.

While Jewishness is absent from discussion of Freud and his patients in "The Freudian Cover-Up," Rush includes a personal anecdote on the article's first page: "I remember that as a child I struggled with a nagging fantasy in which I pleaded desperately with disinterested adults to acknowledge my fears. Considering that I had been told that my tonsillectomy was 'not that bad' or that the dentist whose hands were between my legs was really 'fixing my teeth,' my concern was not unfounded" (31). Rush's personal testimony to abuse at the hands of an authority figure, and the compounding trauma from other adults' refusal to believe her, frame her argument. She revisits this experience in the foreword to *The Best Kept Secret*, but more specific ethnoracial language emerges.

Rush's 1980 book begins with the preface "Growing Up Molested." She reveals that while working as a social worker, she "painfully remembered that I, despite the amenities of a middle-class upbringing, had also been sexually abused as a child" (*Best Kept Secret* x). Rush establishes her familial history in ethnic terms: her "parents left a small town in Czarist Russia to escape my father's imminent conscription into the Russian army and the suffering imposed on their lives by anti-Semitism and poverty" (x). She describes how her parents labored in sweatshops on the Lower East Side, before her father, with the help of relatives and her mother's support, graduated from Brooklyn College and opened up a drugstore. Rush's depiction replicates, almost note for note, an idyllic narrative portrayal of the urban Ashkenazi Jewish immigrant experience.

Rush's narrative choices here are purposeful: by depicting a version of an idyllic home, she forces her reader to grapple with the home's simultaneous existence as a place of sexual vulnerability for children. But Rush roots this contradiction in Jewish terms. She describes Friday nights as "a festive time": "The candles burned for the Sabbath and the dining room table was spread with lace cloth and covered with a variety of cakes, fruits, nuts, wine and tea for guests who customarily dropped in" (x). One guest disturbs the scene: "Among our regular visitors was our family dentist, whom I shall call Dr. Greenberg, and his wife. This couple, along with many others, would share in the warmth and laughter, discussing politics, singing old Russian and Yiddish songs and telling stories" (x). Rush then reveals, with detail, how "Dr. Greenberg" fondled and sexually molested her when she was about seven. And, consistent with the problems of incest testimony that Rush interrogates throughout her book, she reveals how her mother refused to believe her: "I ran home as fast as I could and told my mother everything. Momentarily shaken, she regained composure by reassuring herself that I was lying and had invented the story to avoid the necessary dental work" (xi). Rush indicts her mother's failure to believe her alongside her indictment of "Dr. Greenberg." Rush's choice of milieu and pseudonym anchor her discussion of abuse in specifically Jewish familial and cultural terms.

While this language is far more personal and revealing than the *Chrysalis* article, Susan Brownmiller's memoir provides even more details about Rush's childhood. According to Brownmiller, Rush first remembered her childhood abuse after attending a rape speak-out near the beginning of the women's movement. Brownmiller writes that Rush told her: "I sat there and began remembering that I had been molested as a child. . . . My uncle Willie, our family dentist, the men who exposed themselves in the movie theater, on the subway, in the street" (*In Our Time* 203). Rush makes passing mention of "Uncle Willie" in discussing the consequences children face for speaking out: "She is trapped within a web of adult conjecture . . . while the offender—Uncle Willie, the grocery clerk, the dentist, or her own father—is permitted further to indulge his predilection for little girls" (*Best Kept Secret* 97). The third person and "or" may make these figures seem like representative offenders (excluding the dentist). But Brownmiller makes clear, despite the third person distancing, Uncle Willie was Rush's uncle. Yet unlike in Rush's preface, here, the Jewish home is not associated with sexual abuse.

Rush's text portrays Jewishness as one meaningful cultural construct among many. She portrays child sexual exploitation as universal by discussing various religious and ethnoracial cultural traditions. Chapters include "Greek Love," "A Victorian Childhood," "The Christians," and "The Bible and the Talmud: An Infamous Tradition Begins." Regarding Judaism, Rush mentions the Talmud holding that "a female child of 'three years and one day' could be betrothed by sexual intercourse with her father's permission" (17), and Maimonides approving this in the Mishnah during the twelfth century. She traces rabbinical practice regarding child marriage through to the eighteenth and nineteenth centuries, in the context of European pogroms, and discusses contemporary Israeli state law regarding the age fathers could contract their daughters for marriage.

The chapter on the Bible and Talmud does not discuss incest, but it explores historical contexts that may have contributed to antisemitic discourse stereotypically associating Jews with incest and child sexual violence.[12] A subsequent chapter, "Fathers and Daughters," also interrogates Mosaic and Judaic law and uses biblical stories to contemplate father-daughter incest specifically. Part of the structural accomplishment of Rush's book is its ability to interrogate a set of distinct histories related to sexual exploitation and yet to lean most heavily on those histories associated with "Western" cultures, largely avoiding the result of pathologizing nonwhites. While there is a chapter on child marriage in India, it is just six pages long. In contrast, the sustained attention to Jewishness in the preface, the chapter on the Bible and Talmud, and the chapter on father-daughter incest stands out. Rush made a choice to engage Jewish child sexual exploitation in specific terms, and while she never mentions the taboo or stereotype regarding Jews and incest, or child sexual predation, her text is still unique in not simply disappearing Jewishness into whiteness. The chapter on Freud is the exception. A republication of the *Chrysalis* article, it may signal that while pogroms, Israeli laws, and the Mishnah helped contextualize aspects of how Jewish history intersected with cross-cultural trends in sexual abuse, a Jewish Freud represented the limits of this specification.

This limitation brings us to an intersection between Rush's criticism of "Aetiology" and Weinbaum's invaluable analysis of Freud's racialized, genealogical metaphors in "Aetiology." Weinbaum argues that Freud's use of language and genealogical metaphor in "Aetiology" signals Jewishness by using imagery of a "genealogical tree" to illustrate potentially intertwined branches that would symbolize inbreeding or incest. In writing about the phenomenon of fathers/father figures sexually abusing their children, the tree metaphor connects father-daughter abuse with close lateral (and vertical) endogamies. Freud's mobilization of this metaphor might seem to reify these antisemitic associations, but Weinbaum emphasizes Freud's limited options:

> Although Freud's genealogical metaphors make his conclusions about the sexual nature of hysteria appear inevitable, it is imperative to note that assertion of the "universal validity" of his findings for all the psychoneuroses and all neurotic people would have been viewed as outrageous by the Austro-German medical and scientific establishment. Not only were Freud's findings audaciously sexual, but incest, far from being regarded as a "universal" experience, was within the scientific and medical literature of the period invariably cast as a Jewish racial trait characteristic of a people who were thought to be mired in tribal exclusiveness. (164–165)

As Weinbaum makes clear, "Aetiology" spotlighted Jews and incest not simply because it utilized a genealogical metaphor that connected father-daughter abuse with lateral close endogamies; it spotlighted Jews and incest because it dealt with incest. This alone signaled "Jews."

In Freud's sociohistorical context, the ubiquity of antisemitic associations connecting Jews and incest was unavoidable, and so, in "Aetiology," he utilized that discourse as best he could: "Rather than creating psychoanalysis as a universal science by purging it of Jewishness, Freud incorporated racialized discourse to new ends and built universal claims out of Jewish particularisms" (Weinbaum 168). A variety of this "racialized discourse" also functions, albeit in different ways, in Jewish second-wave feminist texts. By largely eschewing their own Jewishness (with the exception of Rush), stripping Freud of any identification as Jewish, and moving the focus onto Black male "particularisms," Jewish second-wave feminist rhetoric created the conditions not for building universal claims but instead for the systematic displacement of pathology from Jewish men onto Black men.

Rush was an exception to this rule. While other Jewish second-wave feminists tended to minimize or evade entirely the "particularisms" of their Jewish subjective experiences, Rush builds her own Jewish experience into her text. Rush's writing, unlike so many of her peers, helps shoulder the burden of incest stereotype by acknowledging that Jewish men with connections to the Jewish home may engage in sexual exploitation of children. "Uncle Willie" is mentioned only in passing, but *The Best Kept Secret* forces its readers to reckon with "Dr. Greenberg." Still, even Rush omits Freud's Jewishness.

As Weinbaum makes clear, Freud's Jewishness could not have been more central to his subjective navigation and writing regarding the issues of incest, close endogamies, and antisemitic stereotype. Given that "Aetiology" was so saturated with Jewish signifiers, Freud's subsequent abandonment of the "seduction theory" might be read as its own distinctly Jewish community protective move. As Sander Gilman opines, "his abandonment of the trauma theory, in which the reality of incest was the key to understanding specific hysterical symptoms in specific cases, meant that he was able to categorize incest not as a problem of particular people but of human nature in general" (*Freud, Race* 151). By arriving at the Oedipus theory, Freud could alleviate Jewish fathers from the association with incest unavoidably present in "Aetiology." By the time Jewish second-wave feminists criticized Freud's abandonment of the "seduction theory" without acknowledging Freud's Jewishness, they could further alleviate Jewish fathers (and Freud in particular) from an association with incest by shifting that burden to a different group. It is impossible to know how intent functioned in these choices to minimize Freud's Jewishness or displace stigma onto Black men and Black families. However, it seems eminently plausible that, at some level, these Jewish feminists were aware that a more comprehensive linkage of Freud's Jewishness to his rejection of the seduction theory would have been welcomed by antisemites. Considering this phenomenon as one occurring within a community thinking of itself both as white and as Jewish, we can see how Jewish community protective politics operate: an undiscussed anxiety regarding Jewish vulnerability justifies actions that privilege white Jewish interests over Black and nonwhite interests, even as they utilize flawed logic: white Jews' tenuous white privilege, in this equation, must be protected at all costs.

Subconsciously imagined as a zero-sum game, the impulse to retain white privilege accounts for displacing the felt horrors of sexual antisemitism onto a more vulnerable social group. Only the expression of this anxiety may fully facilitate the sort of conversations necessary for coalition building. The irony is that the unexpressed and unarticulable aspects of Jewish incest anxiety contribute to an often-defensive posture that refuses to engage how anti-Black racism, as displacement, emerges as an unintentional by-product of this anxiety.

Juxtaposing Jewish and Black Approaches to Incest in *Chrysalis*

Jewish-authored feminist texts consistently whitened Freud, frequently operated from a rhetorical subjectivity that minimized or made no mention of their Jewishness, and too often pathologized Black male patriarchy while avoiding mention of identifiably Jewish patriarchy. These patterns arise out of inchoate community protective impulses regarding Jewish men, Jewish fathers more precisely, and anxiety regarding the historical antisemitic incest and child sexual predation stereotypes in particular. This surfaces even more visibly when juxtaposed against Black feminist authors' approach to incest: where Jewish second-wave feminists, other than Rush, tended to eschew Jewish particularisms in deference to male-oriented Jewish community protective politics, Black feminist authors addressed Black patriarchy and the incest taboo in culturally specific terms.[13]

This contrast emerges vividly in *Chrysalis*, where Rush first published her criticism of Freud. Rush's article ends on page 45. Audre Lorde's poem "Chain" begins on page 46. Lorde's poem features the following stanza:

> Two girls repeat themselves in my doorway
> their eyes are not stone.
> Their flesh is not wood nor steel
> but I cannot touch them.
> Shall I warn them of night
> or offer them bread
> or a song?
> They are sisters. Their father has known
> them over and over. The twins they carry
> are his. Whose death shall we mourn
> in the forest
> unburied?
> Winter has come and the children are dying. (47)[14]

Lorde's poetry thematically extends Rush's discussion of incest. The poem features no explicit invocation of race. The father and daughters are not racially or culturally specified. The opening words, "Faces surround me that have no smell no colour no time" evoke a universal, timeless setting (Lorde 46).

Given Lorde's status as a renowned Black author, how would this poem have been read vis-à-vis these questions of universality and specificity? Lorde wrote extensively about her subjectivity as a Third World feminist. While both Lorde's poem and Rush's text contain no direct or explicit reference to the authors' ethnoracial identities, Lorde's poem could be categorized into a literary "subgenre" of Black feminist literature dealing with incest.

The extensive, pioneering poem, fiction, and memoir treatment of incest by Black feminist authors serves as a literary counterpart to white (and Jewish) nonfiction approaches. However, Black feminist authors who chose to depict incest in recognizably Black milieus risked what Jewish feminists avoided: direct implications of in-group patriarchal transgression. Black feminist authors portrayed incest despite the risk of reifying associations of incest with Black families. Judith Herman alludes to this problem of associating Black families with incest in *Father-Daughter Incest*: "White people have indulged for too long in discussion about the sexual capacities, behaviors, and misbehaviors of black people. There is no question, however, that incest is a problem in black families, as it is in white families. Many of the first, most daring, and most honest contributions to the public discussion of incest were made by black women, and much of our work has been inspired by theirs" (67). While Herman acknowledges the problem of racist discourse and stereotyping, she praises Black feminist authors as inspirations, naming Maya Angelou, Anne Moody, Toni Morrison, and Gayl Jones in her footnote.[15] However, while these authors address incest in narratives rooted in the simultaneous diversity and specificity of Black American experience, Herman (and, excepting Rush, most other Jewish second-wave feminists) "universalize" their criticism of patriarchy by removing any ethnoracial identifiers other than a white/Black binary.

Contemplating Black and Jewish feminist approaches to incest and patriarchy over the long 1970s illustrates how rhetorical choices shift that burden. Incest scholars Janice Doane and Devon Hodges have observed that American racism and classism set the conditions that "made it easy for the prosperous and white to understand incest as a problem of the poor and black" (31). But within that construct of "prosperous and white" exists a subgroup of American Jews for whom incest had been, historically, a problem associated with them. During this era, white Jewish second-wave feminists rarely wrote about specifically Jewish instances of incest or Jewish patriarchy. By simultaneously writing as "white women" (per Brownmiller), these authors articulated an inchoate, but palpable community protective discourse that shifted the burden of pathologized behavior off of their collective shoulders.[16]

My argument is speculative and certainly does not rule out alternative explanations for why Freud's Jewishness or the authors' Jewishness might be so consistently omitted in these texts. But the notion that Freud's Jewishness was unknown to these authors simply does not seem plausible; these texts are remarkable, thorough, crucial intellectual undertakings. While they are (like all texts) imperfect, the notion that a shared ethnoreligious identity with a central figure of their studies would escape their attention is unlikely.[17] That these authors chose not to mention Freud's Jewishness due to their finding it irrelevant is more likely, but this illuminates how this functioned as an arbitrary, deliberate, disruptive wedge between the notions of personal and political. These community protective politics may also function as a form of assimilation. Not identifying Freud's Jewishness, for fear of reifying an antisemitic stereotype, may be an assimilative statement articulating that Jews are, essentially, no different from other white people. But assimilation is often invoked as suggestive of a minority losing some aspect of its culture in order to blend in. Here, the phenomenon functions less as a loss of cultural identity and more as an active investment in whiteness and anti-Blackness; a melding of white identity with Jewish community identity.

Though Herman appears to acknowledge the problem of Black families bearing the burden of the association with incest, her (and others') choice not to historically contextualize that Jews also bear this burden reveals the problem with this rhetoric: even without intent, and even with earnestly stated concern regarding anti-Black stereotype, it prioritizes the disassociation of Jews from incest over the emulation of the "most daring and most honest" strategies of the Black authors she praises.

Jewish second-wave feminists operated according to Jewish community protective politics in their rhetorical whitening of Freud, which simultaneously protected the image of white Jewish masculinity from the criticisms they lodged against patriarchy. While Freud's iconic status ostensibly played an important role in securing him such treatment, even far less famous Jewish men—like Firestone's father—were omitted from second-wave feminist texts in order to spare Jewish patriarchy from pathologizing. The next chapter focuses on Roseanne Barr's allegations regarding her similarly not famous father, Jerry Barr, and the autobiographical storyline involving Roseanne Conner's abusive father on the initial run of *Roseanne*. While Roseanne Barr's Jewishness is well established, the Conners are almost uniformly described, in cultural criticism and scholarship, as a specifically Midwestern, white working-class, self-consciously "white trash" family. But Jewish community protective politics help explain how the show's incorporation of pseudo-incest storylines, and particularly the sitcom's extended meditation on the fictional Roseanne Conner's abusive father, influenced the show's Jewish content being largely read out of its narrative.

2

Incest, Exogamy, and Jewishness on *Roseanne*

In a segment of CBS's *60 Minutes* that aired April 17, 1994, Morley Safer reported on daytime television's fascination with confessions, recovered memories, and adult allegations of childhood abuse. As Safer put it, "the more bizarre the confession, the more airtime you get." Dr. Elizabeth Loftus, a central figure in the 1990s "memory wars," who consistently challenged the credibility of recovered memories of sexual abuse, framed the issue starkly: "People are remembering sexual abuse in ways that is [*sic*] absolutely impossible; being abused in the womb, being abused in a prior life, being abused by an alien . . . on a UFO" (Safer).[1] Safer also interviewed Roseanne Barr's siblings and her parents, Jerry and Helen Barr, whom she had accused of physical, emotional, and sexual abuse in 1991. Then known as Roseanne Arnold, the actress and comedian disclosed her memories of abuse, and her identification as a survivor, at an incest survivor meeting at a church in Denver, Colorado, and in *People* magazine in October of 1991. Roseanne Barr stated, "My father molested me until I left home at age 17. He constantly put his hands all over me. He forced me to sit on his lap, to cuddle with him, to play with his penis in the bathtub" ("A Star Cries Incest").[2] Describing her difficulty in coming to terms with the trauma, Roseanne Barr wrote, "I clung to my fantasy of our happy, quirky family, a bit off-kilter, but colorful, all-American, Jewish" ("A Star").

The *60 Minutes* interview allowed Jerry and Helen Barr, along with Roseanne's siblings Geraldine, Ben, and Stephanie, to publicly deny these (and other) allegations, as the sitcom *Roseanne* drew to the close of its sixth season. While the denials are forceful, Roseanne Barr's parents and siblings also acknowledge some truths. When Safer brings up Roseanne Barr's daughter's contention that her grandfather molested her at her mother's wedding, Jerry Barr responds in an equivocal fashion: "And then my children asked me, 'Dad, did you pinch her on the tush?' And I said, 'I can't recall,' but knowing me? Probably, probably." Roseanne Barr's sister Geraldine confirms this: "My parents are guilty of being tushy touchers. They are. And that, I believe, is the genesis of a lot of Roseanne's claims. And I think, however, as tushy touchers, the punishment should fit the crime" (Safer).

Geraldine Barr's allusion to punishment fitting the crime is more than idiom. In her second memoir, *My Lives*, Roseanne Barr divulged that her then-husband Tom Arnold "filed police reports in three states" against Jerry Barr based on her daughter's allegations (226). While Jerry Barr was never convicted of any crime, the tabloid and news media fascination surrounding Roseanne Barr's "crying incest" was enough for Safer to describe Jerry and Helen Barr as "the most famous accused molesters in the country." While Safer presents Roseanne Barr's words with skepticism, the Barr family, and Jerry Barr in particular, are treated sympathetically. Yet, as we have established, only a hundred years earlier, antisemitic stereotypes associating Jewish men with incest and sexual predation were prevalent, especially in Europe. The historical context reveals an extraordinary transformation: a white Jewish man like Jerry Barr, historically decidedly vulnerable to these stereotypical associations, in the 1990s appears to benefit from white privilege in the face of such allegations.

This rare televised appearance of Roseanne Barr's parents and siblings frames the ensuing reading of her eponymous television show. This chapter demonstrates how *Roseanne* directly engaged issues of memory, abuse, and incest with the Conners, a working-class white family whose representative qualities invite consideration next to Barr's assessment of her own working-class family as "all-American, Jewish."[3] The show's depictions of the fictional Roseanne and (her sister) Jackie's memories of physical abuse at the hands of their father dovetailed with ongoing media coverage of Barr's actual family allegations, blurring the lines between fiction and autobiographical fiction. While *60 Minutes* cast doubt on Barr's credibility, *Roseanne* presents a complex incest narrative with vertical and lateral components, offering a sophisticated rendering of how abuse (and memories of abuse) could affect siblings in different ways, and portraying the possibilities and limitations of reconciliation. Jewish signifiers and class politics also intersected with the show's consideration of incest. The rare but meaningful depictions of Roseanne Conner's Jewish paternal heritage challenged contemporaneous normative depictions of Jewishness, and Jewish masculinity in particular, by evoking the specter of the pedophilic, incestuous Jewish male. While the Conner family's class status contributed to cultural critics' and scholars' resistance to identifying Roseanne Conner as having Jewish familial heritage, Jewish community protective politics likely also played a role: the show's one recurring Jewish character, Roseanne's father, was a violent and abusive figure implicitly associated with Barr's allegedly sexually abusive father. While Jewish community protective politics are observable in how critics omitted mention of Roseanne's paternal Jewish heritage, the show's writers also used the relationship between pseudo-siblings (and eventual married couple) David Healy and Darlene Conner to displace (lateral) Jewish incest anxiety onto white working-class Americans categorized by the show (affectionately) as "white trash."

While subsequent chapters focus on how these displacements can occur with nonwhite figures, this chapter reveals how Jewish community protective politics contributed to racial formations distinguishing middle-class white Jewishness from a socioracial construct commonly referred to, in contemporary political parlance, as the "white working class." The very fact that Barr has been less commonly considered a Jewish icon than Woody Allen or Henry Roth owes significantly to the sort of myth-building that serves both antisemitic purposes (a preference to imagine Jews as rich and powerful) and community protective ones (a preference within the Jewish community to imagine themselves as economically self-sufficient). The comparative reticence to recognize the Jewish content in *Roseanne* contrasts with exceptionalist tendencies to emphasize the Jewishness of iconic art and artists. But *Roseanne* reveals how constructions of Jewish whiteness inform modern conceptions of whiteness precisely because the show is so rarely seen as meaningfully depicting any representative aspect of Jewishness.

In accounting for *Roseanne*'s depictions of the Conner family's ethnic and religious heritage, I draw attention to specific episodes, while conceding the original nine-year television series' inconsistent approach to continuity.[4] The show featured numerous writers, well-publicized battles regarding creative control, and two actors playing the role of Becky Conner. In a move consistent with the series' humor, the show self-consciously drew attention to this bodily inconsistency.[5] In mining this territory for humor, *Roseanne* draws attention to the limits of the form, confidently invoking its concessions while asserting that Becky (played by Lecy Goranson and Sarah Chalke) always remains Becky. Similarly, my approach to the show's depiction of the Conners' ethnicity proceeds from a commitment to taking the show's fictional world building seriously: where others might see throwaway lines, inconsistent with the broader world of fictional, working-class Lanford, my intent is to examine, first, why we might find these moments "inconsistent" and, second, what they reveal about the world that Barr, along with a large staff of writers, producers, and actors, collaboratively created.

"Can Jews Be Trailer Trash? Apparently So"

Season 6's "I Pray the Lord My Stove to Keep," which aired on May 3, 1994, establishes the Conners' ethnoreligious heritage with specificity but their present identification with ambiguity. DJ, the Conners' then youngest son, rebels by secretly attending church. Roseanne and Dan intervene, and DJ asks a straightforward question:

DJ: What religion are we?

ROSEANNE: I have no idea. Dan?

DAN: Well, my family's Pentecostal on my mom's side, Baptist on my dad's. Your mom's mom was Lutheran, her dad was Jewish.

DJ: So what do we believe?

ROSEANNE: Well, we believe in, uh, being good. So basically, we're good people.

DAN: Yeah, but we're not practicing. ("I Pray the Lord")

This exchange occurred on the first episode of *Roseanne* to air after the *60 Minutes* interview with Barr's parents and siblings, immediately reminding viewers of the fictional Roseanne's Jewish father just weeks after Barr's Jewish father was defended as a "tushy toucher." The episode establishes Dan and Roseanne's parents' religious backgrounds explicitly, poking fun at the vague, not-quite-ecumenical religious world of the show. Roseanne's claim to have "no idea" of her family's religion mirrors what close viewers of the show might have concluded. Despite numerous Christmas-oriented episodes and extensive Christmas decorations, *Roseanne* was largely secular: Christmas, like Halloween and Thanksgiving, emerges as a family holiday, but religion remains peripheral. A Christmas episode dealing with gender wage inequality engaged the holiday in a civic fashion, as Roseanne performs in drag as Santa in order to earn more than playing Mrs. Santa ("Santa Claus"). Furthermore, a menorah appears as part of the Conners' self-consciously tacky Christmas decorations earlier in season 6 ("White Trash Christmas").

In "I Pray the Lord," though, the Conners dodge DJ's question. Roseanne defers to Dan, who cites their parents' religions but avoids identifying *their* religion. And for one grandparent, Dan cites a religion that often doubles as an ethnic identity. The scene establishes Roseanne as a product of intermarriage. She may not identify as Jewish—and to be clear, she never does—but she grew up with a Jewish parent.

In contrast, Roseanne Barr frequently asserts her Jewish identity. Her first memoir declares itself a book "about being Jewish in America" (*My Life as a Woman* xi). She cites the combination of being Jewish and from Salt Lake City in multiple stand-up routines, as early as the late 1980s.[6] Her engagement with Israel has moved from deeply critical to exclusively celebratory over the past decade or so.[7] While her ideology has shifted, her Jewishness has remained a loudly proclaimed piece of her public persona. Each of her three memoirs—*Roseanne: My Life as a Woman* (1989), *My Lives* (1994), and *Roseannearchy* (2011)—mobilizes Jewishness as a significant component of her life narrative. And her assessment of her family as "all-American, Jewish" in *People* aligns Jewish Americanness with normativity. While the religious or ethnic self-identification of the many writers, performers, and creative talents working on the show over its nine seasons is impossible to report, or draw meaningful conclusions from, one writer, Mark Rosewater, claimed that nine of the thirteen writers were Jewish during his tenure (Rosewater). And yet, midway through the first season, Walter Goodman wrote in the *New York Times*, "although Ms. Barr was wont to make quite a megillah in her stand-up routines about being Jewish, that, too, is an unmentionable on the tube." The number of Jewish writers on *Roseanne* was not uncommon for sitcoms generally, but there is a meaningful tension between the number of Jewish creative forces behind the show and assessments, like Goodman's, that explicitly Jewish content would be prohibitive.

All of this is to contextualize my focus on Barr as the central figure behind the show's creative energy, alongside a suggestion that multiple figures involved in the show likely had some investment in the show's depictions of Jewishness, or rather, Jewish heritage/inheritance.[8] However, while the fictional Roseanne Conner's explicit invocation of Jewish familial heritage comes six years in, there were precedents. Season 2 features Roseanne using Yiddish words on three occasions, and while these terms had largely crossed over into "Yinglish" by this time, the circumstance of their usage still merits attention. In the Halloween episode "BOO!" (aired October 31, 1989) she calls Dan a *schmuck* after he deliberately frightens her. She also calls a muscle-bound hunk a *mensch* in a dream sequence on "Sweet Dreams" (aired November 7, 1989), and in that season's first episode ("Inherit the Wind," aired September 12, 1989) corrects her friend Crystal when they discuss an acquaintance, Edna.[9] Crystal knows Roseanne dislikes Edna because she's "a whining, complaining, sniveling kletch." Roseanne (misquoted) corrects Crystal: "*Kvetch*!" Each moment of linguistic "Jewishness" expressed through Yiddish occurs during a private moment: alone with her husband, in a dream sequence, and in a recounted, off-screen conversation. Despite the Roseanne character's bold, public, outspoken persona, Yiddish expression occurs privately. Chronologically, these were the first, seventh, and eighth episodes of the second season; Yiddish on *Roseanne* disappears after "Sweet Dreams."

What do we do with these moments, especially given their apparently haphazard deployment—Yiddish early, a random menorah later on? Rosalin Krieger, discussing the Jewishness of *Seinfeld*, suggests that "Jewish-Yiddish symbols come in the form of historical and cultural references, names, foods, verbal and body language, phenotype, and religious rituals, all of which rely upon individual viewers to identify these clues that represent things Jewish and elements that can be read as possibly Jewish" (388). The menorah in the window in "White Trash Christmas" is as close as we get to religious Judaism—that is, not particularly close. And using three lone Yiddish (or "Yinglish") words cannot and should not be cited as incontrovertible evidence of a speaker's Jewishness. But how does Barr's use of language (verbal and body) contrast with her Jewish and non-Jewish contemporaries vis-à-vis Jewish performance?

A *Saturday Night Live* sketch from February 1992 reveals something of how Barr fit within that prescribed space. Barr and then-husband Tom Arnold hosted, and Barr appeared in the recurring, popular "Coffee Talk" sketch, alongside Madonna and Mike Myers ("Coffee Talk: Barbra Streisand Stops By"). Myers, who based Linda Richman on his Jewish mother-in-law, mixes actual Yiddish with made up words, continuously primping his wig and becoming momentarily overcome with emotion in his drag rendering of a specific form of stereotypical, well-to-do, New York–rooted Jewish femininity (Witchell). Madonna follows suit, while Barr, playing Madonna's character's Jewish mother, visiting from Arizona, occasionally breaks as she struggles with a Yiddish-inflected New York Jewish accent. The choice to make Barr's character from Arizona is itself an interesting reflection of Barr's own southwestern biography. But while Barr is the only Jewish performer in the sketch (prior to a cameo by Barbra Streisand), her performance of Jewishness is far milder than that of her non-Jewish collaborators.

We might infer that Barr made choices as a performer to temper, or counter, expectations regarding "Jewish" performance. This may provide useful context for considering Barr's performative choices on *Roseanne*, and adamant scholarly claims regarding the non-Jewishness of the Conners, despite Barr's Jewish identity. Scholarship on *Roseanne* has tended to foreground the show's Marxist content and feminist politics. However, Joyce Antler, Alessandra Senzani, David Marc, and Kathleen Rowe also mention the significance of Barr's Jewish upbringing. Antler and Marc touch on Barr's Jewishness extensively, making compelling arguments that *Roseanne* subverted antisemitic depictions of Jewish mothers.[10]

However, Antler also claims that "Roseanne Conner had no specific ethnicity and was never portrayed Jewishly" (175). Antler offers this observation directly after alluding to Barr's own contrary reading of her show, as Barr described Roseanne Conner as "actually a Jewish mother" (175). David Marc states, "Roseanne is a Jewish performer who . . . self-consciously constructed an American—as opposed to a Jewish-American—persona" to build a "transdemographic audience" (199). Marc contends that Barr "created not only public masks, but also fictional domestic sitcom milieus that in no way indicated background, culture, or religion," noting that Barr never used "phonetic or phonemic Yiddishisms" (199). Senzani identifies the Conners as a "working-class white family," noting: "There is no other ethnic reference, though it is widely known that Roseanne comes from a poor Jewish family" (237, 248n5). Rowe claims, "*Roseanne* leaves the issues of race, ethnicity, and its own whiteness unexamined," before noting that the show instead "mines the issues of class and gender" (84).

These last two quotes from Senzani and Rowe illuminate one aspect of what may read so convincingly as non-Jewish about the Conners: they were contemporaneously working class. Popular depictions of Jewish American families are largely consistent in depicting white Ashkenazi-descended Jews as middle class or, at the very least, upwardly mobile. The Conners joke about being "white trash" and the harsh reality that their children will not have it as good as they have. These "white trash" riffs echoed jokes about Barr: her husband Tom Arnold (whose Jewish identity also merits extended focus) joked that he and Roseanne were "America's worst nightmare . . . white trash with money" (Elkin 9X).[11]

But the pejorative "white trash," which has its own anti-Black racist undergirding, is not often associated with Jews. As the comedic/exclusionary website *Jew or Not Jew* inquires on its Barr page, "Can Jews be trailer trash? Apparently so" ("Roseanne Barr"). The entry reveals a problematic intersection between Jewish exceptionalism, classism, and assessment of secular Jewish "authenticity." This supposed incongruity, though, finds vivid expression in Barr's stand-up. In her first HBO special, *The Roseanne Barr Show*, Barr leaves the stage to tend to her kids' complaints about their father, played by Tom Arnold. The camera cuts to Barr in a trailer behind the theater, reprimanding Arnold by berating him with Yiddish curses (including an imperative that he should catch the cholera) (*The Roseanne Barr Show*). Years before the *Jew or Not Jew* website's question, Barr's comedy was emphatically challenging the notion of Jewish middle-class normativity. The same stand-up set also explicitly establishes her "domestic Goddess" persona as being part of an intermarried family: "We got like a mixed marriage, me and my husband, on account of like I'm Jewish and he ain't, and everything, so like at the wedding we each tried to please the other person's family, like for my family he crushed a beer can under his heel, and for his family I pretended I was a virgin, so that went really well" (*The Roseanne Barr Show*).

Sut Jhally and Justin Lewis's study of *The Cosby Show* suggests how class might function for white viewers of *Roseanne*. Jhally and Lewis reveal some middle-class white respondents expressing disgust at the Conners' class position, preferring the Huxtables' middle-class milieu. Said one respondent, "I just don't like the way they look" (78). Jhally and Lewis do not account for white ethnicity here, and so this is speculative, but taken alongside the *Jew or Not Jew* website's expression of disdain for Jewish "trailer trash," we might ponder whether Jewish anxiety about class position and perception yields a form of Jewish exceptionalist classism resistant to Barr's attempts to collapse differences between Jews and working-class non-Jewish white people.

None of this suggests working-class secular Jews are absent in Jewish American cultural production. But in the late twentieth century they tend toward existing in a nostalgic past, signifying upward mobility.[12] Consider Woody Allen's *Radio Days* (1987) and Neil Simon's *Brighton Beach Memoirs* (directed by Gene Saks, 1986), films released just prior to *Roseanne*'s run. Though Neil Simon and Woody Allen had notoriously difficult relationships with their parents, the films nostalgically portray sympathetic, working-class fathers. These sensitive, thoughtful souls are nothing at all like Al Harris, Roseanne Conner's fictional father, played by John Randolph.

Born Emanuel Hirsch Cohen, John Randolph made only two appearances on *Roseanne*, though his character (in absence) would dominate an important storyline over several seasons. In his first appearance, Al greets Roseanne affectionately, calling her "kapushka" as he embraces her. The moment seems to immediately announce Al as being, in some fashion, ethnic; *kapushka* is a dialectical variation of the Russian or Polish *babushka*. Though the line is stepped on, he also seems to call Roseanne's sister Jackie "bubela." Roseanne and Jackie happily hug Al here, but later episodes portray their relationship quite differently. They remember the razor strop he kept by the front door, with which he beat them ("This Old House"). They discuss how displaying the strop meant their friends saw it, publicizing their abuse, adding another layer of traumatization. Another episode finds Roseanne spanking and even kicking her son DJ after he steals the family car. In tears, Roseanne apologizes while eating cookies, explaining that her father hit her, but that she would not hit DJ again ("The Driver's Seat"). The distinctive, sobering scene invites the audience to connect abuse with eating habits as an emotional salve—Roseanne eats as she speaks, focusing her eyes on the cookies as much as DJ. Sitcoms commonly feature performative eating, but Roseanne speaks while chewing and the clarity of the dialogue suffers. The scene meaningfully draws attention to the choice to eat cookies while discussing abuse, and in so doing, evokes Judith Herman's work on trauma theory and sexual abuse, which mentions eating disorders as a potential symptom of survivors of sexual abuse (*Trauma and Recovery* 108).[13] But what bears emphasis here is that the show's celebrated critique of patriarchy—which targets male politicians, male bosses, abusive husbands, and corporate entities—also targets Roseanne Conner's Jewish father, Al.

As I demonstrate in chapter 1, the relationship between feminist critique of white patriarchy and white Jewish feminist critique of Jewish male patriarchy is fraught with tension. This may constitute a reason why some viewers read the Conner family as decisively non-Jewish. If discussing a Jewish child abuser as a Jewish child abuser reeks of antisemitism, rhetorically, the community protective impulse demands the figure either not be identified as Jewish, or be innocent. *Roseanne* presented Roseanne and Jackie's remembrance of abuse in sympathetic fashion. As such, ignoring, forgetting, or denying Al's Jewishness emerged as the only viable method of accommodating a protective impulse toward Jewish masculinity. Jewish community politics functioned not to defend Al Harris as innocent, but rather to omit him—functionally, to secularly excommunicate him—from the scholarly and cultural criticism record.

Reading *Roseanne* as unengaged with Jewishness permits celebration of Barr as a Jewish artist without her art being considered at cross-purposes with Jewish community protective politics. Consider Jonathan Freedman's observation regarding how Philip Roth and Tony Kushner challenged sexual antisemitism in their "triumphant transformation of the culturally loaded figure of the Jewish pervert into a culture hero" (6). In *Roseanne*, Barr's eponymous character attains the status of "culture hero," while the one "recurring" Jewish character depicted on her show is the culture hero's physically abusive (and, because of the autobiographical themes, sexually abusive signifying) antagonist. This leaves the audience with the choice of either reconciling the loaded associations with the Jewish assignation or—much easier—choosing to ignore the Jewish component altogether. Withholding Al Harris's Jewish significance equates to removing a nonheroic instance of the problematic "culturally loaded figure of the Jewish pervert."

The obvious danger here is collapsing the fictional world of the show, which chronicled physical violence, but made no mention of sexual abuse, into the real world. But the show always played with the boundaries of real and fiction. Not only did the show playfully draw attention to its two Beckys, it also relied on audience awareness of Barr's love life, which was covered extensively in the tabloids. One post-credit scene features Tom Arnold approaching John Goodman about Dan Conner having kissed Roseanne passionately earlier in the episode ("Less Is More"). The brief sketch requires the audience to know that Barr and Arnold were married and, furthermore, to know something about Arnold's tabloid persona. Otherwise, Arnold's self-deprecating performance (clueless, jealous, powerless, yet convinced of his own importance) would not hit the same comic notes. The fact that *The Roseanne Barr Show* had already established Arnold as a non-Jewish marital foil to the Yiddish-speaking Barr in her HBO stand-up special also suggests that the alluded-to Arnold/Barr romance registered as an intermarriage plot; perhaps one that mirrored the Roseanne Conner/Dan Conner marriage. The autobiographical tensions saturate the show, informing the viewing experience through to the two-part series finale, which revealed the entirety of the series to have been conjured by the fictional Roseanne (Conner), who was writing a book about her family. Some critics expressed ambivalence about the finale, but it functioned as one final expression of the show's meta commentary. The fictional Roseanne explained why she fictionalized aspects of her "real" life (such as swapping her daughter's husbands and portraying her mother as gay when actually her sister was): "As I wrote about my life I relived it, and whatever I didn't like I rearranged" ("Into That Good Night, Part 2"). The fictional Roseanne speaks to her autonomy in utilizing creative license in telling her ostensibly nonfiction story. The rhetorical move also creates space for understanding Barr's assessment of her ownership of the show, despite its collaborative authorship and its fictional construct.

This deliberate mixing of fiction, real life, and metafiction helps account for why Al Harris's stature in the show is so charged. Tabloid and mainstream news coverage of Barr's abuse allegations regarding her father (covered in *TV Guide*, *USA Today*, *60 Minutes*, *Sally Jessy Raphael*, and *People*, among other print and television outlets) was widespread. Undoubtedly, many viewers watched the Al Harris storyline on *Roseanne* knowing that Barr herself alleged that her father had been sexually abusive. And any viewers of the aforementioned *60 Minutes* segment would have been reminded of Al Harris's Jewishness on the subsequent episode of *Roseanne*. Barr herself has indicated how carefully she and the show writers chose what issues would be addressed (Williams 191). Television programming addressing issues of abuse was not unusual at the time.[14] But *Roseanne* moved that conversation to the heart of a highly rated primetime network sitcom. Given the extensive coverage of Barr's sexual abuse allegations by mainstream media, the real-life allegations of sexual abuse very plausibly informed how segments of the audience viewed the Al Harris storyline, especially considering how the show blurred the line separating Barr the actress from Roseanne the character. Some of the textual references to abuse were very general. In the episode where Al dies, Roseanne confronts his mistress, who assumes Roseanne is angry at Al for having cheated on her mother. Roseanne says, "You think this is about the affair? You don't know nothing. You don't know nothing about my childhood. I could tell you stuff about my dad that you couldn't even handle" ("Wait Till Your Father Gets Home").[15] The scene draws attention to what is left unsaid, and like the apology scene with DJ, possesses what Ien Ang calls "emotional realism." Despite the sitcom format, the scene speaks to Roseanne's anger at her father (and those who protect or idealize him). The show's autobiographical elements consistently intersect with what many of Barr's fans would have recognized as an intensely personal matter involving the star's actual life and contested memories.

"Oh, Look, Honey, Our Kids Are Necking"

To fully appreciate the complexity of *Roseanne*'s incest narrative, though, consider that the Al Harris storyline (with its layered depiction of physical abuse, memory, trauma, and extratextual allusions to sexual abuse) represents only one vector of the show's exploration of incestuous themes and their intersection with Jewish stereotypes. The romance between Roseanne and Dan's daughter Darlene Conner and her boyfriend David yielded numerous sibling incest jokes. Season 4 introduces David Healy (played by Johnny Galecki) as Becky's boyfriend Mark's younger brother. Darlene and David begin dating shortly prior to Becky and Mark eloping; when Mark sees David and asks how he is, David replies, "Pretty good, except thanks to you now I'm related to my girlfriend" ("Terms of Estrangement, Part 2"). The Conners invite David to move in with them after Roseanne sees David's mother subject him to emotional abuse. At the episode's conclusion, Darlene and David share an affectionate moment observed by Roseanne, who comments to Dan, "Oh, look, honey, our kids are necking" ("It's a Boy!").

The Conners welcome David into their home in the same season (1992–1993) that Al Harris dies. The humor elicited from the laterally incestuous dynamic of Darlene and David sits against the drama of the vertical (father-daughter) dynamic of the Al Harris storyline. The lack of consanguineous relation between David and Darlene facilitates their pairing (it keeps the incest "pseudo"), but the show establishes David as a son to the Conners independent of his relationship with Darlene. Incorporated as family, David is representative of how *Roseanne* articulated family possibilities involving nontraditional kinship.[16] But while the lateral incest dynamic is positively charged, and the vertical one with Roseanne's father is negatively charged, they are ethnically charged in contrasting ways. Al Harris's Jewishness is established, yet never explicitly centered alongside the negative revelations about his character. David and Darlene's relationship, though, is utilized as fodder for "white trash" jokes.

Nowhere is the intersection of lateral incest and "white trash" identification more explicit than when Darlene announces her pregnancy and intention to marry David. This episode ends with Roseanne soothing a furious Dan, finally making him laugh by declaring: "Check this out. Not only . . . are we going to have a grandchild who is roughly the same age as our own child, but our daughter is marrying the boy we considered to be our son. I think that means we are now officially *the* white-trashiest family in all the land!" ("Another Mouth to Shut Up"). If the Al Harris storyline ran the risk of associating abuse with a Jewish patriarch, especially for the viewers who were aware of Barr's allegations regarding her father, the lateral dynamic between David and Darlene subsumed this tension by explicitly associating incest with a "white trash" ethnic identity. Barr's memoirs, however, reveal a more nuanced and historic conception of lateral incest as having particular resonances in Jewish communities. Regarding her daughter's marriage to a close family friend (not unlike the Darlene/David romance), Barr wrote: "It was a little too European shtetl for my liking, like marrying your cousin or something, as every one of my overly hairy relatives indeed did. My mother's aunt was married to her own uncle (and by the way, I'm my own grandpa!). Two of my sisters are married to a brother and sister, and both of my sisters' last names are Epstein-Barr. You can't make this shit up, folks!" (*Roseannearchy* 161). A parallel emerges: ethnic Jewishness is invoked in Barr's memoir in a similar fashion to how "white trash" identity is invoked on *Roseanne* ("Another Mouth"). Both examples use self-deprecating humor to negotiate close endogamy. While contemporary incest can exist in a purportedly nonethnic, working-class "white trash" household on *Roseanne*, Barr's memoir casts the incestuous undertones of her daughter's relationship as akin to the Jewish past intruding upon the present. But the nostalgia of contemporary economically privileged Jews for a working-class past also features an ambivalence toward the close endogamies that mark that working-class past as pseudo-incestuous.

Taken together, Barr's writing and show speak to a cultural logic that locates white incest as conceivable only in working-class families. As such, the tendency to view the Conners as decisively non-Jewish may hinge not on the separate points of incest and class but on these two points' crucial linkedness. Essentially, white incest finds itself divorced from middle-class normativity, contemporary or otherwise. Kirstine Taylor observes that in the past two decades, following progress for nonwhites in antidiscrimination laws during the 1970s and amid a rise in neoliberal governance, some poor white Americans have chosen to "positively inhabit" a "white trash identity" (74). The Conners reveal a consistently playful attitude toward this identity, but Barr's show also indicates that ethnic Jewish and "white trash" identity could—and did—intersect in meaningful ways. Chronologically, this post–civil rights timeline also overlaps with the eras discussed by those scholars who trace Jews "becoming" white. Regarding the show's incest narrative, one dynamic could hold more "charge" than the other: the "white trash" lateral incest dynamic, which draws attention away from the negatively charged vertical dynamic involving Al Harris, is ethnically reoriented despite striking biographical consistency with Barr's familial close endogamies (both her siblings and children). Meanwhile, Barr's real-life anxiety about close endogamy seems eclipsed by David and Darlene's almost uncomfortably saccharine wedding vows, in which Darlene states that the "best way we can make it" is to "rely on each other the way *our* parents, Dan and Roseanne Conner, have" ("Another Mouth"; my emphasis). Not only do they marry to begin their own family, their vows reveal a continued effort to normalize the nontraditional family that took in David as an authentic sibling. The resultant wedding vows, in which a bride and groom discuss their affection for "our" parents, is not played for comic effect at all, but rather is presented as a deeply touching tribute from sibling lovers to their parents.

None of this works out well for Dan, who has a heart attack at the wedding. Here, lateral incest anxiety explodes into the storyline. The idea of a daughter's marriage resulting in the symbolic (or literal) replacement of a father reads as deeply Freudian, but this narrative arc merits consideration alongside Juliet Mitchell's *Siblings*, which helps to re-center the lateral dynamics of the incest taboo. Mitchell's theory counters generations of psychoanalytic and Freudian theory that have reinforced the incest taboo as being vertically enforced by parents. If, as Mitchell argues, siblings themselves enforce the incest taboo in order to maintain societal conventions and preserve family connections, the David/Darlene/Dan dynamic takes on added nuance. Darlene and David's marriage reveals a defiant rejection of the notion that siblings themselves enforce the incest taboo, as only Dan seems especially troubled by the marriage (albeit, more for the opportunities it may foreclose for Darlene than for her marrying a brother figure). Sure enough, seeing his daughter and son wed gives Dan a heart attack, and he collapses at the reception. But while the subsequent episodes show his convalescence, the series finale, revealing the entire series to have been written by the fictional Roseanne, asserts that Dan's survival was merely a fictional departure from the "real," to help Roseanne process her grief at Dan's death. Barr commented that this controversial narrative mechanism provided "another dimension, another layer, when you watched the entire thing again" ("Season 9: Breaking the Sitcom Mold"). Dan's death does help account for various ninth season plotlines, where Roseanne's processing of grief through writing accounts for the series' simultaneous and sudden incorporation of extreme escapism alongside melodrama.

However, the notion of a wedding killing or replacing a father is not, by itself, an especially unique narrative. Any marriage, accompanied by a Freudian reading, features a daughter replacing a father with a substitute. Instead, it is the subsequent pregnancy scare, alongside the specter of Dan's death/nondeath, according to the season's narrative conceit, that fixes the link between vertical and lateral incest. First, the marriage of David and Darlene simultaneously kills and does not kill Dan, a paradoxical result achieved by waiting until the last episode to revise the show's history. Second, the sibling agency (and failure to enforce the incest taboo) that might appear as the narrative reason for Dan's death upon the initial viewing is superseded by Roseanne's creative choice to keep Dan alive. Thus, female creative agency establishes whether the incest taboo does or does not result in the death of the father. Especially given the history of silencing surrounding women's storytelling regarding incest, the ninth season's narrative conceit of Roseanne's writing/rewriting of two divergent autobiographical stories seems especially subversive and a provocative challenge to the "truth/lie" binary that limits most incest discussions.

Third, and most important, the indeterminacy of Dan's survival is mirrored by the indeterminacy of David and Darlene's daughter's survival. Indeed, Harris Conner Healy's premature birth intimates that lateral incest is vertically destructive in both directions. *Roseanne*'s depiction of Harris's premature birth and a tearful scene in which Darlene and David wonder what they might have done to "deserve" a prematurely born, near-death infant resonate with narrative conventions regarding the genetic risks of lateral incest. Darlene and David's lack of a consanguineous relationship allows for their pseudo-incestuous bond to be positively charged, but the transgression undergirding that union yields the precise consequence literature so often associates with consanguineous sibling relations (and Jewish ones in particular).[17]

In contemplating *Roseanne*'s thematic approach to vertical and lateral incest, considering the show's audiences along ethnoreligious lines might seem viable. But attempting to delineate *Roseanne*'s Jewish audience from its non-Jewish audience overlooks the show's own rejection of such easy distinctions. Freedman's compelling argument that Jewish American cultural production reflects a "syncretic, hybridizing engagement with a national culture in ways that transform both their own identity and experience and that of the culture at large" seems especially relevant regarding the liminal Jewish space carved out on *Roseanne* (38). The show provides its own critique of even mild essentialism, as Roseanne herself and her family emerge at the center of the liminal space that is often disallowed in conversations of what is or is not Jewish. By crafting a fictional reality that commits to incorporating an only hinted-at Jewish familial history without ever championing Jewish identification, Barr's show speaks most directly to a liminal audience—crucially, a liminal audience that would be defined as decisively not Jewish according to Jewish institutions that privilege matrilineal descent. On *Roseanne*, the Conners function as a family with a history of Jewish intermarriage that expresses ambivalence about their religious and/or ethnic categorization. Yet that very same family emerges as the epitome of "white" in the popular and the scholarly record. Barr's observation that she considered Roseanne Conner to be "actually a Jewish mother" has been taken as ironic or metaphorical, despite the text suggesting that it might have been meant quite literally (Antler 175). Ralph Ellison's paint factory in *Invisible Man*, in which one drop of black paint creates the whitest white, may be instructive here. *Roseanne*'s achievement is depicting a world where the whitest white working-class family has a Jewish father/grandfather. Borrowing from Ellison's critical eye, we might consider that Al Harris's Jewishness is structural, and not incidental, to the Conner family's undeniable whiteness. This is not to suggest that the liminal Jewish content of *Roseanne* supersedes its unambiguous Marxist content, but rather to surmise that some evidence of Jewish identity can exist within this artistic depiction of a purportedly prototypical white working-class family, as long as it accedes to particular cultural logics. But while scholarship has flattened the Conner family's ethnicity into a non-Jewish, nondescript whiteness, not all viewers missed the cues.

A 2006 online fan-fiction piece entitled "Lanford Days Again," by an author using the screen name "CNJ," picks up eight years after the end of the series. The story reveals Jackie still dealing with the trauma of her father's abuse, but situates those memories alongside Nana Mary, Jackie and Roseanne's maternal grandmother, discussing family history over photos of long-dead relatives. About a great-aunt Annika, Nana Mary says, "Their father was killed in the pogroms raging through Eastern Europe then. I remember her telling me about this when I was little" (CNJ). The story ends with Nana Mary's "mostly . . . secular funeral," presided over by a rabbi. In incorporating fan fiction to this analysis, I mean to show how some viewers contemplated the Conners' Jewishness in complex ways invited by the show, despite consistent scholarly assessments of the Conners as decisively "not Jewish." Indeed, a fan-fiction author reading Jewishness into the Harris family background is not altogether surprising, as *Roseanne* explicitly marks Al Harris as Jewish and features the aforementioned signifiers of some Jewish heritage. But Nana Mary is not Al Harris's mother; she is Roseanne's maternal grandmother.

As such, CNJ reads, and subsequently writes, Jewish history into Roseanne's Lutheran mother's genealogy, opening up an entire subtext regarding Jewish conversion, passing, and assimilation. In this respect, CNJ does not seem to be merely "racebending" here, though racebending is characteristic of fan fiction. The choice seems less about departing from the text and more about reading deeply into it. CNJ's choice to make Nana Mary Jewish concretizes Barr's own allusions to the character, as she described Shelley Winters's performance of Nana Mary as representative of one of her Jewish grandmothers, Bobbe Mary, whom she discusses extensively in her memoirs. Winters (who was Jewish) delivered "a good representation of my actual grandmother whose name was Mary. She was very much like that. All the women of that generation who were Jewish from Russia and Europe were kind of like that too" (video commentary on "Thanksgiving 1991"). Barr's commentary here speaks to a simultaneous specification and universalization of the Nana Mary/Bobbe Mary "type"; she pronounces her recognizably Jewish on a show that also presented her as simultaneously recognizably "white trash," clad in trucker hat, sipping hard alcohol. The politics of Jewish representation on *Roseanne* speaks to the flexibility with which some audiences could view the same characters as distinctly representative of some version of non-Jewish "whiteness," even as the other viewers saw a much more complex picture. Reading Nana Mary as

Jewish, and thus her daughter Bev as converted (or as a closet Jew), reveals *Roseanne's* textual receptivity to nuanced analyses of its depiction of whiteness.

Uncle Sol and a New Jerry

Season 8's "The Last Date" speaks obliquely to the charged nature of Al Harris's Jewish patriarchal character through its deployment of Shecky Greene, the Jewish stand-up comedian, as a far more *heimish*, avuncular, Jewish paterfamilias. Yet the episode, which features Roseanne and Dan crashing a bar mitzvah on their final date prior to the arrival of their youngest child, also portrays Dan and Roseanne's encounter with the Jews at the bar mitzvah as so detached and othering as to strain credulity that Roseanne grew up with a Jewish father, or that Dan might have two seasons earlier matter-of-factly disclosed to DJ that his grandfather was Jewish. Ultimately, "Uncle Sol," played by Greene, confronts Roseanne and Dan for having crashed the event. Roseanne protests his outing them as outsiders, asserting, "I know what all this is about. It's because I married a gentile, isn't it?" ("The Last Date").

The line draws attention to Barr's real-life intermarriages, while also remaining true (even in its jest) to the fictional reality of Lanford. Roseanne's identification of Dan as gentile is, ostensibly, funny because it articulates her own in-group membership. But she is not Jewish—except she maybe kind of is? The joke either goes over the audience's heads, or perhaps asks too much of them in terms of making sense of exactly how Roseanne (and Barr) function vis-à-vis the Jewish community. It is the rare sitcom moment where a clear punchline yields no audible laughter. Uncle Sol, however, does not banish them upon learning they are crashing the affair. Instead, he provides sage wisdom and encouragement, alleviating their concerns about once again becoming parents. While Al Harris's fatherly parental authority vanishes in Roseanne and Jackie's memory of his physical abuse, Uncle Sol serves as an idealized, decisively Jewish paternal presence. The episode's mobilization of Jewish stereotypes (the bar mitzvah attendees are depicted as gossips, *fressers*, lawyers, and doctors) ends with Uncle Sol's positioning as a viable, charitable male patriarch—a sort of father-knows-best type—the very archetype the show otherwise deconstructs as sitcom mythology. Read through this lens, the episode may be the most anticanonical in the series run and perhaps reveals something of Barr's (and the show's) anxiety and ambivalence about the show's sustained criticism of patriarchy. Though Al Harris never finds redemption on the show, the figure of the Jewish patriarch does; Uncle Sol, more than any other male figure on the show, is given the authority to bless Roseanne and Dan's pseudo-intermarriage and procreation, even within an episode emphasizing Roseanne and Dan's outsiderness to Jewish traditions. This episode reads very differently if considered outside of a project so attentive to depictions of Jewishness across the show's nine-year duration, and I concede some of its mobilization of Jewish stereotype is quite problematic. But if we consider how Jewish community protective politics played a role in how *Roseanne*'s critique of patriarchy read when it involved Roseanne's Jewish father, we can see how "The Last Date" cedes patriarchal Jewish authority back to Uncle Sol. While this occurs within a cartoonish Jewish space (the over-the-top bar mitzvah party) that emphasizes Roseanne and Dan's unbelonging, it also provides a uniformly positive depiction of Jewish patriarchy, contrasting sharply with the memory of Al Harris.

Though Al Harris never finds redemption on the show, Roseanne finds some muted resolution in confronting him after he dies, giving a speech to his coffin-interred body. Roseanne's last words to him, "I-love-you-goodbye," are muttered quickly as she leaves the room in the funeral parlor ("Wait Till"). Even as she attempts closure, there is ambivalence. But the fictionalized lack of resolution, and heartache, dramatized in the episode pale next to what Barr has said and written, since *Roseanne* first went off the air, regarding her real-life allegations. In a 2000 interview, Barr reflected on her choice to publicly air her allegations, as well as her status as an inspirational figure for having done so: "'It's been 10 years since I spoke to my family. They're not willing to.' Her voice drops and there's a long pause. 'Now I do regret it, yeah. I get letters from people saying: "When you did it, it gave me courage." But I was just thinking about this yesterday, the price that I had to pay is too high. I go back and forth'" (Bradberry). After attributing her decision to go public in 1991 to Tom Arnold's pressure, Barr goes even further, offering the following advice to abused children: "I wouldn't urge any kid to tell. I'd tell 'em not to. I really thought about that a lot. But, knowing what happens, I think the best you can do is grow up and deal with it. Grow up, go to therapy and deal with it" (Bradberry).

In 2011, in her most recent memoir, *Roseannearchy*, Barr again addressed her allegations, and her thoughts regarding them two decades later: "The word *incest* conjures ideas of sex, but there was never any sex between my father and me. There was violence, humiliation, inappropriate words, 'jokes,' and rather grotesque displays that never should have occurred between a father and his daughter, but there was no actual *sex*" (217). She even addresses her parents having passed a lie detector test, stating: "Of course, they passed a polygraph test, proving there was no 'incest.' I still wonder what word would have been better to use. It doesn't seem that there is one that conveys the feelings I had as a young girl in a family that didn't really value women's needs, privacy, shame, or pride" (Barr, *Roseannearchy* 217).

On the talk-show circuit, promoting the book, Barr and Oprah Winfrey had the following exchange:

> "I think it's the worst thing I've ever done," Roseanne told Oprah. "It's the biggest mistake that I've ever made."

> "Calling it incest? Or going public?" Oprah asked.
>
> "Well, both of those things," Roseanne said. "I think what happened was that—well, I know what happened was that I was in a very unhappy relationship. I was prescribed numerous psychiatric drugs. Incredible mixtures of psychiatric drugs to deal with the fact that I had, and still in some ways, have and always will have some mental illness. And the drugs and the combination of drugs that I was given, which were some strong, strong drugs, I totally lost touch with reality in a big, big way." ("Roseanne Reveals New Reality Show")

Here, too, Barr alludes to her relationship with Arnold, while also candidly revealing her battles with mental illness. But the question she arrives at in her memoir merits consideration: what word would have been better than "incest"? The years between Barr's initial allegations and her more recent recantation of their public nature and wording, but not content, featured an even higher profile examination of sexual semantics regarding the word "is," and Bill Clinton's testimony regarding whether oral sex was, or was not, sex. Indeed, Barr's apology is difficult to read; her assessment of having "lost touch with reality" in the Winfrey interview seems to invite complete discrediting. The extent to which these nuanced, regretful meditations were simplified and packaged as clickbait (one article was titled "Roseanne Reveals New Reality Show; Apologizes for 1991 'Incest' Claim") speaks to the continued political relevance of the two-decades-old "memory wars" and the societal predisposition to simplify incest narratives into "truth/lie" propositions. Most disturbing is Barr's frank suggestion that abused children "shouldn't tell." Barr's political transformation from staunch feminist star of a recognizably Marxist television sitcom to hero of the alt-right, Trump supporter, and frequent and viral tweeter and retweeter of racist and Islamophobic content has confused and upset many of her fans. We might consider this political transformation alongside Barr's declaration that speaking out about her experience of abuse was a mistake. I am cautious of being overly determinative, but if Barr believes, at some level, that speaking out against patriarchy cost her a relationship with her father, and that she bears the blame for this, this identification with an aggressor might contextualize her embrace of Donald Trump, despite the many women who have spoken out against him regarding sexual assault (and his own tape-recorded admission) ("Transcript").

On April 18, 2001, the *National Enquirer*, a tabloid Roseanne Conner jokingly referred to as the newspaper "of record," reported on Jerry Barr's death of a heart attack, while noting "his heart was broken years ago when his superstar daughter publicly accused him of molesting her" ("Roseanne's Dad Dies with a Broken Heart"). The article focuses on Barr and her father's failure to reconcile, but an accompanying feature, a "Fast Fact," reads as follows:

"Roseanne's dad, who was Jewish, once sold crucifixes door-to-door" ("Roseanne's Dad Dies"). The sentence is alarmingly dense with subtext regarding the Barr family, the question of their ethnoreligious identity, and their liminal status as Jews. Separated from an "obituary" that only addresses allegations of molestation (avoiding the word "incest"), the "Fast Fact" simultaneously assigns and qualifies Jerry Barr's authentic Jewish identity.

While Jerry Barr and his daughter never reconciled, Roseanne gave birth to Jerry Garcia Conner, named after the lead singer of the *Grateful Dead*, during *Roseanne*'s eighth season. That episode aired directly after Uncle Sol's, and found Roseanne bequeathing her fictional son with the very same first name as Barr's father. The choice to name Roseanne's son Jerry suggests the possibility of integrating flawed father figures back into the family—even if only symbolically. The show's ambivalence regarding closure remains consistent on a thematic and episodic level throughout: problems are not generally solved; they are just replaced by new ones. But in this context, Jerry Garcia Conner seems especially significant, and perhaps radical, in his symbolic importance to generations-long disputes regarding the plausibility and denial of paternal sexual abuse. Despite Barr's public campaign to draw attention to her memories of her father's problematic behaviors and their subsequent estrangement, she seems to have chosen to honor him, however obliquely, toward the end of her show's original run.

Much work remains to be done regarding Barr, *Roseanne*, and the politics of the artist and her eponymous show, particularly given her contemporary "second act" as a reactionary supporter of white nationalist politics. But our understanding of her first act requires some recentering of how aspects of Barr's incest narrative intersected with her iconic television show's navigation of the specter of Jewish incest, and how Jewish community protective politics contributed to the show simultaneously shedding association with Jewishness in the popular and critical imaginary due to Al Harris (and Jerry Barr). Despite his being a fictional character, this forgetting of Al Harris functions like a covert excommunication. A Jewish man is removed from the record discreetly, as opposed to declaratively, but it is a removal, all the same. Significantly, this Jewish community protective phenomenon occurred alongside the development of one of the most iconic and resonant incarnations of the white working class (the Conners) in popular culture.

These first two chapters have showcased how Jewish community protective politics can de-Judaize Jewish men credibly accused of incest-associated behavior, whether iconic historical figures, like Freud, or fictional supporting characters, like Al Harris. The subsequent three chapters focus on scenarios where iconic Jewish artists defiantly celebrated their incest narratives in film and literature. Barr's negotiation of race and incest involved the space between white

Jewishness and the purportedly non-Jewish white working class, but Woody Allen's incest narrative required a more complex negotiation of Asian, white, Catholic, and Jewish identity. Furthermore, where Barr's narrative shows the formidable resistance a Jewish woman faced in discussing and artistically depicting an abusive Jewish father, Allen's incest narrative reveals how much more power and success he had, as a white male Jewish artist and icon, in framing his story to elicit sympathy from his audience.

3

Woody, Wood Yi, and Communion Wafers

Ethnoracial Signifying in the Woody Allen Incest Narrative

While the Woody Allen incest narrative began in the 1990s, it re-emerged in February 2014, when Dylan Farrow, writing under a name that she had not used for years, published an open letter in the *New York Times* detailing two-decades-old allegations regarding sexual abuse by her father. Farrow began by inquiring, "What is your favorite Woody Allen movie," implicating her audience's affinity for her father's art prior to revealing her fraught relationship to his ubiquitous image: "Each time I saw my abuser's face—on a poster, on a t-shirt, on television—I could only hide my panic until I found a place to be alone and fall apart" ("An Open Letter"). Dylan Farrow also made mention of her estranged sister Soon-Yi Previn to whom Allen has long been married (making Allen both Farrow's estranged father, as well as her estranged brother-in-law): "I didn't know that my father would use his sexual relationship with my sister to cover up the abuse he inflicted on me" ("Open Letter").

In this chapter, I demonstrate how Allen, in interviews, press releases, and press conferences, appealed to Jewish community protective politics to cast his Jewish masculinity as sympathetic and vulnerable after Dylan Farrow accused him of sexual molestation. I also explore how even as Allen intimated that he was a victim of an antisemitic smear campaign, he also defiantly asserted his relationship with Soon-Yi Previn as a positive and celebratory development.

Allen successfully weaponized Jewish community protective politics by intimating that his white Jewishness necessarily made him sympathetic and vulnerable in the context of a white Catholic daughter figure, even as that very same white Jewishness privileged his subjective categorization of grooming behavior as "love" in the context of a nonwhite daughter figure.

I begin this chapter with Dylan Farrow's words partly to draw attention to her provocative contention that Allen used his relationship with Previn as a "cover-up" for the sexual abuse she alleges he inflicted on her. Dylan Farrow's words may refer to how media coverage of Allen's affair with Previn displaced coverage of her serious allegations. But the idea of a "cover-up" may also refer to Allen's willingness to publicly assert and counterintuitively celebrate one form of incestuous behavior implicitly functioning as evidence that he must not have committed any other form of incestuous behavior. While this chapter considers how Allen's words and aesthetic influenced news coverage (and comedic commentary) on the incest narrative involving Dylan Farrow and Previn, it also considers how other figures, like Mia Farrow, attempted to tell that story. But beginning with Dylan Farrow's words also signals the importance of Allen scholarship attending to her words, allegations, and presence; a presence that has largely gone unmentioned, or has been alluded to only in passing or in footnotes.

This chapter's primary focus involves how Allen told this story, and exerted influence on how others told it, in nonfictional contexts. But it also considers how Mia Farrow told the story, the implications of popular comedic depictions on *The Howard Stern Show* and *The Ben Stiller Show*, and how race, religion, and racism informed all of these attempts at telling. By unpacking how Allen set the terms for discussing Dylan Farrow's allegations in ways that emphasized his Jewish vulnerability, we can see how his discussions of Previn implicitly stressed his white male privilege in diametrically different ways. Allen used dog whistles to intimate that Mia Farrow and Connecticut law enforcement were antisemitic, preemptively undercutting Farrow's attempt to tell her story in terms of her re-emergent Catholic faith by stressing communal white Jewish vulnerability. Simultaneously, media depictions of Soon-Yi Previn consistently depicted her in overtly sexual and racist ways that normalized Allen's presentation of her as an object of affection, preventing more sustained discussions of how the Allen/Previn dynamic may have reflected predatory grooming. Comedic commentary that readily employed racist and sexualizing humor in portraying Previn also often transmogrified Previn in ways that signified Dylan Farrow, intimating her unspeakable presence as a seven-year-old white girl who had alleged a Jewish man of sexual abuse. To better understand how Allen influenced this media coverage, and the challenges for other parties depicting him, we need to first acknowledge the enormous influence of the Woody Allen persona, a dominant pop cultural iteration of white Jewish masculinity for going on four decades when Dylan Farrow's allegations were made public.

Allan Konigsberg and the Woody Allen Persona

Allen's effective negotiation of early 1990s media reporting makes sense given his decades-long success at crafting an influential and iconic filmic persona. Woody Allen was not born Woody Allen. Allan Konigsberg legally changed his name to "Heywood Allen" at sixteen (Lax 9). From an early age, Allen legally inhabited the role that he first developed as a stage name. Today, "Woody Allen" refers to both the individual as well as the carefully honed comedic and filmic persona that has appeared in over forty movies and countless stand-up routines. From its inception, Allen's early stand-up persona was "an 'exaggerated version' of Allan Konigsberg, one that blurred the line between autobiography and comedy" (Meade 54).[1] Allen himself downplayed his agency creating the persona, stating, "Gradually, the character evolved. . . . It didn't evolve deliberately. I just wrote stuff that seemed funny. But the character was assigned to me by the audience" (Meade 54). Allen's creation myth simultaneously downplays his agency in crafting such an iconic persona and reinforces the ambivalence consistent in the characters he portrays. And yet, as a filmmaker and artist, Allen is famously precise with his authorial choices.

This tension plays out as an ethnoracially significant contradiction: Allen decisively and precisely performs of a version of Jewish masculinity that consistently articulates its lack of agency. This aspect of the persona—the illusory, overstated lack of agency in a supremely successful and precise performer—may account for much of Allen's star appeal.[2] Since *What's New Pussycat* (1965), the Allen film persona has broadcast to millions of viewers a depiction of whiteness, Jewishness, palpable (hetero)sexuality, cosmopolitanism, and middle-/upper-middle-class normativity. Allen's persona was that of an everyman, but a distinctly Jewish one; often characterized as a schlemiel or nebbish. The persona's appeal emerges from its nonthreatening relatability. As John Baxter related in his biography, a French cabdriver characterized his affinity for Allen to a female journalist thusly: "Well . . . look at him, madame. He's short. He's bald. He's ugly. He can't get laid. He's just like me" (30).

Except Allen's filmic protagonists have a lot of sex. The cabdriver suggests that Allen's appeal involves his everyman qualities, but this is another paradoxical aspect of the persona's appeal. The Allen persona presents itself as incapable of attracting women despite countless successful seductions.[3] Allen's persona, however recognizably Jewish, carries appeal across race and nation, speaking to audience desires for alternative masculine archetypes. Allen's cultural impact involves successfully rendering the sexually potent schlemiel as recognizable everyman for non-Jewish audiences.

The Allen persona is also defined by its aspiration to ethics. While Allen's protagonists often sexually transgress, most commonly through cheating on a partner, Allen's early films were known for their protagonists' pronounced superegos. Paula Span notes that "the nebbishy Woody character often agonizes over moral choices, considers good and evil, reflects on life's meaning. He's the stubborn ethicist." Span wrote these words for the *Washington Post* while covering the Allen/Farrow custody trial, and this is characteristic of post-1991 commentary that attempted to discern the man from the persona. However, scholars have widely approached Allen's films with the notion of the actor/director and the protagonists he plays as ethicists. Early in Allen's career, some critics called attention to misogyny in his work (such as Vivian Gornick in her 1976 *Village Voice* article, "Face It, Woody Allen, You're Not a Schlep Anymore"), but Allen's films are widely celebrated by academia for their humor, technical merit, style, and sophisticated engagement with moral questions.[4]

Allen's films engage these moral questions through their mobilization of the schlemiel, a ubiquitous figure dating back to the advent of Yiddish literature.[5] Theorist Menachem Feuer has distinguished between Allen's early and later film iterations of the schlemiel, while reaffirming that "The schlemiel, as is well known, is Woody Allen's staple character" (81). Allen's ubiquity in films and popular culture over decades has made the Woody Allen persona contemporarily almost as archetypal as the historical schlemiel of Yiddish literature. Diane Tobin has even labeled the inability of many Americans, Jewish or otherwise, to fully grasp the intersections of diversity, race, and Judaism as "Woody Allen Syndrome." For Tobin, Allen's ubiquity as a signifier for Jewishness obscures the existence of nonwhite Jews. We might extend this further: Allen's filmic persona normalizes Jews not merely as white but also as male, well-off, heterosexual, urban, neurotic, and secular. Allen signifies "Jewish," but in so doing, signifies (and normalizes) a very limited cross section of contemporary Jewishness. Allen's success signifying a specific form of Jewishness makes the relationship between the Allen persona and Jewish masculinity something of a two-way street. If the Allen persona stands in for a version of Jewish masculine identity, allegations against Allen negatively reflect upon the (limited) conception of Jewish masculinity in popular media. In this regard, Allen's ability to weaponize Jewish community protective politics involves the success he had making his own personal brand synonymous, for many audience members (Jewish and otherwise), with a popular and sympathetic conception of Jewish masculinity.

The Allen persona, as with all schlemiel performances, suggests a comparative powerlessness at the hands of society, police, the state, and, of course, his wife or partner. As such, Allen's attempts to frame Dylan Farrow's allegations as Mia Farrow's and his insinuations that he was unfairly targeted by state authorities in Connecticut were structurally consistent with culturally specific depictions of Jewish male vulnerability and powerlessness. In order to further distance himself from the allegations that he actually operated from a position of patriarchal power and white privilege in a destructive or sexually abusive fashion, Allen drew attention to Mia Farrow's Catholicism and to the state of Connecticut as a site of antisemitic persecution.

Press Releases, Timelines, and Sourcing Allegations

While previous chapters have demonstrated how Jewish community protective politics are mobilized out of a positively valenced effort to protect the image of some external vulnerable Jewish masculinity (a specific father, father figure, or image), Allen employed Jewish community protective politics for his own self-interest. As early as his press conference on August 18, 1992, Allen intimated that Mia Farrow, and not Dylan Farrow, was the true source of the allegations of sexual abuse (Barron). Treating Dylan Farrow's allegations as if they were actually Mia Farrow's facilitated Allen eventually implying that Mia Farrow's ulterior motives involved antisemitism, while simultaneously casting both himself and Dylan Farrow as victims of an antisemitic plot. Allen also intimated that Connecticut law enforcement officials were motivated by antisemitism, but Allen never explicitly said the word "antisemitism" nor that he was targeted as a Jew. Instead, Allen utilized dog whistles, playing up Mia Farrow's Catholic identity in unflattering terms, a strategy that effectively countered her attempts to narrate her experience of her family's dissolution in her own faith-based terms. In short, Allen employed Jewish community protective politics to effectively recast a story about allegations of his predatory behavior into one that exploited historical anxieties regarding communal threats of antisemitism.

A brief timeline of relevant dates helps clarify certain events that led up to the initial public coverage of Dylan Farrow's allegations. Mia Farrow adopted Dylan Farrow in the summer of 1985 (Meade 176). While Allen was not yet Dylan Farrow's adoptive father, and they did not cohabitate, Allen played an active role in Dylan Farrow's life. In 1990, Allen began working with the therapist Dr. Susan Coates to modify behavior that concerned Mia Farrow (including "putting his face in Dylan's lap, encouraging her to suck his thumb, and constant caressing") (Meade 199). Allen "reportedly improved in these areas" after multiple sessions (Meade 199). On December 17, 1991, Allen, with Mia Farrow's support, legally adopted her adoptive children Dylan and Moses (Meade 200). Just weeks later, on January 13, 1992, Mia Farrow found nude Polaroids Allen had taken of Soon-Yi Previn. That same day, Allen and Previn admitted to their affair (Meade 16, 216). Mia Farrow and Allen did not immediately separate; both indicated to each other, at times, an interest in trying to salvage the relationship. On August 5, 1992, Casey Pascal, a friend of Mia Farrow's, informed her that Pascal's baby-sitter recounted witnessing Allen engage in "disturbing" behavior with Dylan Farrow in the Farrows' Connecticut home on August 4, sitting with his head, face-first, in her lap (Meade 225, 227). Also on August 5, Dylan Farrow told her mother that Allen touched her "privates" (227). Mia brought Dylan to her pediatrician, where Dylan refused to repeat her allegation, later telling Mia that she was embarrassed (227). The following day, they returned to the doctor, where Dylan Farrow stated her allegation; the doctor informed Mia Farrow he had to contact the authorities (227). On August 13, Allen filed suit for sole custody of Dylan along with Moses and Satchel (230). On August 17, Connecticut police confirmed to the press that they were investigating allegations of child abuse involving Allen; the very same day, Allen issued a press release affirming his relationship with Previn, "never making reference to the double police investigations in Connecticut and New York" involving Dylan Farrow (232). On August 18 Allen held a press conference denying Dylan Farrow's allegations, suggesting instead they were "a currently popular though heinous card played in all too many child custody cases" (232).

The events of August 17 and August 18 are worth emphasizing: on August 17, the same day that Connecticut authorities publicly confirmed that they were investigating Dylan Farrow's allegations, Allen issued a press release in which he declared his love for Previn: "Regarding my love for Soon-Yi: It's real and happily all true. She's a lovely, intelligent, sensitive woman who has and continues to turn my life around in a wonderfully positive way" (Weber). Allen's invocation of his love for Previn had a profound impact on subsequent media coverage. A story that would otherwise have centered upon the alleged abuse of a seven-year-old white girl transformed, overnight, into one where Allen confidently admitted to a different seeming sexual transgression, albeit one that most commentators considered less severe. The following day, various news reports commented not just on the Connecticut legal investigations regarding Dylan Farrow, but about Allen's celebratory declaration of love for Previn.

As such, Allen's initial denial of Dylan Farrow's allegations, on August 18, consisted of his second press release in as many days. The first release only touched on Previn. By commenting on the Previn rumors a day before addressing Dylan Farrow's allegations, Allen manipulated the timeline of how audiences encountered the narrative. When Allen's second statement cast Mia Farrow as "vindictive," and Dylan Farrow's allegations as "instigated by her," he did so after imposing his own timeline suggesting a "cause and effect" between the Previn affair and the Dylan Farrow allegations (Barron).[6] Furthermore, his insinuation that Mia Farrow "instigated" Dylan Farrow's allegations as a "heinous" strategy given the custody case misrepresented the fact that Allen himself brought the custody case and only did so *after* he learned that Dylan Farrow had accused him of molestation.

If this seems confusing, it owes in part to Allen's deliberate attempt to confuse the issues. Allen was aware of Dylan Farrow's allegation by the time he initiated the custody case on August 13 and consciously chose to go public affirming his affair with Previn first. This played out such that Allen's declaration of love for Previn received mainstream news coverage within the same news cycles in which Dylan Farrow's allegations were first confirmed by Connecticut authorities. In essence, Allen's press release served as an admission to the lesser of two transgressions (in terms of legal risk) and also provided a motive for what he immediately characterized as Mia Farrow's "gruesomely damaging manipulation" of Dylan Farrow (Barron). The initial media reports echoed Allen's declaration that he had found love, and the timing of the press release allowed Allen to suggest, from a very early point in the media coverage, that Mia Farrow's anger over Previn provided motive for a false allegation. The content and timing of the press release helped Allen influence media to frame Dylan Farrow's allegations as Mia Farrow's allegations.

Rugelach and Communion Wafers

While it was less overt than the often explicitly racist caricaturing that accompanied discussion of Previn, media coverage of Allen alongside Dylan Farrow and Mia Farrow also routinely sought to establish their ethnoracial difference. While Previn's Asianness accentuated Allen's appearance as, comparatively, recognizably white, Dylan Farrow and Mia Farrow's white Catholicism mitigated the extent to which Allen could appear simultaneously Jewish and white. Against these comparatively "whiter," Catholic figures, Allen could be read as a sexually threatening Jewish other, in line with nineteenth-century stereotypes of the incestuous Jew/Jewish pedophile. Allen utilized this to his advantage, intimating that the allegations of sexual abuse had antisemitic undertones, conspiratorially attributing this to Mia Farrow and state authorities, but again, never to Dylan Farrow. Meanwhile, Mia Farrow's court testimony and memoir, *What Falls Away*, and Allen/Farrow family childcare provider Kristi Groteke's account, *Woody and Mia: The Nanny's Tale*, emphasized Mia's Catholic faith and correspondingly drew attention to Allen's secularity and reliance on therapy, characteristics that the Woody Allen persona had positively associated with a certain type of Jewish masculinity for decades. Mia Farrow discussed her Catholic faith as helping her overcome the traumatic familial crises involving Allen, Previn, and Dylan Farrow. However, Allen's casting Mia Farrow's Catholicism as antisemitic and fraudulent undercut her ability to use her faith as an appeal for sympathy. Furthermore, Allen's success at crafting a secular moral persona in his films left Farrow attempting to rebut the notion that Allen's secularity was moral. Her assessment of him as amorally faithless amounted to a takedown of the Woody Allen persona that Allen had so successfully marketed as a popular version of clearly coded Jewish secular masculinity. Allen's decades-spanning success crafting films celebrating his sympathetic persona left Mia Farrow in a situation where surface readings of her memoir, and certainly content from her nanny's less sophisticated memoir, might well have struck some readers as antisemitic.

In intimating that Farrow's characterizations of Allen as a sexual predator were necessarily antisemitic, Allen found a rhetorically formidable defense. Allen's strategy involved emphasizing antisemitic undertones without ever explicitly accusing Farrow of antisemitism. In both Allen and Farrow's telling, Allen's celebrated secularity (or, alternatively, his godlessness) and Farrow's Catholic piety (or, alternatively, her cynical faux religiosity) formed an ethnoracial subtext in which the privileges of Jewish secular white manhood were cast against those of religious white Catholic womanhood.

Mia Farrow published her memoir, *What Falls Away*, in 1997, the same year Allen released *Deconstructing Harry*, which I address in chapter 4. The memoir immediately establishes a framework of her Catholic faith, mentioning the Ten Commandments, the Seven Deadly Sins, the Rosary, and her First Communion prayer book all in the first few pages. Farrow describes spending time with her grandparents in Ireland, where she learned stories of "Jesus and His miracles, the cross, the nails, the crown of thorns, an agony beyond comprehension, and out of everything the rising in an exultation of angels, and oh the glory and mystery of all these things" (9).

In contrast, Mia Farrow's treatment of Allen avoids almost any religious or ethnic signifiers. A rare exception occurs when Farrow discusses her work in *Broadway Danny Rose*: "Woody the actor had long ago invented his screen persona: a lovable nebbish, endlessly and hilariously whining and quacking, questioning moral and philosophical issues great and small" (216). She then dismisses this persona as "a guy who is nothing like the real Woody Allen" (216). While "nebbish" is the book's only explicit Jewish signifier, virtually no readers would have required cues to Allen's Jewishness.

Mia Farrow does allude to Allen's secularity, though, establishing a contrast between her faith and his lack thereof. She includes a letter she wrote to a friend after discovering Allen's affair with Previn: "I have spent long years with a man who had no respect for everything I hold sacred—not for my family, not for my soul, not for my God or my purest goals" (285). At the American Booksellers Association convention in June of 1996, Mia used similar language in promoting the book, saying, "Very quickly I learned that this man had no respect for everything I hold sacred—not for my family, not for my soul, not for my God or my goals" (Meade 309). Farrow crafts an exogamy narrative with an incestuous subtext; in her telling, Allen's religious difference accounts for his failure to abide by religious proscriptions against incest. What is less clear here is whether Farrow intimates that this religious difference involves Allen's Jewishness or secularity. Regardless, antisemitism poses dangers to religious and secular Jewish identities alike, and as such, Farrow's statements here may conjure up antisemitic notions of a "godless Jew." And yet, if we consider Farrow's subjective experience of Allen's amoral, or immoral, behavior, alongside her reliance on faith to navigate his behavior's consequences for her and her family, we might also conjure a sympathetic reading in which we acknowledge that Farrow had an enormously narrow rhetorical path available to her in plainly describing her experience of Allen without her comments registering as antisemitic in a broader sociohistorical context. Suggesting that Allen's screen persona was a fraud did not equate to suggesting that secular Jewish ethical masculinity was a fraud; and yet, for many people, Allen's persona occupied the space of "secular Jewish ethical masculinity" in popular culture.

In addition to painting Allen as spiritually bereft, Mia Farrow also paints a picture of Allen's reliance on psychotherapy as a sort of false faith: "Looking at the place psychoanalysis had occupied in Woody Allen's life, it seemed that it had helped to isolate him from people and the systems we live by, and placed him in the center of a different reality—one that exists only after he has bounced his views off his therapist" (288). The notion that Allen revealed the limitations of psychotherapy as an alternative to religious faith found frequent expression for those of various faiths who found Allen's behavior problematic. A September 1992 editorial in the *Jewish Advocate* opined, "The psychiatrist's couch, which has an important place in medical treatment, apparently has become skewed into an idol for him" ("Elul for Woody").

While the *Jewish Advocate* casts psychotherapy as representative of Allen's betrayal of Jewish traditions, sympathetic portrayals of Mia Farrow routinely juxtaposed her Catholic faith against Allen's Jewish secularity. Maureen Orth's November 1992 article for *Vanity Fair* ends with a jarring juxtaposition, suggesting the uncertainty surrounding how Farrow, Allen, and the children could move on from the events:

> Left unresolved, however, is the healing process—how Mia and Woody and these 11 children can ever be reconstituted as a family.
>
> In March, Mia Farrow had all of her children who were not Catholics—including Soon-Yi—baptized.

Orth's article makes no explicit mention of Allen's Jewishness, but intimates that Allen, famous for being Jewish and secular, has no place in this baptized familial reconstitution.

Kristi Groteke, also Catholic, frames her time as a nanny for the Allen/Farrow family as a testament to faith. Groteke's 1994 book begins with an account of the day she testified in the Moses/Dylan/Ronan (then Satchel) custody case, when she felt like a "big, scared, clumsy Catholic girl from Bridgewater, Connecticut. . . . I saw Mia sifting through her mammoth straw pocketbook, finally picking out the heavy wooden rosary beads with the silver cross, beads that had once belonged to her father. 'Here, Kristi, do you want these while you testify?' she asked, holding them out to me" (22). Groteke invokes her shared Catholic faith with Mia Farrow at the moment of testifying against Allen. In Groteke's words, Farrow emerges as a devout Catholic with an "angelic smile" (49) who wanted to be a nun as a child, who "really *lived* her religion," (53), who told her, "Catholicism is tattooed on your soul. You never get rid of it" (53).

But where Mia Farrow and Orth minimize direct invocation of Allen's ethnoreligious difference, Groteke's depiction of Farrow's Catholic faith finds colorful juxtaposition in Allen. Groteke suggests that "Woody was as different from Mia as rugelah [*sic*] from communion wafers" (56). Subsequent depictions of physical difference were more loaded: discussing (pre-breakup) pictures of Allen and Farrow in tabloids, Groteke writes, "Always, there would be an angelic smile on her face. And we couldn't help wondering, who is this brainy little troll who has managed to captivate Beauty's heart?" (49). Groteke again draws attention to her perceived discrepancy in attractiveness by referring to "the Gentile goddess and the Jewish nerd" (51). However, describing Allen as a "brainy little troll" is an unmistakably dehumanizing effort; it is worth stressing how a textual moment like this can recast the ways in which Orth and Farrow's engagement with Allen operates in the broader media coverage of the incest narrative. Scholars and cultural critics might consider this a moment in which Allen's antisemitic detractors say the quiet part loud. But while Groteke's role in the narrative should not be minimized (a TV movie would be optioned from her memoir), her treatment of Allen's ethnoreligious difference doesn't accentuate Farrow and Orth's prose, to my reading, so much as it reveals the difficulty of their more careful attempts to frame Allen's actions as immoral without coming across as antisemitic.

While Groteke, Orth, and Mia Farrow all positively stressed Farrow's faith, Allen actively denigrated it. In a *60 Minutes* interview with Steve Kroft that aired November 22, 1992, Allen connects Farrow's supposed faith in God with her newfound association of Allen with the devil: "I started getting phone calls all night long, and death threats, and—and calling me the devil and evil incarnate, and—and—and she ran out and adopted two kids, and suddenly ran out and you know, baptized a number of kids. She was never religious for 60 seconds in all the years I knew her, then suddenly ran out and baptized the kids and told me that she had found God, and now everything was going to be directed toward a richer life and a greater life, and she was at peace and she was forgiving. And 24 hours later, she was threatening my life, threatening to stick my eyes out" ("Woody Allen Defends Himself"). Allen's appearance on *60 Minutes* presents Farrow's Catholicism as inauthentic and hypocritical, stressing Farrow's violent threats.[7] Both Farrow and Allen allude to faith and Catholicism in telling their stories, but in oppositional ways. Farrow uses religious iconography to privilege her faith-driven subjectivity over that of Allen's secular appeal. Allen, correspondingly, draws attention to Farrow's very same allegations of godlessness, but characterizes the accusation as irrational and dehumanizing, stressing that she considered him not merely a threat, but an inhuman one: "the devil and evil incarnate." Further, by challenging Farrow's ever having been religious, Allen defends his own secularism by casting her own supposed faith as inauthentic.

To whom, exactly, is Allen appealing here? He seemingly forsakes any attempt to gain sympathy from those who consider religious awakening a reasonable response to a family trauma. Instead, he insists there was no trauma, appealing to an audience that would find a characterization of Farrow's behavior as irrational (perhaps hysterical) as compelling. And in drawing attention to Farrow's use of religious language, he intimates that being called evil incarnate and the devil by a nonauthentically faithful Catholic is problematic, without overtly naming antisemitism. Allen presents himself as victim, threatened by an irrational, inauthentic Catholic who (mis)expresses her faith by not demonizing, but devilizing, a Jew. He also alludes to the baptisms. Allen's secular Jewish continuity is severed by what Allen presents as a forced, insincere conversion. Orth presents baptism as Farrow's attempt to reconstitute (without Allen) "the family." Allen invokes the baptism to mark the point at which his family is taken from him. In his reference to Farrow having baptized "a number of kids," and later "baptized the kids," Allen's awkward wording reflects the complicated task he makes for himself: how do you refer to a collective including *his* children without folding Previn into that group (despite the fact that she, too, was baptized)? Lamenting that Mia baptized "our" kids would make for a stronger condemnation of Farrow's unilateral decision. But Previn's presence rules that language out.

Mia Farrow's belief that Allen was "evil" emerged in coverage of the custody trial as well. Susan Coates, one of Allen's therapists, reported that Mia Farrow called Allen "satanic and evil" prior to Dylan Farrow making her allegations, regarding his relationship with Previn (Marks, "Doctor Recounts"). Mia Farrow's lawyers responded by inquiring if it was unusual "for a mother under the circumstances to believe that the man she had brought into the family, introduced to her children as a lifetime partner, who was having an affair with one of her daughters, is evil?" (Marks, "Allen and Farrow"). The judge was sympathetic to the question, and the judge, lawyers, and witness actually discussed what distinguished a "bad man" from a "bad act," in the context of Allen's affair with Previn. Meanwhile, the *New York Times*'s reporting described Mia Farrow as looking "like a Roman Catholic schoolgirl" while under cross-examination by Allen's lawyers (Grimes).

Outside of the courtroom, Allen exerted more control over the narrative. His most overt allusion to antisemitism occurred in a televised press conference after Frank Maco, the Connecticut prosecutor assigned with the abuse case, announced that he would not press charges. Standing in front of cameras reading from a statement, Allen chose to speak directly to Dylan Farrow, assuring her that "the dark forces will not prevail. . . . Not second-rate police or judicial setbacks, not tabloid press nor those who perjure themselves nor all who rush to judgment, not the pious or hypocritical, the bigoted" (Henneberger). Allen groups "pious," "hypocritical," and "bigoted" together, suggesting that those who proclaimed faith were both hypocritical and antisemitic.[8]

Though Allen remarked that he intended the words for Dylan Farrow, remember that at the time, just over a year after the alleged abuse, she was just eight. Allen also implied that Connecticut authorities had nefarious reasons for even conducting an investigation: "Is it possible they were prejudiced against me because I'm a diehard New Yorker and all that that implies, and Ms. Farrow a Connecticut local?" (Groteke 263). Allen's reference to "prejudice" and use of the phrase "and all that that implies" asks his audience to connect "diehard New Yorker" with his own vulnerable Jewishness.[9] This conflation of "New York" and "Jewish" is nothing new, but worth considering alongside contemporaneous discussion of Allen. The aforementioned *Jewish Advocate*'s critical op-ed about Allen also lamented that "Allen's ideas, intonations, mores, as depicted in many of his pictures, have been instead narrowly 'culturally' New York, but confused with being Jewish in content because of his identity" ("Elul for Woody"). Though the *Jewish Advocate* bemoaned Allen's role in transforming "New York" into a signifier for secular Jewishness, Allen embraced this conflation, utilizing it to suggest his victimization by antisemitic forces. That the eight-year-old Dylan Farrow would be sensitive to these insinuations seems unlikely; Allen directs his appeal to those, Jewish or otherwise, who might be sympathetic to Allen casting himself as vulnerable as a Jew.

Theorizing Fatherhood and Incest in the Allen/Farrow Family

While Allen used a dog whistle to imply that antisemitic forces rendered him vulnerable to allegations involving Dylan Farrow, his defense of his relationship to Soon-Yi Previn involved him making bold, defiant, assertive claims. This different approach allowed Allen to exploit specific cultural norms involving how white fathers, historically, have been privileged to subjectively assert who is or is not their relation.

In an interview with *Time*, August 31, 1992, Allen defended his relationship with Previn by stating that he had no paternal relationship to her: "I am not Soon-Yi's father or stepfather" (Isaacson). When the interviewer asked, "What about how it would affect her siblings?" Allen dismissed the possibility, responding, "These people are a collection of kids, they are not blood sisters or anything" (Isaacson). But just a year earlier, when Eric Lax published his official biography, Allen declared, "Mia's been a completely different kind of experience for me, because the predominant thing has been family" (312). Allen's protestation that his affair with Previn was not incestuous required denying a paternal relationship with Previn, but also depicting the Farrow family as *not* a family. Previn echoed Allen's points in *Newsweek* in August 1992, stating, "He was never any kind of father figure to me" ("Soon-Yi"). And yet, by 2015, Allen matter-of-factly stated in interviews that he and Previn's successful marriage owed in part to the fact that "I was paternal. She responded to someone paternal" (Fragoso). While Allen's recent comments undercut the integrity of these earlier characterizations, the custody case he brought in 1992 required him to convince the court that he should be given custody of Previn's siblings Moses, Dylan, and Ronan (then Satchel). Allen had to make a case that *he* was the component that created "family"—but just for his children (thus excluding their siblings, including, crucially, Soon-Yi Previn). To set conditions for a new family, Allen had to deny (if not destroy) the existence of a previous one.

Incest scholars might recognize these familiar, problematic dynamics. While both Allen and Previn's claims to not viewing their relationship as incestuous convinced many that the relationship was nonincestuous, Judith Herman stresses that "paternal authority" overrides paternal biology and "paternal feeling" in accounting for how power dynamics function in incestuous families. Furthermore, Herman's attention to how incest frameworks develop when older female children become "their fathers' confidantes" matches Allen's own presentation of the Allen/Previn dynamic (80). Juliet MacCannell suggests that viewing father figures as Freudian father figures (akin to powerful "tyrants" or bad dads) obscures how male familial privilege operates in a post-Freudian context in which men often rail against their own "tyrant" fathers. MacCannell's reading is especially helpful for thinking about a celebrity figure like Allen, given how his iconic filmic and comedic presence, and particularly his ubiquitous invocation of Freud and therapy, resulted in the fundamental unlikelihood of his being perceived as typically tyrant-like. Instead, MacCannell's theorizing helps us see how Allen's citing of multiple mitigating factors reflects a narcissistic, shape-shifting quality typical not in tyrant fathers, but in "brothers": "the modernized fraternal superego is both ego and *It*, changing roles whenever it suits him" (17).[10] We grant Allen's nonconsanguineous paternity of some of Farrow's children but happily accede to his denial of paternity for Previn, whom he claims to love differently.

MacCannell's observation about the dangers of "brothers" (as opposed to "tyrant fathers") helps theorize Allen's patriarchal behavior, but specific rhetorical and societal conditions also facilitate Allen's subjective, inconsistent, categorization of "family." As we have observed, Allen emphasized his Jewishness in framing his vulnerability to Mia and Dylan Farrow's white Catholicism. But if Allen's whiteness also juxtaposed with Previn's nonwhiteness in a fashion that permitted Allen to selectively, and for many viewers, plausibly, frame his own relationships with her as nonfamilial, specific historical conditions facilitated this privileging of white American paternal subjectivity. The legal theorist Zanita Fenton provides insight into why audiences might have lent credibility to Allen's selective pronouncements about paternity and family despite their logical inconsistencies. For Fenton, understanding American incest narratives involving white men requires considering a particular overlooked historical and legal context: a plantation system in which "incest and miscegenation were inseparable and socially and politically synonymous" (324): "White slave masters could enjoy unrestricted sexual access to their black children that breached the underlying objective of both the incest and miscegenation taboos: he could have relations with his biological child because she was not white; he was not . . . expected to interconnect (read: marriage / read: sex) with non-related individuals from the subordinated black slave community" (323). Fenton builds upon Werner Sollors's assessment of how American racism confused the "structural symmetry" of "too close" (signifying incest) and "too far" (signifying miscegenation) (Sollors 320). Fenton theorizes that this confusion actually served to hide incest in plain sight. "Racial politics," she argues, "created the hidden exhibition of incest" (324).

Fenton's assessment of how white male subjectivity navigates intersections of family and racial difference may be applicable with Allen, especially as it pertains to his inconsistent employment of the concept of "family": simultaneously denying the Farrow family as family, even as he protested that his family was being taken away from him. Fenton theorizes that white patriarchal supremacy is built upon a refusal to recognize these contradictions, as societal proscriptions against both miscegenation and incest accommodated the racist, illogical notion that one ruled out the other. The inability to recognize this inconsistency facilitated these transgressions. In effect, white men's preferred subjective perspective on who was or was not their family member trumped any other consideration, biological, legal, or otherwise.

In applying Fenton's hypothesis to the Allen family construct, I acknowledge the decidedly different sociohistorical and legal contexts. And yet, in contemplating the institution of slavery's various historical legacies, the credibility still afforded white fathers in dictating whom they claim as children and how they inconsistently conceive of family, plausibly originates in this plantation context. Understanding Allen's subjectivity in a sociohistorical American context, and not merely a Jewish one, helps illuminate how whiteness functioned for white Jews, like Allen, in the 1990s. If white male American privilege historically involved the freedom to commit incest with nonwhite children, Allen's incest narrative emerges as an important case study for how this privilege functioned for contemporaneous white Jewish American men.

One last aspect of Fenton's theorization invites application onto the Allen incest narrative. Fenton suggests that "once there was silent condonation for the liaisons between a white father and his reflection in brown, it must have become more psychologically plausible that such liaisons could also occur, with impunity, with his reflection in white. The commonsense progression within this power dynamic includes the unchallenged access of these same fathers to their white children" (321). For Fenton, the way a white father conceives of the incest taboo regarding a nonwhite child inevitably impacts his conception of what might be plausible with his white children. Allen's relationship with Previn, by all accounts, began well before Dylan Farrow accused him of sexual molestation. While Allen's alleged transgressions with the of-age, or nearly of-age, Previn may seem categorically different from the alleged transgressions with Dylan Farrow, this aspect of Fenton's theorizing is also applicable to contemporary society: for a white male father, the ability to get away with incest with a nonwhite child might embolden that father in testing boundaries regarding his white children.

While Fenton's work helps us think about how Allen's whiteness and maleness operated given the history of American interracial family units, Allen's celebrity also played a role in how he was successful at making audiences read Previn as *fortunate* to be the object of his attention. The extended quote from the August 1992 *Newsweek* interview in which Previn denied a paternal relationship with Allen is instructive here: "He was never any kind of father figure to me. I never had any dealings with him. He rarely came to our apartment before his own children were born. Even then, he never spoke and the truth is I never cared that much for him. He was always preoccupied with work and never talked to me. Not really to any of us" ("Soon-Yi").

Cultural critic Lili Loofbourow analyzed Previn's statement by considering how the above dynamics actually facilitate eventual romantic connection: "This is a completely devastating portrait. A painfully quiet, socially awkward girl comes of age with a stepfather figure who never showed any interest in her or acknowledged her presence. Instead, he lavished his attention on her mother and her blond little sister. She develops, and suddenly this man who has been in her house for years but seemed not to see her notices her! Her!" Loofbourow's reading reflects a dynamic that Judith Herman explores in *Father-Daughter Incest*. Furthermore, the very qualities that Loofbourow conveys as so emotionally gratifying to a "quiet, socially awkward girl" are amplified when the stepfather figure is not just mom's partner, but one of the most iconic movie stars of his generation. The theoretical dynamic that incest scholars like Herman discuss, and cultural critics like Loofbourow identify within the psyche of a daughter figure like Previn, echoes the affinity Allen's moviegoing audience felt for him, finding him desirable, countercultural, and aloof.

At a narrative level, then, by publicly declaring his love for Previn, Allen also effectively tapped into powerful audience fantasies premised upon his desirability as a movie star. (The fact that the Allen persona consistently, and disingenuously, rejected the premise of this desirability via self-deprecation amounted to an aspect of the specifically packaged appeal.) But here, too, race had an important function. Audiences were more predisposed to privilege Allen's subjectivity asserting that Previn was the object of his love and affection and not a victim of predatory grooming because of race. Kimberly McKee, whose work on incest also importantly focuses on power dynamics as opposed to consanguinity, notes: "Notions of Asian and Asian American women's hypersexuality aligned with discourses of promiscuity linked to the circumstances of her life in South Korea. This coupling results in a lack of compassion or empathy for considering how she was vulnerable for abuse. Soon-Yi is never considered the subject of predatory behavior; rather, she is viewed as an instigator or at least a complicit party" (163). McKee's observations also intersect with popular, raced conceptions of childhood. Reporters and entertainers often struggled to keep Dylan Farrow and Soon-Yi Previn separate, though, in their coverage of these intertwined stories. Especially as it involved questions of age and ideas associated with childhood and sexuality, Soon-Yi Previn and Dylan Farrow were conflated in ways that underscored the racist presuppositions facilitating tacit acceptance of Allen's behavior with Previn.

"His Real Life Is Not So Different From His Art"

Allen's status as a heroic and iconic artistic figure influenced the media to reinforce his characterization of his relationship with Previn as a positive development. This bias toward Allen's subjectivity can be seen in how media outlets used his films to frame the events. Once Allen issued his press release affirming his love for Previn, local and national news immediately began covering the story. Both the local Fox affiliate in New York City and CNN featured clips from Allen's 1979 film *Manhattan*, where Allen, playing protagonist Isaac Davis, declared, "I'm dating a girl who does homework" ("Woody Allen Affair"). CNN correspondent Cynthia Tornquist arrived at the same point as many commentators: "in *Manhattan*, Woody Allen portrayed a 42-year-old writer who has an affair with a 17-year-old prep school student played by Mariel Hemingway. Now, the filmmaker reveals that his real life is not so different from his art."

The significance of *Manhattan* being used to contextualize the story of Allen's relationship with Previn cannot be overstated. CNN utilized clips from Allen's film's sympathetic presentation of a protagonist played by Allen discussing predatory behavior to frame reports that Allen was in a relationship with a girl who had just come of legal age.[11] The sensationalistic engagement with the surface-level similarities of the story facilitated the Overton window shifting far beyond any meaningful news media engagement with questions of grooming or predation, because *Manhattan* treated the material as (highbrow) romantic comedy. Furthermore, the introduction of the specific line "I'm dating a girl who does homework" almost obliterates any meaningfully objective attempt to consider questions of consent, age, and predation by turning the act of sexual predation into a fictional male protagonist's self-deprecatory joke. Alluding to *Manhattan* in reporting on Allen's press release presented the appealing, readily available cliché of life imitating art. But in fact, these reports suggested life was imitating a romantic comedy that normalized sexual predation on high school girls. Allen's influence manifested itself in how his films were employed by reporters, comedians, and late-night talk-show hosts as blueprints for how they told the story, and these blueprints were enormously generous to grown men whose behavior with girls was indulged, even treated as indicative of an idealized, sensitive, intellectual masculinity preferable to typical Hollywood alpha males. The minute Fox and CNN (and other broadcasters, pundits, and commenters) covered Allen's press conference by comparing his life to *Manhattan*, comparing Allen the man to Allen's fictional, beloved filmic alter ego, they all but endorsed his relationship with Previn.

While media reports used Allen's own filmic texts in ways that implicitly privileged Allen and his worldview, they were far more explicitly racist, sexist, and objectifying in their characterization of Previn. Consider New York Fox affiliate newscaster Rosanna Scotto's choice to refer to Previn as "the Korean-born beauty" when first reporting on Allen's press release ("Woody Allen Affair"). While this sexualization had the effect of depicting Previn as an "instigator" (McKee 163), comedic commentary shows how jokes ostensibly made at Previn and Allen's expense not only deliberately targeted Previn with racist caricature, but frequently evoked Dylan Farrow without naming her. While jokes demeaning Previn were ubiquitous, the prospect of making jokes about a seven-year-old white girl who might have been sexually molested by her adoptive Jewish father were too charged (and disturbing) for many mainstream comics and comedy writers. Marion Meade's biography of Allen comments on the racism in jokes made at Previn's expense (243, 317); *Saturday Night Live* and *Mad TV* featured multiple sketches throughout the 1990s depicting Previn in various degrees of yellowface caricature or sexual objectification, while rarely making direct reference to Dylan.[12]

The racist humor at Previn's expense was especially explicit on *The Howard Stern Show*, which reached the largest radio audience in both New York City and Los Angeles by the end of 1992 (Puig). After Allen's press release of August 17, 1992, Stern and cohost Robin Quivers emphasized the racial difference of the parties with attention to their sexual relationship during their news segment:

QUIVERS: Woody uncharacteristically issued a statement through a spokesperson yesterday confirming the tabloid reports that he, yes, is in love, [Stern: with what's her name] with his stepdaughter.

STERN: And what is her name?

QUIVERS: Um, Bang Some—

STERN: Bang Some Schmuck.

After Stern suggests "Lick Some Jew" and "Two Jew Wang" as alternative names, Quivers quotes Allen directly (but for the name changing), citing the press release:

QUIVERS: The fifty-six-year-old movie maker avowed his love for the Korean-born girl, saying "Regarding my love for . . . [Bang . . . Some Schmuck], it's real, and all happily true."

STERN: Can you imagine this? This is so depraved. ("Howard Stern")

Quivers and Stern utilize racist, mock-Asian names that draw attention to Allen's Jewishness, emphasizing difference, and framing Allen and Previn's relationship as purely sexual. This undermines Allen's comparably lofty discussion of love, but also leaves unexamined what, exactly, Stern finds "so depraved." Ostensibly, it is Allen's paternal relationship to Previn (which Quivers approximates by referring to Previn as his "stepdaughter," though, technically, she was not). However, in racially demeaning Previn and reducing her to a sex object, the humor implicates the interracial element of the relationship as transgressive.

Stern's ostensible confusion of the interracial sexual taboo for the incestuous sexual taboo is not unusual. Werner Sollors's observation about nineteenth-century American interracial incest narratives helps to unpack Stern's humor: "interracial alliances are often perceived to be the opposite of, or antidote to, closely endogamous ones" (318). If incest is "too close," and interracial sex is "too far," the logical gaps thus precluded interracial incest from reading (to white men, and fathers in particular) as incest (Sollors 318). But Stern has it both ways; he mocks Allen for failing to recognize the logical gaps and also explicitly draws attention to the interracial aspect of his affair with Previn while only making minimal mention of their familial relationship. While the humor may function by displacing what Stern (and his writers) find most disturbing (incest), the effect is an explicitly racist emphasis on racial difference.

The introduction of a recurring character called "Wood Yi," played by Steve "The Engineer" Fried, provided a vessel for Stern's show to repeatedly mock Allen and Previn (and their interracial relationship) in explicitly racist terms. The premise of the character was simple: Steve Fried, a microphone-shy member of Stern's staff with a vague New York accent and no comedic timing, read lines written for him, performing an ostensibly unintentionally terrible Allen "impression." Wood Yi was an utter failure at capturing the Allen persona, making it a unique comic takedown. Allen, so commonly mocked as a brilliant intellect with a troubling capacity to rationalize any transgression, found himself transformed into a dim-witted cipher.

But while removing all wit and superego composed a crucial aspect of the bit's humor, the premise demanded further transmogrification. The implication of Wood Yi is that Allen's interracial relationship transforms his own racial and gender identity. His relationship with a Korean American woman manifests itself in Allen's name being Koreanified and simultaneously feminized. Reborn as a gender and racial hybrid, Woody as Wood Yi makes jokes that focus on sex acts with Asian women, and, most frequently, younger versions of Previn: self-love and love of racial other are merged. Sollors's logical gaps of "too close" and "too far" thus find perverse, literal expression.

The sketch resonates not only with incest theory, but also with Zygmunt Bauman's theory of proteophobia. The sketch's negotiation of racial exogamy and incest as simultaneous acts "blurs the borderlines which ought to be kept watertight and undermines the reassuringly monotonous, repetitive and predictable nature of the life-world" (Bauman 144). While Bauman uses those words with ethnoracial and religious qualities in mind, they also apply to concepts of family, sexuality, and gender. In essence, the sketch's proteophobic response to Allen's incest narrative is to collapse all of the vexing complexities (involving Allen's whiteness and Jewishness, Previn's Asianness, the contested paternal or nonpaternal qualities of their relationship, and Allen's vulnerable Jewish masculinity alongside Previn's Asian hypersexuality) into a single body. Wood Yi manifests a proteophobe's nightmare.

While Previn is incorporated into Wood Yi, she also functions as the predominant sexual target of the Wood Yi jokes. In this external role, though, she also stands in for the otherwise erased Dylan Farrow. Even Stern, never one for self-censorship, avoided explicit reference to Dylan Farrow in these early sketches. But Stern's writers evoked her in the Wood Yi routine: numerous jokes referenced recess, lunch boxes, and even diapers (in each case signifying a daughter figure younger than Previn). One joke is especially specific: "What goes into seven twice?" Wood Yi asks, before answering, "me" ("Howard Stern"). This joke clearly indicates the writers' awareness of Dylan Farrow, and her age, when making pedophilia jokes. Stern and his writers depicted Previn as younger than she was in order to signify the presence of a younger figure whose sexual vulnerability or ostensible "innocence" could not be directly invoked. This phenomenon transpired in other media coverage (comedic and otherwise) regarding Previn and Allen. James Kincaid, for instance, noted that "the twenty-one-year-old Ms. Previn somehow gets younger and younger, folds into the body of the seven-year-old Dylan" (227). Kincaid correctly categorizes this displacement as a function of a broad sexual fascination, but race also facilitates these transmogrifications of Previn and Dylan Farrow.

Notions of childhood informed by race and sex help illuminate Dylan Farrow's ostensible absence alongside racist and sexualized portrayals of Previn. Kathryn Bond Stockton's work on childhood, as a raced, classed, and desexualized concept helps elucidate how Soon-Yi Previn and Dylan Farrow both operate in archetypal fashion. In Previn and Farrow, the media had two distinctly different versions of "children" to situate versus Allen. Farrow, who might be read as "pre-sexual," and the older Previn, who emerged as "the Freudian child . . . remarkably, threateningly, precocious: sexual and aggressive" (Stockton 27). Race undergirds this dichotomy, though, and Stockton's theorizing here aligns with McKee's earlier referenced observations about Previn being "viewed as an instigator or at least a complicit party" (McKee 163). If, as Stockton suggests, "children, as an *idea*, are likely to be both white and middle-class" (31), the question of when Allen and Previn's relationship began, or whether Allen's prior behavior might be considered grooming, becomes moot. Just as whiteness and middle-class status are privileges, the idea of a sheltered childhood—a childhood deserving of such protections because of its implicit "innocence"—becomes raced and classed. For poor nonwhite children, the experience of poverty, violence, and racism signifies a lack of innocence. In addition to being Korean, and thus subject to a broad, racist discourse of hypersexualized Asianness, Soon-Yi spent her earliest years impoverished in Seoul, and, according to the nuns at the orphanage from which Mia Farrow adopted her, she was the child of a physically abusive sex worker (Meade 205). Various forces contributed to Previn being unlikely to read as capable of having experienced a traditional childhood, but Allen played a role in this process. Allen referred to Previn (affectionately) as the "kid who was eating out of garbage pails in Korea" (*Wild Man Blues*) and also characterized the nude photographs he took of Previn as her idea (Meade 15). His (self-serving) characterizations have helped render her as "too advanced for innocence" (Stockton 32).

By characterizing Previn in this fashion, Allen signaled to audiences that he could not have acted inappropriately. How do you hold someone accountable for corrupting someone who is already too experienced? And yet, by casting the relationship in lofty terms of love, Allen also shifted focus away from power dynamics and functionally championed Previn amid racist media coverage that sexualized her. Even though Allen occasionally stressed Previn's "too advanced for innocence" qualities, he also simultaneously occupied the posture of a white liberal defender of his racially demeaned Asian partner. For viewers inclined to think of Allen in sympathetic terms, this framework provided a plausible alternative to seeing Allen as a predator. If he was a predator, why was he the only one on television seeming kind to a woman of color who was being routinely demeaned in racist and sexist media coverage?

Comedians' sustained focus on his relationship with Previn helped Allen by keeping the presence of an allegedly abused white Christian girl at bay and by making Allen appear, to viewers sensitive to the media's racist coverage, as Previn's champion. On April 10, 1993, a *Saturday Night Live* sketch featuring Jason Alexander served as an exception proving the rule, providing rare, mainstream, explicit comedic commentary on Dylan Farrow ("Season 18: Episode 17"). While the Previn/Allen jokes erase, or only signify, Dylan Farrow, the *SNL* sketch suggests that audiences (and comedy writers) were well aware of her allegations, given the attention national news outlets like *Newsweek*, the *Washington Post*, and *USA Today* were paying to the custody case. While the trial did not end until May, and the verdict was not released until about one month later, the *SNL* sketch envisions a dwindling number of Allen fans' absurd suspensions of disbelief at Allen's actual testimony, suggesting Allen's strategy had alienated some significant portion of his fans and debased the remaining ones.

Set at a "Woody Allen Fan Club" meeting at the 92nd Street Y, multiple cast members do their best Allen impressions as they discuss the trial. As each Allen fan recounts one disturbing piece of court testimony after another, they rationalize each behavior and reimagine it as good parenting. Kevin Nealon's character remarks, "It's all coming out now. He's a very affectionate father! I mean, sticking his face in his daughter's lap. I mean, you know, my parents have kissed me in all kinds of places. It's completely natural!" ("Season 18: Episode 17"). Other performers would make reference to similarly specific court testimony, such as Allen's supposedly inappropriate placement of sunscreen lotion on Dylan Farrow's "tush" ("He's a concerned father. What, he's gonna let it burn?"), and, in the one Previn reference during a Dylan-centered sketch, his rationalization of his sexual relationship with Previn ("And so what if he had sex with Soon-Yi? He was right. It gave her more confidence").

The sketch is clear-eyed and unapologetic in presenting testimony casting Allen in a disturbing light. By featuring so many performers' impressions of Allen, the sketch stresses just how easily Allen's supposed rationalizations and statements, whether corroborated by his testimony or not, could be imagined in his voice. Unlike when comedians or news programs made *Manhattan* references that framed Allen's wrongdoing as nonfamilial, the "Fan Club" sketch intimates that Allen's transgressions involved their incestuous nature within a family construct. And the sketch directly engaged Allen's alleged behavior with Dylan Farrow, which was rare. But the sketch also pays artistic homage (referencing *Annie Hall* and *Manhattan*) even as it registers disillusionment. As such, the homage also subtly defangs the criticism; it suggests that Allen may have done horrible things, but its nostalgic engagement with his aesthetic renders Allen an uncredited author of the sketch. Furthermore, the sketch's premise and maudlin crescendo intimates that whatever Allen may have done to Dylan

Farrow, the more salient tragedy is that fandom of Allen has been corrupted. The white male fans and comics who have perfected their Allen impressions and idolized a flawed man are those who deserve sympathy.

Coda: Husbands and Wives and Monsters

While this chapter explores Allen's influence on how various figures told the nonfictional, contested story of Allen's relationships with Mia Farrow, Dylan Farrow, and Soon-Yi Previn, Allen asserted far more control over how he incorporated autobiographical material into the films he subsequently wrote, directed, and starred in. In these movies, Allen (literally) recast his incest narrative, revealing an underappreciated ability to appeal to audience appetites for patriarchally sympathetic incest stories. The following chapter close reads three Allen films to demonstrate how Allen included readily identifiable, specific allusions to his incest narrative in his movies. In setting that up, I want to discuss one last sketch, which deals, obliquely, with exogamy, Jewish community protective politics, and what it means to be (or to be associated with) a "monster."

The Ben Stiller Show's "Woody Allen's Bride of Frankenstein" makes no direct reference to Dylan Farrow or Soon-Yi Previn. The sketch, a shot-for-shot parody of scenes from Allen's *Husbands and Wives*, came out just months after Allen made his public denial/confirmation. It makes no mention of incest. The premise is simple: Allen and his demonstrably Jewish cast of characters (à la *Husbands and Wives*) are monsters. Except, as with any Allen production, two want to have affairs—one with a human. The sketch might be read as a straightforward Allen film parody poking fun at exogamy. However, considering the timing of the sketch, its transformation of Jews into monsters feels particularly resonant with both historical sexual antisemitism as well as the specific charges levied against Allen. If sexual molestation of a seven-year-old girl is monstrous, what would it mean for Allen to be a monster?

Stiller's sketch attempts to answer this question: Allen is depicted as a typically nonthreatening, charming, banal neurotic . . . and literally monstrous (he is "the Mummy"). But the entire cast, other than Frankenstein's blonde, non-Jewish girlfriend ("she's not even one of *us*—she's *alive*"), is also made up of monsters. At surface, the sketch suggests that, Jewish or otherwise, sexuality makes all of us potentially monstrous and yet simultaneously not particularly scary.[13] But the sketch also intimates that identifying with Allen is facilitated by the incongruity of imagining him as a monster. If Allen's film catalog consists of thirty-plus depictions of the Allen persona as driven by a nonthreatening but potent id, the sketch underscores just how bizarre it is to imagine that id as threatening.

The allegorical depiction of white Jewish difference as unmistakable, and bodily, however, shows that even as Stiller's writers engage with the problem of Jewish sexuality as a form of "monstrosity," they still blatantly reject the proteophobic anxieties that *The Howard Stern Show* considers with Wood Yi. Frankenstein's monster, the Mummy, the Bride of Frankenstein, and zombies are "fixed." They do not shape-shift. Whatever transformation renders them undead has already occurred. The Wolfman, or Dr. Jekyll and Mr. Hyde—monsters who demonstrate proteophobic anxiety—are metaphorically too charged for a sketch meditating on 1990s white Jewish identity when a beloved icon was alleged to have sexually molested his white Catholic daughter. Woody Allen as the Mummy is funny because Woody Allen is nothing like the Mummy. Woody Allen as the Wolfman or Dr. Jekyll, on the other hand, suggests Allen's capacity for the transformation into (and importantly, out of) monstrous form that Mr. Hyde and the Wolfman dramatize.

The sketch thereby reminds us of the limits of depictable forms of monstrosity and also societal expectations regarding monstrosity. On February 7, 2014, shortly after Dylan Farrow wrote her open letter re-articulating her abuse allegations, a victim of child abuse named "William Warwick" (a pseudonym) addressed Dylan's accusations by noting how society brands child abusers as monsters, when, in fact, they are merely humans—including loving fathers—who have committed reprehensible acts. Warwick writes, "Those of us who were abused by a family member, or a family friend, have shared banal time and space with the sort of people who molest kids."

Warwick's observations help our reading of Stiller's sketch. The premise of "Woody Allen's Bride of Frankenstein" is the absurdity of watching monsters sharing "banal time and space" together. But while Stiller and his writers broached the topic of Allen's monstrousness in 1992, Allen would as well, most audaciously in 1997's *Deconstructing Harry*, one of (at least) three films where Allen engages his incest narrative in specific terms.

4

Blood Libel Humor and Incest Easter Eggs

Family and Destruction in *Deconstructing Harry*, *Irrational Man*, and *Blue Jasmine*

In a March 2016 appearance on the daytime television show *The Real*, Malcolm Jamal Warner suggested a media double standard in the treatment of Bill Cosby's collaborative work. Warner did not defend Cosby, but stood by *The Cosby Show*, the television show on which he (and so many other Black actors) appeared, noting that corporate entertainment industry responses to allegations that Cosby sexually abused more than fifty women (including more than twenty allegations of rape) seemed quite distinct from those concerning white male artists also accused of rape (Holpuch et al.). Referring to Woody Allen, Roman Polanski, and Stephen Collins, Warner claimed, "it's very clear the crimes they've committed. . . . But there is no one that's calling for Woody's movies to be pulled off the air" (Lutkin).

In mentioning Polanski and Allen, Warner might make an unintentional second distinction: not just between white and Black entertainers, but also between white and white Jewish entertainers. However, Warner does not take this step; his comparison suggests that white Jews, like Allen and Polanski, group easily with non-Jews like Stephen Collins—even though Allen and Polanski are celebrated world-famous directors, while Collins has comparatively limited acclaim as an actor.

I begin with this anecdote because of the limits of Warner's juxtapositions, in which Allen's (and Polanski's) whiteness subsume their Jewishness, despite the historical parallels between threatened Black masculinity and threatened Jewish masculinity. Warner observes a double standard, but it's one that writes off the possibility of antisemitism that Allen alluded to in press conferences and interviews in the 1990s. While historical and contemporary antisemitism certainly informs conversations and media coverage of Jews and incest, it does not operate as a perfect parallel to anti-Black racism. Within these stories, racism, antisemitism, and white privilege intersect in complex ways. As we have observed, racism, and anti-Asian racism in particular, operated within media representations of Allen's incest narrative to cement Allen's whiteness as compatible with his Jewishness.

Returning to Warner's assertion, and leaving aside his assessment of the clarity of Allen's guilt, Warner expresses exasperation regarding why Allen's movies continue to be celebrated, while *The Cosby Show* has been pulled from the air. Warner's complaint merits consideration especially when we take into account the content of the artists' work. While *The Cosby Show* depicted a fictional well-to-do Black family, and, per the sitcom formula, rarely touched on questions of sexual assault (unlike Cosby's stand-up), Allen's films are saturated with allusions to child sexuality, sexual predation, incest, and literal and metaphorical destruction of families. In the years since Allen and Farrow's custody case, Allen's films have consistently, even obsessively, engaged these themes in hyperspecific terms clearly evocative of his incest narrative. And many of his films have engaged the theme of getting away with a serious crime.[1]

In this chapter, I demonstrate how post-custody-trial Allen films consistently engage the Allen/Previn/Farrow familial incest dynamic as central to Allen's creative process, telling and retelling a patriarchal incest narrative for mass consumption. Allen's films routinely draw on his autobiographical experience in ways that package his incest narrative in recognizable filmic vignettes. Despite Allen's repeated denials of incestuous transgression, his films reveal a vicarious invitation, if not insistence, that his audiences celebrate stories that consistently suggest the plausibility of Allen's incestuous transgressions. Similarly, despite Allen's repeated denials of his films being at all autobiographical, the stories are so specifically targeted and detailed in their layered references to his incest narrative that they undercut his denials. While my previous chapter shows how Allen mobilized Jewish community protective politics to displace a narrative of contested sexual predation with one of Jewish communal vulnerability to antisemitism, this chapter shows how Allen's films consistently engage the story of Allen's incest narrative despite Allen scholarship almost never commenting on this crucial characteristic. Here, Jewish community protective politics dictate the critical silence. The choice not to address themes Allen transparently incorporates into his films reveals a deferral to Allen, who gets to have it both ways: he can repeatedly deny wrongdoing, and deny that he autobiographically addresses allegations of personal wrongdoing in his films, even as the films actively re-engage, and even provocatively celebrate, specific aspects of his incest narrative. If Jewish community protective politics work elsewhere to shield ostensible Jewish male vulnerability, here, they function to enable Allen's thinly veiled commercial marketing of the possibility that he incestuously transgressed, which the moral universe of his films intimate is far more plausible than either his denials allow or his critics concede.

I conduct close readings of scenes in *Deconstructing Harry* (1997), *Blue Jasmine* (2013), and *Irrational Man* (2015) to reveal how Allen repeatedly draws on his own autobiographical incest narrative in recognizable fashion, always in plots where figures accused of committing a crime are, in fact, guilty of having committed said crime.[2] While two of these films postdate the 1990s, they touch on particular components from the 1990s incest narrative (Mia Farrow's call to a doctor to report Dylan Farrow's allegations and the family court judge Elliott Wilk). In concluding the chapter, I consider Allen's approach to storytelling alongside that of Jim Trueblood, the infamous narrator of his own father-daughter incest violation from Ralph Ellison's *Invisible Man*, who markets his incestuous transgression to eager audiences that financially compensate Trueblood for facilitating their vicarious celebration of his acts.

Incest in the Early Work, via Leviticus

The close readings in this chapter involve films Allen made in or after 1997, but Allen regularly engaged incest in his prior work. Most famously, *Hannah and Her Sisters* (1986) tells the stories of two men who have affairs with sisters/sisters-in-law. Though not consanguineous, sexual intercourse with a spouse's sibling is prohibited in Leviticus and historically considered an incest prohibition within Jewish communities.[3] *Shadows and Fog* (1991) also features a protagonist (Kleinman) who has an affair with the sister of his fiancée. *Deconstructing Harry*, which I discuss in greater detail later in this chapter, begins with a depiction of a sexual affair between a novel's autobiographical protagonist and his sister-in-law. Allen's fiction also delved into the subject, as his short story "Retribution" (1980) finds its protagonist falling in love with his girlfriend's mother and marrying the mother, which makes him (as stepfather) sexually irresistible to his ex-girlfriend. "Retribution" delves into the incest theme along distinct vectors: first, the protagonist's sexual attraction to members of the same family (Leviticus 18 and 20 prohibit multiple iterations of such sexual relations); and, second, the Electra complex (the daughter/father version of the more commonly discussed Oedipus complex). Meanwhile, *Stardust Memories* (1980) and *Anything Else* (2003) also engage the Electra complex, as both films feature the protagonist's love interest discussing her sexual attraction to her father. (*Stardust Memories* also features Dorrie [Charlotte Rampling] accusing Sandy [Allen's character] of flirting with her thirteen-year-old cousin.) Most recently, *Café Society* (2016) features Bobby (Jesse Eisenberg) in a love triangle with his uncle Phil (Steve Carell). After Phil marries Bobby's love interest Vonnie (Kristen Stewart), Bobby confides his continued feelings for her: "I was in love with you, and you decided to marry my uncle, which makes you my aunt . . . Aunt Vonnie. I think I still have a crush on you, Aunt Vonnie."

Incest emerges thematically in much of Allen's work, and it emerges with remarkable consistency. Stephen Marche, writing for *Esquire* in 2014, around the time that Dylan wrote her letter to the *New York Times*, compiled a list featuring several of the aforementioned scenes, as well as others with "newly-chilling themes" involving sexual transgressions. Regarding incest in particular, Allen's works mine the attraction men feel for nonconsanguineous members of one's family, as well as the Electra complex. (Curiously, even keeping "Oedipus Wrecks" in mind, straightforward Oedipus complex narratives are correspondingly rare in his work.) Allen consistently examines the incest or incest-associated proscriptions set forth in Leviticus that feature no consanguineous consequence. This facilitates Allen's protagonists engaging incest prohibitions and exogamy taboos in the very same person. *Hannah and Her Sisters*, *Stardust Memories*, *Café Society*, and "Retribution" all depict the forbidden "family" members as "shiksa" types—they are never Jewish.

Close reading of Allen's films with these relationships in mind permits a more thorough analysis of these films' considerations of family, difference, sexual attraction, and legal marriage. In avoiding these issues, scholars risk dismissing contradictions and inconsistencies that, ironically, Allen demands his audience engage. Consider Lloyd Michaels's word choice for introducing a limited reading of Allen's personal life in considering his "cinema of regret": "Allen's place as the epitome of artistic integrity and icon of intellectual hipness met its demise with the scandal over the breakup with his star and longtime romantic companion, Mia Farrow, following the revelation of his affair with Farrow's adopted daughter, Soon-Yi Previn (who, it *still needs to be said*, was not Allen's legal stepdaughter), and the subsequent custody battle over their children in 1992" (469; my emphasis). Michaels's idiomatic insistence that "it still needs to be said" that Allen was not Previn's legal stepfather sits problematically aside Michaels's choice *not* to say anything about Dylan Farrow's abuse allegations, which, as I have argued, cannot be separated from the Previn affair. But this choice to so curtly dismiss any audience inclination to consider Previn as a daughter figure seems especially ironic given the content of an article that mines the artist's consideration of regret. Christopher Knight, on the other hand, decisively labels Allen's behavior with Previn as immoral, on account of "entering into a sexual relation with a very young Soon-Yi, the daughter of his partner" (77). However, in his examination of themes of melancholy, regret, and despair in Allen's post-1991 films, Knight makes only very cursory reference to Dylan, and instead of dealing straightforwardly with the nature of her allegations, tends toward vague euphemisms (regarding Allen's custody case, "the matter, as we know, became more complicated, with the result that Allen lost custody of his natural male child" [77]).[4]

This tendency to avoid mentioning Dylan Farrow in scholarly assessments of Allen's work, even regarding the "scandal," is relatively common. Colleen Glenn and the aforementioned Christopher Knight are the only scholars to make even passing reference to Dylan and her allegations in 2013's *A Companion to Woody Allen*, a compendium that comes in at over six-hundred pages. Vincent Brook and Marat Grinberg's more recent collection, *Woody on Rye*, which focuses on Jewishness and Allen's films, features essays that refer to the "scandal" but only makes very brief mention of Dylan in Brook's essay ("The Gospel" 12).[5] That said, Brook and Grinberg's introduction notes the importance of the "scandal" to Allen's work, "particularly in regard to depictions of women and romantic relationships" (xxviii). The acknowledgment highlights the corollary gap: any corresponding notion that depictions of children and fatherhood might also be significant are left to be inferred by readers familiar with the significance of Dylan Farrow's allegations or skeptical of Allen's inconsistent claims that his relationship to Previn was not paternal.

We might also consider the term "scandal." Certainly, it makes for a convenient shorthand, and a less awkward one than "incest narrative." But referring to "scandal" may intimate voyeuristic engagement that subsumes serious consideration of the transgression—indeed, the extent to which Allen scholarship refers to the Allen/Previn or Allen/Mia Farrow "scandal" reminds us of the comparative difficulty of characterizing the alleged sexual abuse of a seven-year-old as "scandal." This term functions quite euphemistically, suggesting a prurient preoccupation with sexual transgressions that cannot be named, leaving the incestuous or pedophilic quality unspoken. By referring to the "scandal," but neglecting to speak to the specifics of the alleged behavior, these scholars seem to exemplify Toni McNaron and Yarrow Morgan's assessment: "We believe that there is not a taboo against incest; merely against speaking about it" (15).[6]

Among those creating scholarship about Allen's life and work since 1992, Samuel Dresner addresses the incest narrative most directly. In "Woody Allen and the Jews," Dresner approaches Allen's films and his personal life from a religious Jewish perspective. The piece makes a thoughtful and compelling case for understanding Soon-Yi Previn and Allen's relationship as incestuous, defining the incest taboo as serving to "prevent the power relations and emotional ties of the family from being abused" (195). But this comes directly after the observation that "for some, it took the tragedy of Mia and Woody to demonstrate the value of marriage" (194). Dresner also laments Allen's filmic depictions of "the lusting of the Jew for the Gentile woman" (193). Dresner's critique of Allen also essentially invokes conservative "family values" when he asks, "Once we abandon the strictures of marriage, family, the home, the bulwarks of Jewish and Christian morality, why not approve pedophilia and incest?" (197).

Dresner's scholarly consideration of Allen and incest, in many respects, is the exception that proves the rule (along with Jeffrey Rubin-Dorsky's essay on *Deconstructing Harry*, which I consider shortly). In the subsequent close readings, we will see how Allen's post-custody-trial films frequently invite the audience to consider his art alongside the public incest narrative that so comprehensively impacted Allen's public image. That is, the axiom of "separating the art from the artist," even were we to grant it as an ideal for considering an artistic aesthetic, is something Allen himself coyly forswears, as his art so clearly draws on aspects of his real-life incest narrative and custody case. Thinly veiled allusions to specific allegations, along with the question of how to come to terms with getting away with a moral transgression, emerge as singular points of focus in many of Allen's post-1992 films.

"Getting Away with Murder"

Crimes and Misdemeanors, released in 1989, predates the public incest narrative. But it marks the beginning of Allen's decades-long engagement with the theme of getting away with murder. It has also been considered one of Allen's more "Jewish" films, given its religious content and preoccupation with faith, sin, and moral judgment. While various scholars have explored Allen's engagement with the "getting away with murder" theme, the extent to which plot points in these films intersect directly with his autobiographical incest narrative has not been sufficiently interrogated, despite the thematic parallels.

Allen's *Deconstructing Harry* is rarely grouped in the "getting away with murder" genre. Far more conventionally, the film is analyzed for its layered depictions of fictions within fiction: the plot involves an author dealing with custody issues and self-loathing retreating into his own fictional worlds for respite from the "reality" in which he has failed to forge meaningful relations. Sam Girgus analyzes the autobiographical components of the film in some detail, including an allusion to protagonist Harry Block's custody situation with his ex-wife: "As a profound reminder of the relationship between Allen's life and his fictional characters, in a scene near the end of *Deconstructing Harry*,

Harry sits in jail after being accused of kidnapping his son, a distressing reminder of accusations of molestation and abuse that were made against Allen just a few years earlier" (152). Girgus identifies an important intersection—the specific issue of custody that comes up again in *Irrational Man*—but uses passive voice, ostensibly to avoid attaching the claims of abuse to Dylan Farrow. But Girgus later makes clear that considering the sexual content of Allen's films "compels some reference" not just to Allen's affair with Previn, but to Dylan Farrow's allegations as well (162). Girgus analyzes the film in the context of the significant personal criticism Allen had received since 1992, suggesting that by "embodying Harry's horrible qualities of character, Allen mitigates somewhat the effectiveness of . . . attacks on Allen's own moral character" (152). Essentially, by having Block concede his immorality, Allen the artist can succeed at creating art delving into Block's introspection and artistic struggles, even if the film is marked by "nihilism and cynicism" (163). Mary Nichols also reads the autobiographical elements of *Deconstructing Harry* as serving a defensive purpose, suggesting that Harry Block provides Allen's "most vociferous critics, who confuse his art with his life and judge both harshly, a version of the despicable person they imagine that he is. He holds out bait, and critics bite" (x). Where Nichols indicates more of Allen's playful, or perhaps defiant, mode, both she and Girgus read the film as responding to negative coverage of Allen.

But the depths of the nihilism and cynicism in *Deconstructing Harry* may extend farther than even Girgus allows. Among the film's set pieces, the Max Pinkus story finds Allen engaging complexly, and disturbingly, with the blood libel and sexual antisemitism. A close reading of the vignette compels acknowledgment of Allen's status as a Jewish man accused of child abuse. That precise intersection exponentially increases the provocative nature of the scene.

The Max Pinkus story begins with an accusation. The film's protagonist, Harry Block (played by Allen), has been called a self-hating Jew by his sister. As evidence, the film jumps from the "real" (Block's visit with his sister) to a bar mitzvah scene in which Block narrates Pinkus's story, about an elderly Jewish man admitting to his wife that years ago he had killed his first wife and *her* children (not *their* children) and ate their bodies. All of this is consistent with blood libel, but Allen mines the territory for comedy. The bar mitzvah scene has a *Star Wars* theme, and Darth Vader's disembodied head sits as a centerpiece of nearly every shot. Allen's imagery suggests bad fathers as a universal problem, though the setting entails a specifically Jewish context. Jeffrey Rubin-Dorsky identifies these tensions and contemplates Allen's choice to depict "Jewish primitivism" (22) and whether the story's use of antisemitic themes ought to offend his "fiercely loyal" (28) Jewish audience. Rubin-Dorsky's nuanced analysis considers the type of community protective impulses that inform Block's sister's emphatic rejection.

Though Rubin-Dorsky correctly identifies the charged nature of Allen engaging antisemitic stereotype, he avoids mention of the scene's intersection with Dylan Farrow's allegations. But the scene begs for analysis in the context of Allen having been accused of sexually molesting a white Christian girl. The blood libel, the notion that Jews killed Christian children and consumed their blood, invites contemplation alongside sexual antisemitism, and pedophilia in particular. Cannibalism (bodily consumption) echoes sexual threat, especially when the assailant is an adult and the victim a child.[7]

Pinkus literally destroys a family that he is at once a part of and apart from (the children are from a previous marriage) by devouring a wife, her two children, and a neighbor.[8] Allen, of course, also contradictorily pronounced himself as both a part of and apart from a Farrow family that he moved from elevating to denigrating. And Mia Farrow's assessment that Allen's behavior played a role in destroying that family certainly bears mention. Rubin-Dorsky suggests that Allen's Jewish audience might find his mining the blood libel for comedy offensive, but this prompts us to consider precisely what a "fiercely loyal" Jewish audience does or does not find offensive in Allen's scene. By referring to his audience as "fiercely loyal," Rubin-Dorsky ostensibly identifies those Allen fans who remained loyal after the events of 1991 and 1992. The offense Rubin-Dorsky signifies, without actually identifying, may be Allen's reminding this audience that, in choosing loyalty, they overlooked credible allegations regarding Allen's behavior with his previous, non-Jewish family.

On that note, for all its autobiographical intersection, the scene is devoid of regret or remorse in arriving at its amoral punch line. When confronted by his wife of thirty years about his murderous past, Pinkus offers, "If I tell you why I did it, will you promise not to nudge me?" Pinkus's defiant, dismissive defense is, "So what are you making a fuss? Some bury, some burn, I ate!" The supposed apologia is satirized. Having set up the suspense of Pinkus finally revealing why he committed an unspeakable act, he instead affirms cannibalism as his preferred method of disposing of bodies. In his filmmaking choices, Allen also bypasses any impossible, pointless attempt at earnest apologia for a clear, defiant assertion of his preference to satirize it. Some apologize, some go on *Oprah*, Allen makes jokes.

Pinkus's demeanor and name also merit scrutiny. The scene's comedic energy necessitates him being utterly unthreatening. Allen reveals Pinkus in the vignette's final scene, and all he wants is to eat his dinner. The buildup yields an old schlubby man, an unconvincing monster, and yet a murderer nonetheless; his flippant admission seems all the more horrific and thus comedic. This too brings Allen to mind. How much evidence of sexual transgression would Allen have to present for his adamant defenders to find him morally culpable, or capable, of committing such transgressions? In many respects, the Pinkus scene echoes Stiller's "Woody Allen's Bride of Frankenstein" sketch. But where Stiller's sketch obliquely engages the question of the Allen abuse allegation vis-à-vis Jewish community complicity and protective politics, Allen's vignette is defiant and aggressive.

Regarding the name, the *pinkas* refers to the book of records in Yiddish-speaking Eastern European Jewish communities. The scene may comment on the relationship between immoral actions, history, and stereotype. Some actions, including, perhaps, some of Allen's, cannot be removed from the record.

A Consequential Phone Call in *Blue Jasmine*

Blue Jasmine (2013) functions as a metaphorical "getting away with murder" plot, but with a twist. The Bernie Madoff-esque financial transgressions of Hal (Alec Baldwin), ex-husband of the film's protagonist Jasmine (Cate Blanchett), ostensibly serve as the film's pivotal crime. Toward the end of the film, though, we learn that Jasmine turned her husband in to the FBI. This reveal indicates how his eventual suicide and the devastation his arrest wreaked on her and her son's lives continue to weigh on her conscience.

The viewer learns this information from Jasmine's estranged son, who introduces the relevant flashback after defiantly telling her, "I know the whole story; I found it out, so don't act surprised." The flashback depicts the moment when Hal tells Jasmine of his affair and his plan to leave her. Blanchett performs Jasmine's emotional devastation, while Alec Baldwin's Hal is calm, collected, and direct. He tells her, "Lisette and I are in love," and "I know this comes as a shock but I have to be honest with you." Hal's calm only accentuates Jasmine's state of distress. When Jasmine exclaims, "She is a teenager for Christ's sake!" there are echoes of both Mia Farrow's and Allen's descriptions of her reaction to learning about Allen's affair with Previn.

Reviews occasionally commented on this evocation. Anisse Gross observed, "The scene where she confronts Hal about his affair with [a teenage] au pair, she is portrayed in classic Woody Allen 'hysteria' but really she's only responding naturally to a horrific scenario. My friend Larry pointed out that while watching the scene he couldn't help but wonder if this wasn't more or less the exact exchange between Woody Allen and Mia Farrow when he told her he was leaving her for her daughter." Allen covered this betrayal territory before.[9] But this portion of the scene is merely prelude. Hal leaves, unwilling to continue interacting with Jasmine during what he characterizes as her "tantrum." Jasmine finds the phone and, wrought with emotion, calls the FBI. The next scene shows Hal being arrested.

We then return to the present, where Jasmine's son Danny says, "As disillusioned as I was with him, I hated you more." Through tears, Jasmine responds,

"The moment I did what I did I regretted it." Danny replies, "You can't take back that phone call." Michaels's cinema of regret is on full display. The twist reveals Jasmine's responsibility, and its consequences.

As Gross and others have observed, an autobiographical reading of the Hal/Jasmine relationship, especially the affair with the teenage au pair, invites consideration against the Allen/Mia Farrow/Previn triangle. Vincent Brook also makes the case that Allen revisits the "Mia Farrow/Soon Yi Previn scandal of 1992" in direct fashion: "Hal's high profile scandal itself, which, though of a more serious nature (legally and ethically) than Allen's affair with, and later marriage to, Soon-Yi (discounting unproven charges of sexual abuse of his adopted daughter Dylan), has clear associations with it" ("Woody's Revenge"). Brook proceeds to comment on the parallels between Jasmine's relationship with her estranged son and Moses Farrow's public declaration of siding "with Allen on the child molestation charge" ("Woody's Revenge").[10] Brook's reading into the autobiographical intersections in Allen's work fuels his analysis. However, "discounting" Dylan Farrow's "unproven" allegations prevents a more comprehensive engagement with Allen's biography's significance to the plot.

Jasmine's phone call, and the idea of a phone call that puts catastrophic events in motion and cannot be taken back, echoes descriptions of phone calls (in Mia Farrow's memoir and Marion Meade's biography of Allen) that Mia Farrow made to her lawyer, Dylan Farrow's pediatrician, and one of Allen's therapists (Susan Coates). These were phone calls in which Mia Farrow relayed Dylan Farrow's allegation that Allen had touched her inappropriately.

Unlike other aspects of the incest narrative, nobody contests that these phone calls took place, though Allen and his apologists insist that Mia Farrow fabricated or somehow implanted Dylan Farrow's allegations. However, according to Marion Meade, after Dylan Farrow communicated to her mother that Allen touched her "privates" during a visit at their Connecticut home, Mia Farrow called Eleanor Alter, the divorce lawyer who would represent her in the subsequent custody case. Alter, according to Meade, "advised her to take Dylan to the family pediatrician immediately" (227). She did so, and though Dylan Farrow did not repeat her abuse allegations at that first visit with her physician, the following day they returned to the doctor, who "was able to elicit the story Dylan had told to her mother" (228).

While the phone calls and the visits are uncontested, Allen and his lawyers and supporters have consistently suggested that Dylan Farrow fabricated her testimony on account of Mia's brainwashing, bullying, or "indoctrination" (a term Allen used in his February 2014 *New York Times* op-ed response to Dylan Farrow, "Woody Allen Speaks Out").[11] But for this reading of *Blue Jasmine*, the question of whether Mia Farrow did or did not "implant" memories is moot. Following the second visit, the pediatrician "phoned Mia to say he would be notifying the authorities. *Surprised, she tried to dissuade him, but Dr. Kavirajan had already checked with his lawyers*" (Meade 228; my emphasis). Meade reports that Mia Farrow then called Susan Coates, who told her she also legally had to contact New York City authorities if Dylan Farrow's pediatrician was contacting Connecticut authorities and that she would also contact Allen. Meade reports, "Mia burst into tears. Fearing Woody's anger, she begged Coates not to tell him" (228).

In her memoir, Mia Farrow conveys the same information, though she provides dialogue for her conversation with Coates: "'Don't tell him,' I said. 'I'm scared of what he'll do. Can't you just deal with it? Don't report it to the authorities. That will destroy everything. It's too big. Terrible things are going to happen!'" (300). Mia Farrow's real-life calls are conveyed not as impulsive so much as protective, in her and Meade's telling. However, Mia Farrow, even more than Meade, reveals a sense of foreboding regarding the inevitable consequence of her choices and, to be sure, a sense of regret—if not remorse, to keep Lloyd Michaels's relevant distinction in mind.

Blue Jasmine suggests that Jasmine's call does indeed "destroy everything," including any chance that she and Danny might end their estrangement. Yet while we are not privy to Jasmine's call, at no point does the plot suggest she lies in providing information to the FBI. Allen casts Jasmine's act as immoral because, previously complicit, she only implicates her husband for his illegal activity once she becomes jealous of his new lover. Essentially, the film asks us to see Jasmine for what she "truly" is—a hypocrite who brought her downfall upon herself. The same scene essentially exonerates Hal of hypocrisy, as he clearly and forthrightly admits his affair. But Hal *is* a criminal. And while Brook contends that Hal's crimes are more serious than Allen's transgressions with Previn, this is a subjective minimization (and one that discounts Dylan Farrow's sexual abuse allegations).

Again: I am not suggesting that *Blue Jasmine* functions as autobiography. However, it engages the question of guilt and consequence in highly specific terms that intersect with a pivotal moment in Allen's life that hinged on someone else's choice. In drilling down into the parallels, we see that if Jasmine is a Mia Farrow surrogate, she is one that Allen reveals not as a liar but as a hypocrite. This is unexpected. According to his public and courtroom testimony, Allen swore that he never touched Dylan Farrow in the fashion alleged in Mia Farrow's initial phone call. He suggested that Mia Farrow fabricated Dylan Farrow's allegations. Yet as an artist, he writes a story that suggests Jasmine sins by telling the FBI the truth. If we take seriously the notion of Jasmine functioning as a Mia Farrow surrogate, and read *Blue Jasmine*'s moral universe onto real life, Allen's complaint with Mia Farrow's call to the pediatrician is not that she reports anything untrue, but, rather, that the call is motivated by her jealousy regarding Allen's affair with Previn.[12]

I emphasize that I offer this reading only in the context of considering Jasmine as a Mia Farrow surrogate. I am not claiming that Allen molested Dylan or citing *Blue Jasmine* as evidence. However, this is the type of reading that numerous Allen film scholars attempt with his films and that Allen himself implicitly solicits: an attempt to understand his films in the context of his life and stardom. Glenn reminds us that Allen's fans have difficulty discerning the movie character from the man himself, and while I agree, I also want to foreground that this confusion involves Allen's purposeful crafting of a viewing experience that demands that confusion. Allen's public insistence of his innocence functions as a prerequisite for reviewers and critics lauding films that consistently reveal Woody Allen surrogates getting away with serious crimes. The disconnect resides in departing from the premise of Allen's innocence and the choice to ignore Allen's simultaneously disturbing and "playful" suggestion that, perhaps, he is guilty.

Irrational Reading of a Custody Case Conversation

Elliott Wilk presided over the custody case that Allen brought against Mia Farrow for sole custody of their children Moses, Ronan (then Satchel), and Dylan Farrow. His decision not only denied Allen custody but undercut the findings of the Child Sexual Abuse Clinic at Yale-New Haven regarding Dylan Farrow's allegations of abuse, as Yale-New Haven suggested that her claims were fantasy.[13] Wilk wrote, in his opinion, "Unlike Yale-New Haven, I am not persuaded that the videotape of Dylan is the product of leading questions or of the child's fantasy" (M. Farrow 362). By the time *Irrational Man* (2015) hit theaters, Wilk had been dead for over a decade.

Irrational Man's plot revolves around philosophy professor Abe Lucas (Joaquin Phoenix) murdering a family court judge after overhearing a conversation at a diner. Lucas hears a woman accuse the judge of denying her custody of her children due to the judge being "cozy" with her ex-husband's attorney. Joan Ullman, writing for *Psychology Today*, connected Allen's autobiography to the plot, noting that because Wilk "sided with Mia in almost every particular," Allen had "every motive to wish any biased family court judge—real, or fictional—dead." While Ullman found Allen's use of the autobiographical material justified and entertaining, other critics found it disturbing. As entertainment journalist Kate Aurthur put it, in a conversation with film critic Alison Willmore, "it's a shocking autobiographical reference on Allen's part. Is there a term for an inside joke . . . when it's something about that time you were accused of incestuous pedophilia?" (Willmore and Aurthur).

The plot point may register as shocking because reviews and scholarship have, for more than a decade, taken pains not to engage the number of inside jokes Allen has included about the time he was accused of incestuous pedophilia, such as in *Deconstructing Harry* and *Blue Jasmine*. *Irrational Man*'s specificity, though, stands out: Lucas poisons Judge Thomas Augustus Spangler when he sits down on a bench at a park after his morning jog. Meade's biography of Allen refers to Wilk as "the jogging jurist." The unexpected nature of the relatively young Spangler's death at sixty-one factors into suspicion that he was murdered. Wilk died at sixty from cancer (Martin). The mother, in the diner, says of Spangler, "I hope the judge gets cancer." Allen returns to the specifics of the incest narrative with disconcerting precision here.

Taken as a body of work, we might think about Aurthur's sense of "inside jokes" and consider the observation alongside a feature of film fandom dating back to *The Rocky Horror Picture Show*. The presence of discernible Easter eggs in various scenes of *Rocky Horror* accounts for the name of a film-viewing phenomenon involving particular details rewarding attentive viewers. Because these references are immaterial to the plot, they demand no exposition and neither disturb nor complicate the viewing experience for the broader audience. However, for the discerning viewer, Easter eggs augment the viewing experience, providing a sense of being in on something inaccessible to other, less informed viewers. *Deconstructing Harry*, *Blue Jasmine*, and *Irrational Man* all contain incest Easter eggs. Now, Allen himself has contradicted this premise, stating that "people are always making these crazy parallels between my life and my films" (Girgus 149). But we cannot take Allen at face value in making this claim. The specificity of these intersections—these "crazy parallels," as he puts it—defy categorization as mere creative coincidence.

Allen essentially hides these Easter eggs in plain sight, and his assertion that they are *not* there provides the cover for him to incorporate such blatant references. The notion that these choices are mere coincidence defies reason; not merely because of their specificity, but because ignoring them also requires diminishing Allen's intelligence and artistry. Acknowledging them would force audiences to honestly reckon with how his films consistently suggest the plausibility of the incest allegations in terms of the moral quandaries and ambivalences of the various Allen/Farrow surrogates. Even when scholars assert amoral or nihilistic structures in *Deconstructing Harry*, for instance, these studies depart from an assumption that Allen operates with a functioning moral compass in rendering his view of nihilism or amorality. This presupposition requires a blindness to how the amoral logic of Allen's films extends to excusing, justifying, or defiantly accommodating abusive, even monstrous, adult male behavior. But consider Max Pinkus: Allen depicts monstrosity as paradox; unthreatening, familiar, and familial. Allen is well aware of how these dynamics function and how his own persona operates as a shield against allegations.

If we concede that Allen consciously incorporates these moments into his films, we must acknowledge that he trades on his autobiographical incest narrative. On the one hand, this makes sense; the material provides a window into his thinking on allegations about which he is often circumspect in interviews. But it seems odd, given the extent to which Allen scholars go out of their way to avoid engagement with the incest narrative, ostensibly premised on a notion that addressing it would be either lurid or libelous, that Allen returns to it time and again. And yet, it reaffirms what incest scholars like Gillian Harkins have argued persuasively: incest narratives invite mass consumption. Allen's incest narrative is no exception.

Gillian Harkins has observed that the 1990s found an increase in female-authored (and broadly, female-consumed) incest narratives: "Once the publishing industry grasped the possibilities of this new market, more and more women were empowered to speak out and contradict the masculinist silencing of incest in print" (3). Harkins's analysis examines how many of these texts simultaneously reified and resisted, in subtle ways, patriarchal neoliberal logics regarding sex and family. But Harkins importantly distinguishes between types of sexual abuse narratives—she notes that incest narratives were largely consumed during the 1990s, while pedophilia narratives were often litigated. Allen's narrative, as established in the previous chapter, simultaneously linked and unlinked incest and pedophilia in its telling; the family structure was constantly being qualified as not *truly* a family. Previn's age was constantly confused, deliberately or subconsciously, with Dylan Farrow's age. Race also played a role in affecting the extent to which Previn was depicted as capable of having ever had a "childhood."

Thinking about Allen as an author of incest narratives forces us to consider, first, the subjectivity of his films and, second, the amount of Dylan Farrow references within his work. He purposefully returns to those autobiographical intersections that evoke her, and time and again engages the trope of a protagonist getting away with crime. We might also think of the particular scenes he revisits time and again, such as the betrayal scene. In *Deconstructing Harry*, Kirstie Alley plays the role of the scorned adult lover, who yells and screams at Allen's Block. In *Blue Jasmine*, Alec Baldwin's Hal dismisses the emotional response of Cate Blanchett's Jasmine as a "tantrum."

These scenes play on the trope of a "woman scorned" and emerge regularly within masculinist incest stories. While Harkins focuses on female-authored texts that "contradict . . . masculinist silencing" (3), Allen's films give voice to "hysterical" women. This reveals a particularity of how masculinist incest narratives appeal to their audiences: incest needs to have consequence. It just doesn't have to be a big consequence. Being yelled at, in Allen's films, generally suffices. For fragile masculinities, being yelled at by a woman may seem authentically terrorizing.

Consider Jim Trueblood's role in Ralph Ellison's *Invisible Man*. Trueblood follows up the unbelievable story of his having supposedly unintentional sex with his daughter, Matty Lou, with an account of how his wife, Kate, accosts him with an ax afterward. The consumable aspect of Trueblood's incest story, in order to successfully solicit financial donations from his white audience, requires a particular framing. First, he has to successfully convince his audience that having sex with his daughter was an accident, and, second, he has to reveal that his wife was severely angry with him afterward. The Trueblood incest narrative has a built-in excuse (I didn't mean to do the thing you're paying me to tell you about) and a built-in point of sympathetic engagement (my wife was unreasonably angry with me when she saw what I "accidentally" did; your wife probably would have been, too).

Allen's storytelling resembles Trueblood's. He repeatedly revisits the scene of betrayal, and he consistently denies agency. He does this by referring to the autobiographical content of his films as "crazy parallels." With Allen, it is not the sex that is accidental, but the autobiographical intersections that are. He insists we suspend disbelief. But his manner of appealing to a predominantly masculinist audience's vicarious interest in incest is familiar: he just replaces Kate's ax with Kirstie Alley's (and others') traumatized, furious, screams.[14]

Café Black Guys Playing Jazz and Jewish Guy Being Exotic

In closing this chapter, I turn to a moment in Allen's recent film *Café Society*, one of Allen's period pieces. Set in New York City and Los Angeles in the 1930s, its protagonist, Bobby Dorfman (Jesse Eisenberg), falls in love with a young woman also romantically involved with his uncle. Bobby confides his continued feelings for Vonnie (Kristen Stewart) to her even after she and his uncle Phil (Steve Carell) wed, calling her "Aunt Vonnie." But the scene I want to focus on features Bobby and his eventual wife, Veronica (Blake Lively), at a jazz club on the night they meet.

The scene has no overtones of incest. But it features an explicit discussion about antisemitic stereotypes, layered onto conversation rife with sexual tension. The topic of their conversation, in essence, is Bobby's exotic sexual appeal.

The scene begins with the camera panning across a small nightclub before focusing in on Bobby and Veronica, as the band plays Ralph Rainger's composition "June in January." With the possible but unlikely exception of the light-skinned standing bass player, everyone else in the club is Black. As Bobby and Veronica flirt, she shares her political philosophy, saying, "I hope you don't mind a Democratic liberal." Bobby explains his family is Jewish, and Veronica teases him, "How quaint," before sharing (and flirting) about antisemitism growing up in Oklahoma:

VERONICA: Plays right into my rebellious streak! You know, in Oklahoma, we weren't even allowed to mingle with Jews growing up!

BOBBY: Really?
VERONICA: Yeah, you guys are moneylenders!
BOBBY: No, we control everything, actually.
VERONICA: I didn't even see a Jew until I moved to New York.
BOBBY: No horns, so.
VERONICA: I find Jews exotic, mysterious. I wouldn't mind if you had horns.
BOBBY: You wouldn't?
VERONICA: No.
BOBBY: OK, come on, let's go.
VERONICA: What?
BOBBY: We'll go to my place. (*Café Society*)

Veronica declines his advances, but her reply expresses antisemitic stereotype alongside flirtatious banter: "It's true what they say, you people are pushy!" Eisenberg plays Bobby's emotional response to Veronica with nuance. His jokes draw attention to the absurdity of Veronica's comments but also cut the tension regarding her immense familiarity—he seems, between jokes, to sip his drink and arch his eyebrows in ways that suggest annoyance and amusement with her flirtatious othering. But the scene explicitly connects sexual attraction with Jewish exoticism drawn from antisemitic stereotypes. It is Veronica's vocalized exoticizing of Jews ("I wouldn't mind if you had horns") that directly spurs Bobby to proposition her.

That line, in particular, evokes how Allen presents Jewish masculinity throughout his films. Jewish masculine potency as derived from its historically marginalized status serves as a challenge to, and not an affirmation of, Bobby's individual sexuality. For Veronica, Bobby's attractiveness may center his Jewishness above his other human qualities. Furthermore, while Veronica explicitly references the Jew's horns, she may also allude to cuckoldry (the cuckold's horns), a theme that Allen also explores in *You Will Meet a Tall Dark Stranger*.[15] Her othering of Bobby simultaneously hypersexualizes him and emasculates him; he becomes her object. Propositioning her directly after her "horns" statement facilitates Bobby confirming some of her flirtatious insinuations as to his sexuality, while refuting others.

But the scene's setting speaks to another set of contradictions for which Allen's films have received significant and important criticism: Veronica sexualizes Bobby in a jazz club with a Black band and Black audience members surrounding them. Bobby brings them to the club after Veronica confirms her love for jazz, and the jazz facilitates their sexual banter. Allen's films, so many of which are set in New York City, have consistently eschewed depicting the city's considerable nonwhite population. Spike Lee stated in an interview in 1987, "Woody Allen, he can do a film about Manhattan—it's about one-half black and Hispanic—and he doesn't have a single black person in the film"

(Mieher). In *Café Society*, Allen films Black jazz musicians and customers, but they say nothing as a non-Jewish white woman communicates her sexual interest with the help of Black music.[16]

Set in the 1930s, Veronica's antisemitic flirtation carries foreboding qualities. In that sense, the scene echoes aspects of Philip Roth's *The Plot against America*. Both Roth's novel and Allen's film engage, though briefly and ambivalently, the problem of contextualizing antisemitism alongside American racism. African Americans play a very small role in *The Plot against America*, but for a thought-provoking, discomfiting scene in which Walter Winchell, the Jewish anti-fascist presidential candidate, attempts to rouse audiences with his pro-democracy, anti-Lindbergh rhetoric. On September 8, 1942, Winchell campaigns across New York City, with varying success, and finally arrives in Harlem, "where, in the crowd of several hundred Negroes who gathered at dusk to hear him speak at the corner of Lenox Avenue and 125th Street, a few laughed and a handful applauded but most remained respectfully dissatisfied, as though to work his way into their antipathies would require his delivering a very different spiel" (P. Roth 260–261). The crowd is relatively unmoved, and the narrator seems at ease with this. While American Jews of European descent earnestly pursued the promise of democracy, due to their legal whiteness, Roth suggests that appealing to these ideals might leave Black citizens "respectfully dissatisfied." The Harlem crowd's reaction to Winchell's speech implies skepticism regarding his attention to their oppression. We might reasonably be skeptical of whether Black voters in Harlem would have been so indifferent to Winchell's appeal; Black voters distinguishing among politicians with varying degrees of insincerity and fascistic intent was nothing new in the 1930s. Yet Roth, to his credit, seems to wrestle with the very presuppositions of his historical novel, which departs from the premise that the absence of Roosevelt in the presidential race clears the way for fascism. But this type of historical fiction obscures Jim Crow (among other systems of distinctly American fascist oppression) to achieve this contrast.

Read sympathetically, Roth's novel acknowledges the irony of a Jewish American candidate failing to rouse moral indignation from an American population whose rights had never been fully granted. *Café Society* seems more cynical. Black extras sit in the club, play music, and provide "atmosphere" to accentuate Bobby's catch-22: his "seduction" of Veronica has less to do with Bobby as a person than it does his membership in an exoticized group. And while Bobby struggles with whether the beautiful woman flirting with him will acknowledge his humanity, his citizenship rights are far more assured and protected than his fellow club-goers. But in focusing solely on Bobby's experience, Allen does not address the irony of Bobby's masculine insecurities being exposed while sitting among a Black audience and performers who have no dialogue, muted such that they cannot even be "respectfully dissatisfied." For

Allen, these Black faces serve merely as backdrop, augmenting the "authenticity" of the jazz club scene in which Jewish male sexual insecurity can be explored.

In bookending this chapter with scenes in Allen's films that deal directly with Jewishness and sexuality, I concede that the content of *Blue Jasmine* and the murder of the family court judge in *Irrational Man* do not actively engage questions of Jewishness or Jewish-identified characters. Perhaps, by deracinating the characters and content in *Blue Jasmine* and *Irrational Man*, Allen more comfortably engages with his personal incest narrative. But even in this deracinated form, the intersections are so particular as to demand that we consider Allen's incorporation of these moments as deliberate engagements. As a writer and director, Allen tells his own stories and constructs his own settings: time and again, the ethnoracial significance of Jewish male sexuality demands, for Allen, that it be foregrounded in a New York City that never accurately reflects the city's demographic realities. That loose framing, that sense of what moves, as Toni Morrison puts it, at the margins, sets up my final case study of Henry Roth's *Mercy of a Rude Stream*.

5

"Till a *Khusin* Comes Along"

Cousins, American Africanism, and Rape in Henry Roth's *Mercy of a Rude Stream*

For a book eponymously engaged with incest as Jewish taboo, this chapter departs from a counterintuitive premise: when a text gains notoriety for its provocative, explicit engagement with autobiographical Jewish incest, what deeper taboo might that celebration obscure? If previous case studies reveal how Jewish community protective politics disassociated Jewish icons with incest, Henry Roth functions as a stress test for the proposition, as he was never alleged to have committed incest. Rather, he essentially confessed to it. In Roth's mid-1990s autobiographical novel *Mercy of a Rude Stream* (*MORS*), the protagonist reveals a sexual relationship with his sister, a component of the plot that has generated significant critical and scholarly commentary. Here, I investigate two underexamined facets of the text: the protagonist's sexual relationship with his first cousin and the structural role played by hypersexual Black characters. Jewish community protective politics, as enacted by the novel's editor and critics, played a discernible role in sensationalizing the text's engagement with approximately lateral sibling incest in ways that obscured the novel's depiction of more deeply felt Jewish taboos: pedophilia and anti-Black racism. Jewish community protective politics reveal their adaptability here, salvaging an iconic figure's problematic autobiographical depiction of white Jewish masculinity by disguising taboos arguably more dangerous to how the Jewish community conceives of itself. While everyone presumably agrees that sibling incest is bad, this chapter shows that it is less taboo than white Jewish investment in white supremacy or the prospect of a Jewish teenager raping his eleven-year-old first cousin.

I examine these themes via close reading *MORS* along with its manuscripts and spotlighting the editing process, overseen by Robert Weil at St. Martin's Press, that substantially altered Roth's original text. The editorial process abided a version of Jewish community protective politics by removing the racist language Roth used to describe Black characters and changing the age of a character the novel's protagonist repeatedly rapes. While Jewish community protective politics typically act to disassociate Jewish men from incestuous stereotypes, this case study reveals that the same principals—the importance of protecting a particular image of white Jewish masculinity—could accommodate the invocation of Jewish incest if that deflected attention from an even greater taboo. In *MORS*, graphic renderings of sibling incest and pronounced homophobia were deemed permissible, yet Roth's equally explicit depictions of pedophilia and the protagonist's racism were omitted, thereby revealing those behaviors as better fitting the definition of "taboo."

Though Henry Roth was best known as the author of *Call It Sleep* (1934), widely considered a classic of modernist immigrant American literature, *MORS* garnered significant critical and scholarly attention for its depiction of an autobiographical protagonist's sexual relationship with his sister. *MORS* was published by St. Martin's Press in four volumes from 1994 to 1998 (with the final two volumes released after Roth's death) and follows the story of Ira Stigman, Roth's autobiographical surrogate. The main narrative begins with Ira as an eight-year-old and follows him through his twenties, when he wrote a novel that would bring him great acclaim. A secondary narrative finds the elderly Ira commenting on his long-lost youth, the writing process, and his perspective on the world as he approaches death: his heartfelt idealization of his wife M; his identification with Israel; his rejection of James Joyce as a literary forebear; his rightward political trajectory; his ambivalence about his first novel; and his declining physical health. Roth conducts this largely in third person, but occasionally, first-person narration survives into the final publication. Roth also employs a third narrative voice, the postmodern, disembodied voice of Ira's computer's word-processing program, dubbed Ecclesias. Ecclesias exists as a sort of alter ego, or literary conscience, serving as interlocutor and therapist for the elderly, often obstinate Ira character.

A four-volume epic originally designed with a six-volume arc, the plot features multiple components. I read the published novel as structured intently around Ira's sexual trauma and his subsequent struggle to come to terms with his incestuous relationship with his sister, cease the serial raping of his cousin, and (ironically) establish the conditions for his authoring the novel he distances himself from in the secondary narrative. A summary of specific, pertinent plot points will help frame this approach: volume 1 finds Ira being molested by adults on two occasions; once in Fort Tryon Park by a stranger named "Mr. Joe" and later by his Spanish teacher, Mr. Lennard. Mr. Joe gropes Ira's buttocks while masturbating, while Mr. Lennard simultaneously masturbates himself and Ira. Volume 2 reveals the presence of Ira's sister Minnie, named "Ruthie" in drafts, a name ultimately changed because it was too similar to Roth's actual sister's name (Rose). Minnie appears midway through volume 2, verbally instigating a sexual encounter with Ira. This revelation ostensibly accounts for the elderly Ira's frequently stated anxiety about content he had omitted from the narrative. Volume 2 also depicts Ira's sexual relationship with his fourteen-year-old cousin Stella, though unlike with Minnie, Roth graphically portrays their initial sexual encounter. Volume 3, largely due to Roth's sister Rose Broder's legal challenge, features no sexual contact with Minnie, but follows Ira's continued sexual relationship with Stella, his friendships with Larry Gordon and Edith Welles, and his intellectual awakening.[1] In volume 4 Ira moves out of his parents' apartment in Harlem and moves in with Edith, now his lover.

Before continuing with *MORS*, I should provide background on Roth's first novel. *Call It Sleep* (*CIS*) cemented Roth as an iconic, almost mythical figure in American Jewish literature, and *MORS* deals extensively with Ira's psychological navigation of having written a celebrated novel that he artistically disowns. The novels are inextricably linked. As Rachel Rubinstein observes of *MORS*, "*Call It Sleep* haunts both the narrative and the metanarrative: Stigman explicitly refers to the traumative effect of the writing of the novel during his metanarrative, and the narrative itself is rife with quotes and references to *Call It Sleep*, as scenes, images, and phrases are reproduced, and often implicitly explained, in the sections that recount Ira's childhood and young adulthood" (143). The novels overlap extensively, and both feature a child protagonist, though Ira Stigman eventually grows older than *CIS*'s David Schearl does. But while *CIS* was largely well received upon its publication, Roth was devastated by a review in a Communist journal (*New Masses*) he considered negative (Kellman 132, 134).[2] In 1960, Harold Ribalow bought the rights and arranged for the novel's first reprinting (Kellman 220). Four years later, Irving Howe reviewed *CIS* in the *New York Times Book Review* and the paperback edition became one of the year's best sellers (Kellman 226). Even then, though, Roth felt alienated by his first novel, suggesting that he felt like it was written by someone else (Kellman 233). Since the publication of *MORS*, scholars have tended to accept the premise that Roth's shame regarding incest largely accounted for the period of relative literary silence.

While both novels are autobiographically influenced, *MORS* sits more precariously on the precipice of novel and memoir. Volume 1 includes photographs of Roth as an adult and a child on its back cover, and its front and back endsheets feature a posed family picture from his youth, ostensibly indicating the prose's autobiographical engagement. The Library of Congress categorizes the book as fiction, but the design creates ambiguity. Close examination of manuscripts and drafts, as well as previously published materials, reveals how much Roth's creative process blurred the lines between fiction and memoir. A character strikingly similar to *MORS*'s Larry Gordon, based on Roth's real-life friend Lester Winter, appears with the name Lester Winter in a story called "Itinerant Ithacan," published in 1984. The same story also features a character named Eda Lou, who would be called Edith in *MORS*. But only in *MORS*, with the legal advice of his editors, does Roth change the name of his real-life friend and mentor Eda Lou Walton to "Edith Welles." The overwhelming autobiographical content motivated Hana Wirth-Nesher to refer to *MORS* as a "meta-memoir." For Wirth-Nesher, Roth's approach to carving out space between autobiography and fiction involved the challenges of writing about a life that was a subject of public fascination, and his status as a supposedly representative Jewish American writer. By writing a meta-memoir, Roth provides a "self-reflexive" response "to public discussion of . . . [his] career" (Wirth-Nesher 260).

While Wirth-Nesher's analysis creates a vocabulary for considering Roth's navigation of fact and fiction, I consider Roth's choices alongside those of his editors, who fundamentally transform Roth's text. Alan Gibbs also considers Roth's editors' impact on the characterization of Ira's sister, focusing on aesthetics, but I am most interested in the political ramifications of these revisions. What accounts for some of the manuscripts' supposedly unspeakable sexual taboos finding artistically celebrated expression, while others remained beyond the pale of representation? How did these tensions and seeming inconsistencies play out in the context of the expanded mainstream acceptability of explicitly sexual content characteristic of the 1990s?

In focusing on the sibling incest content in the novel, Roth scholars have left the first-cousin sexual relations less examined. The fixation on sibling incest has actually obscured the novel's portrayal of close endogamy, a phenomenon that was very common through to the early twentieth century, and not just in Jewish communities, but across a range of ethnoracial groups. Unlike sibling incest, first- and second-cousin marriage is identifiably extant in many family genealogies, Jewish or otherwise. Also not uncommon are ancestors who married at young ages. *MORS* allows for the important consideration of historical rape laws, ethics of representation of rape, and cousin relations, in addition to sibling incest. The focus on sibling incest has also provided scholars a seemingly plausible and convenient premise to account for Roth's long literary "silence." Suggesting that Roth waited half a century to write his second opus to process his shame at consensual incest facilitates a more uplifting account than suggesting that even with decades to reflect, Roth never truly processed the implications of his repeated rapes of an eleven- or twelve-year-old first cousin for whom, in his editor's estimation, he felt no respect (Gibbs, "Conversation" 157).

The Significance of Two Years

Unlike Ira's sister Minnie, who shockingly appears mid-narrative in volume 2, Stella, Ira's first cousin, shows up early in the first volume of *MORS* as a little girl. In a scene following Ira's bar mitzvah, Ira briefly introduces the various members of his extended family and then describes Stella as she leans out a window: "Mamie was admonishing her seven-year-old daughter, Stella, not to lean out so far, and Ira, stealing glances at his cousin's plump legs, slumped further down in his chair so that he could see up further, and fantasizing with fierce intensity that Stella was older" (1: 162). The scene is set in "the early summer of 1919" (1: 161). Having just had his bar mitzvah, we know that Ira was thirteen, and we can calculate that Stella was born in either 1912 or 1913.

This six-year age difference shifts in volume 2. In conversation with his friend Larry, Ira refers to "a cousin who's nearly fourteen years old. Stella" (2: 194). Stella's next appearance, and the first episode in which she and Ira interact, occurs at a family bris, where he either seduces her, coerces her, or rapes her. What you call it depends on a number of factors, including legalities (and the temporality of those laws), and how to assess sexual consent for an act conveyed by the narrator/rapist. But before close reading that scene, consider the prose that precedes the sex act. Upon seeing her at the bris, Ira thinks to himself: "Stella. For Chrissake. How old was she? Fourteen? Was he crazy or was he right?" (2: 282).

Note the attention that Roth has already devoted to establishing Stella's age. She is seven when she first appears in volume 1, and even at thirteen, Ira's gaze is lustful, as he wishes that the seven-year-old Stella were older. In volume 2, she goes from "nearly fourteen" to "fourteen?"—a distinction significant in highlighting Ira's uncertainty as well as historical consent laws.

Despite the question mark, Roth documents his timeline with relative precision when it comes to Stella: "The year 1924 waned into the Christmas holidays. In the Farb family a *bris* was to be celebrated on a Sunday during the Christmas holidays" (2: 278). Ira, born in 1906 (like Roth), having been bar mitzvah in 1919, would be approximately eighteen during this scene. This means a six-year age difference has collapsed into four years. Ira's wish "that Stella was older" (1: 162) has been granted.

Drafts for volume 2 reveal the precise moment this revision occurs. The copy-edited version features strikethroughs over the word "twelve" whenever Ira speculates as to Stella's age, with the word "fourteen" written in its place (Roth Collection, box 7, folder 49, vol. 2, p. 299/305).

This revision changes our reading of the novel and also calls into question Roth's documented history. Steven Kellman states in his biography that at another cousin's bris, Roth "led his fourteen-year-old first cousin, Sylvia Kessler, downstairs into a freshly cemented basement and seduced her" (68). We can presume that Kellman is writing about the act that served as source material for the scene in Roth's autobiographical fiction, but additional documents suggest that Sylvia Kessler, like Stella in the original drafts, was either eleven or twelve years old at the time of this bris. Alan Gibbs consults records from the 1920 U.S. census, which reveal that Sylvia would have been eleven at the time of the 1924 bris, consistent with Ira's uncertainty as to whether Stella was indeed twelve in the original drafts (*Henry Roth's Semi-Autobiographical Tetralogy* 19). Further, in January 1971, Roth's sister wrote him about the death of their cousin Sylvia Ackerman (Kessler's married name). Lamenting that she "never made it to her 58th birthday," Broder's letter implies that Ackerman was born after January 1913 (Roth Papers, box 1, folder 19). This also indicates that Sylvia Kessler was eleven years old at the bris.

The historical record sheds light on Roth's imprecise language regarding Stella's age in Ira's interaction with Stella, as well as his depiction of sex/rape. Despite scholarly accounts casting the scene as a fictionalized version of a seduction (to use Kellman's term), we may more accurately consider the scene as a literary depiction of a rapist's mind-set. The draft questions ("How old was she? Twelve? Was he crazy or was he right?" [Roth Collection, box 6, folder 46, fourth version, vol. 2, pp. 429–430]) take on new meaning; they indicate Ira's attempt to convince himself, or rationalize, that she's twelve. But why would twelve have been a meaningfully more acceptable age for sex with an adolescent girl than eleven?

In the early twentieth century, twelve signified a common age at which girls could be understood to give consent. Carolyn Cocca, a historian of statutory rape laws, notes that English common law assessed the age of consent as ten by 1576, and American colonies "basically imported" this legal language, though the age of consent was set at ten or twelve in the United States until late nineteenth-century legal reforms increased the age of consent drastically (11). This means that at the time of Ira's sexual conduct with Stella, the age of consent across the United States was sixteen or eighteen, meaning that according to laws contemporaneous with the scene, Roth definitively depicts Ira raping

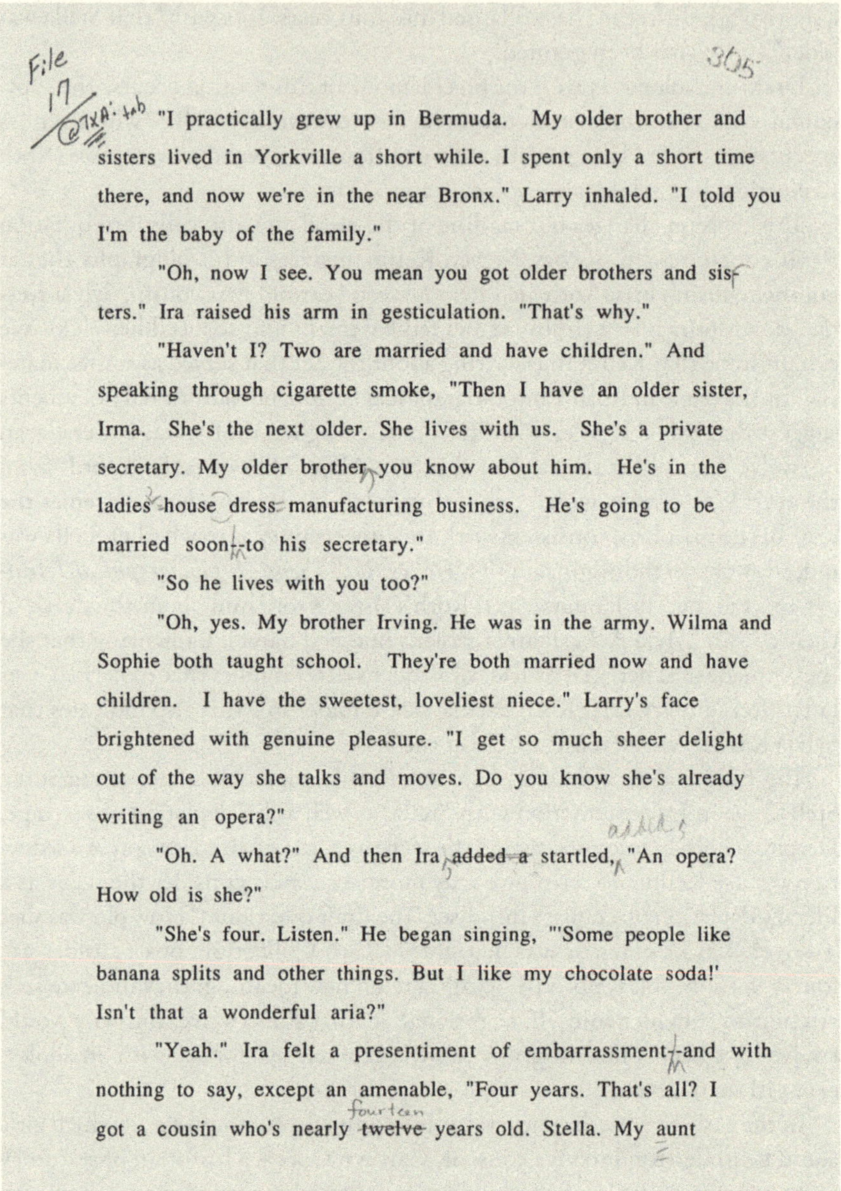
File 17

305

"I practically grew up in Bermuda. My older brother and sisters lived in Yorkville a short while. I spent only a short time there, and now we're in the near Bronx." Larry inhaled. "I told you I'm the baby of the family."

"Oh, now I see. You mean you got older brothers and sisters." Ira raised his arm in gesticulation. "That's why."

"Haven't I? Two are married and have children." And speaking through cigarette smoke, "Then I have an older sister, Irma. She's the next older. She lives with us. She's a private secretary. My older brother, you know about him. He's in the ladies' house dress manufacturing business. He's going to be married soon--to his secretary."

"So he lives with you too?"

"Oh, yes. My brother Irving. He was in the army. Wilma and Sophie both taught school. They're both married now and have children. I have the sweetest, loveliest niece." Larry's face brightened with genuine pleasure. "I get so much sheer delight out of the way she talks and moves. Do you know she's already writing an opera?"

"Oh. A what?" And then Ira ~~added a~~ adds startled, "An opera? How old is she?"

"She's four. Listen." He began singing, "'Some people like banana splits and other things. But I like my chocolate soda!' Isn't that a wonderful aria?"

"Yeah." Ira felt a presentiment of embarrassment--and with nothing to say, except an amenable, "Four years. That's all? I got a cousin who's nearly ~~twelve~~ fourteen years old. Stella. My aunt

FIG. 1. The first instance of Stella's age being changed in the manuscript for Henry Roth's *Mercy of a Rude Stream*, volume 2 (copyedited version, p. 299/305 [1994]; Henry Roth Collection, AJHS Archives P-694, box 7, folder 49, American Jewish Historical Society, New York).

Stella (whether she was twelve, as in the drafts, or fourteen, as in the published version).[3] Furthermore, no age span provisions, today far more common in statutory rape laws, existed at that time. Instead, in the original drafts, Ira's focus on Stella being twelve conveys a meaningful preoccupation with an age that, up until quite recently in the novel's temporality, had been a widely utilized age of consent. The revision makes Ira preoccupied with an arbitrary age, as opposed to a historically significant one. The legal history supports a reading in which Ira's imagining of Stella as twelve accounts for why he considers his sex with her acceptable, as opposed to prohibitive.

The revision of Stella's age changes Ira's rationalization of the sex act. And yet, no concomitant revisions are made to Stella's characterization, even though not-yet-twelve-year-olds are, ostensibly, different from not-yet-fourteen-year-olds. The changes to Stella's age were made quite late in the process, on the fourth draft of the manuscript, and are not in Roth's handwriting. While Roth's editor, Robert Weil, has discussed aspects of the editing and revising process he undertook with Roth, this revision of Stella's age has not come up in the published record. But changing Stella's age without changing any other aspect of her characterization has stark, problematic implications: the revision suggests that age, in the context of rape and consent, functions merely as a number indicating legal status, and not as a reflection of adolescent human development. Yet Ira himself diagnoses the act as rape in both versions. He depicts Ira musing, after the scene, that he is "doubly liable to indictment for statutory rape" (2: 287). An excised portion of volume 2's manuscript also calls it rape, while juxtaposing it with Ira's sexual relations with his sister: "Incest [*sic*] a cut higher—or was it a cut less, cutless—than with Ruthy: screwing your kid first-cousin, statutory rape. She was only thirteen" (Roth Collection, box 4, folder 32, edited version, vol. 2, p. 980).[4] An early draft that did not cross Weil's desk for editing refers to Ira's sex with Stella as "semi-rape" (Roth Papers, box 26, folder 3, "Book II: 1928–1932 B," p. 308).[5]

Contemporarily, some states' legal designation of statutory rape can be mitigated by certain age gaps. This legal development helped clarify power dynamics and preserve sexual agency for adolescent girls. Age spans as a legal concept were widely introduced during the 1970s, at the apex of the women's movement, as a reform of previous consent laws that, in many cases, dated back to the nineteenth century. Considering the depiction in this legalistic light, the fact that Ira was only four years older than Stella in the published version makes the two parties read as more akin to peers than if Stella was eleven or twelve. New York actually changed statutory rape laws to account for age span earlier than other states. In 1950, New York passed a law making a five-year age gap the boundary distinguishing a sexual act between consenting parties and statutory rape (Cocca 38). By adjusting the age difference between Ira and Stella from six years to four, the revisions ensured the narrative does not necessarily

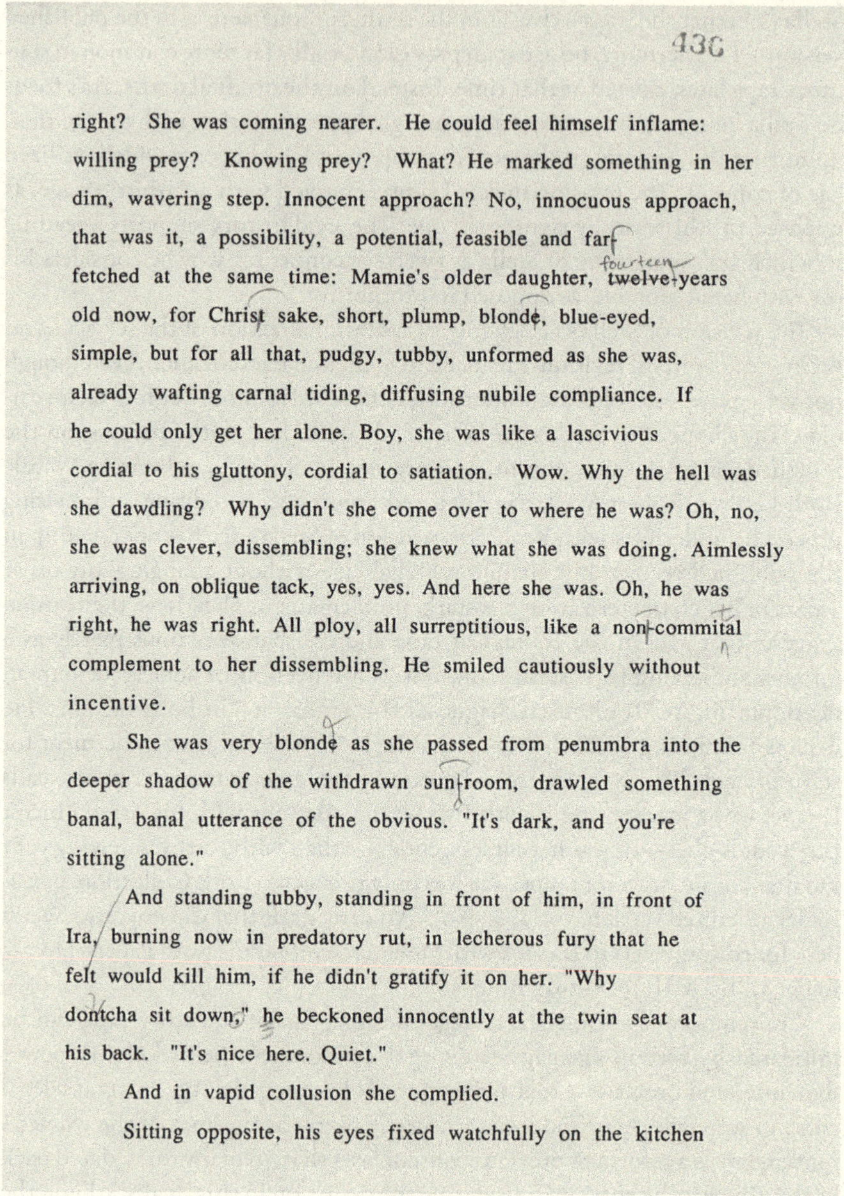
430

right? She was coming nearer. He could feel himself inflame: willing prey? Knowing prey? What? He marked something in her dim, wavering step. Innocent approach? No, innocuous approach, that was it, a possibility, a potential, feasible and far-fetched at the same time: Mamie's older daughter, ~~twelve-~~ fourteen years old now, for Christ sake, short, plump, blonde, blue-eyed, simple, but for all that, pudgy, tubby, unformed as she was, already wafting carnal tiding, diffusing nubile compliance. If he could only get her alone. Boy, she was like a lascivious cordial to his gluttony, cordial to satiation. Wow. Why the hell was she dawdling? Why didn't she come over to where he was? Oh, no, she was clever, dissembling; she knew what she was doing. Aimlessly arriving, on oblique tack, yes, yes. And here she was. Oh, he was right, he was right. All ploy, all surreptitious, like a non-commital complement to her dissembling. He smiled cautiously without incentive.

She was very blonde as she passed from penumbra into the deeper shadow of the withdrawn sun-room, drawled something banal, banal utterance of the obvious. "It's dark, and you're sitting alone."

And standing tubby, standing in front of him, in front of Ira, burning now in predatory rut, in lecherous fury that he felt would kill him, if he didn't gratify it on her. "Why dontcha sit down," he beckoned innocently at the twin seat at his back. "It's nice here. Quiet."

And in vapid collusion she complied.

Sitting opposite, his eyes fixed watchfully on the kitchen

FIG. 2. Another instance of Stella's age being changed in a manuscript for Henry Roth's *Mercy of a Rude Stream* volume 2 (copyedited version, p. 430/436 [1994]; Henry Roth Collection, AJHS Archives P-694, box 7, folder 50, American Jewish Historical Society, New York).

depict rape according to present-day (i.e., post-1950) New York law. In order to read the published scene as something other than rape, the reader would have to apply present-day New York law, with the age-span corollary, to a sex act that occurred twenty-five years prior to that law taking effect.

The age revisions take on a separately insidious quality given that Stella's characterization is never revised. A close reading reveals that Ira's sex act with a thirteen- or fourteen-year-old girl resembles the rape of an eleven- or twelve-year-old girl because Roth wrote the scene to physically and emotionally depict Stella as eleven or twelve. The revisions imply that the theoretical differences between the literary representation of an eleven- or twelve-year-old girl versus a thirteen- or fourteen-year-old girl were meaningful only to the extent that the age proved problematic for the male protagonist, male author, or publishing house. The patriarchal logic is so deeply ingrained that the revision of Stella's age challenges our assessment of whether it meaningfully revises anything. The intended literary characterization of an eleven- or twelve-year-old remains. The age revision actually disguises the *absence* of revision.

Consider the physical characterization of Stella as Ira plots the sexual assault:

> She was coming nearer. He could feel himself inflame: willing prey? Knowing prey? What? He marked something in her dim, wavering step. Innocent approach? No, innocuous approach, that was it, a possibility, a potential, feasible and farfetched at the same time: Mamie's older daughter, fourteen years old now, for Chrissake, short, plump, blond, blue-eyed, simple, but for all that, pudgy, tubby, unformed as she was, already wafting carnal tiding, diffusing nubile compliance. If he could only get her alone. Boy, she was like a lascivious cordial to his gluttony, cordial to satiation. Wow. Why the hell was she dawdling? Why didn't she come over to where he was? Oh, no, she was clever, dissembling; she knew what she was doing. (2: 282)

Ira's gaze reveals his predatory psychology: he refers to Stella as "prey" twice, problematically uses adjectives like "willing" and "knowing"; and suggests, "Oh, no, she was clever, dissembling; she knew what she was doing." The prose also reveals Ira's own real-time revision of Stella's sexuality; after observing her "innocent approach" he quickly reinterprets: "No, innocuous approach, that was it." Catharine MacKinnon's contention that rape is legally theorized by adjudication as to whether an accused *perceives* consent, finds literary explication here: Roth depicts Ira projecting consent onto a figure he simultaneously labels "prey."

The physical descriptions of a girl on the verge of puberty sexualize that transition: "unformed as she was, already wafting carnal tiding, diffusing nubile compliance." Later, upon bringing Stella to the cellar, Roth once again depicts

Stella's physicality in early pubescent terms: "She pulled aside the skimpy sling of her teddy to reveal elemental, adolescent fuzz" (2: 284). Bodily, Roth portrays Stella as having just begun puberty.

Roth's depiction of Stella's physicality, and what it reveals about Ira's sexuality, invites contextualization amid historical literary portrayals of pubescent girls—in particular, Dolores "Lolita" Haze, from Vladimir Nabokov's *Lolita*. Kathryn Bond Stockton's scholarship on *Lolita* and its filmic adaptations helps illuminate how popular media consumption of child sexuality navigates the contradicting impulses toward moral condemnation and lustful celebration (of what James Kincaid refers to as "erotic innocence"). Stockton argues that while the novelistic Lolita is twelve, both filmic versions of *Lolita* cast older actresses and employ different strategies for adapting Nabokov's story. Sue Lyon and Dominque Swain were both fourteen years old when they were cast in Stanley Kubrik's and Adrian Lyne's respective films, which appeared in 1962 and 1997 (Genzlinger; Thomas). Stockton observes that the difference in age is less important than the different approaches to filming the actresses: Kubrick depicts Humbert's fascination with Lolita in "normal" terms: the viewer's eyes, like Humbert's, tell "us that she is not a child: she is a sexy cinematic still" (149). Stockton indicates that Kubrick shows the viewer a woman, even though the story is ostensibly about a "child." Lyne's approach, in contrast, is to "carefully spoil our viewing pleasure—literally to give it for a certain interval, then take it away" (Stockton 151). Lyne accomplishes this by showing Lolita's retainer, for instance, and showing her move with "the frenetic kind of motion we cannot associate with beautiful women" (Stockton 151). As Stockton puts it: "Adrian Lyne, feminist nemesis . . . makes us feel the comfort of our usual perversion, our Playboy-channel gaze as it extends to the beauty of a girl, before he rips the rug of our perversion out from under us, so that he may offer a sexual child" (151).

Unlike with Kubrick and Lyne's directorial choices, replacing the word "twelve" with "fourteen" does not change Roth's imagery of the character. Moreover, Roth never has to "spoil our viewing pleasure" because he never depicts Stella as beautiful, unlike, for instance, how he describes characters like Edith. By denigrating her appearance, Roth's descriptions conflate Ira's disgust with Stella's physical characteristics with his erotic obsession, a very different approach to rendering pedophilic fascination from what Kubrick or Lyne provide. Like Lyne, Roth reminds us of Stella's girlishness, but Roth's approach does not demand that the reader "see" a woman whom he spoils by revealing as a child. He presents Stella as a girl consistently, and this is why the age revision is legally meaningful but otherwise meaningless: whether twelve or fourteen, the depiction is of a girl who has just begun puberty, *not* a girl who could be reasonably mistaken for a woman. If Lyne suggests that the pedophilic gaze sits uncomfortably close to the heteronormative gaze and surreptitiously indicts the audience as complicit, Roth's text reveals how misogynistic physical degradation can function as part of a pedophilic gaze, while still indicting his audience as complicit. Ira's expressed disgust purports to mask Ira's (and the complicit audience's) lust for a pubescent girl's body. But while Lyne operates as a "feminist nemesis" who "rips the rug of our perversion out from under us" (Stockton 151), the revisions to Stella's age mask the extent to which the audience is forced to confront their own complicit engagement of a pedophilic gaze. In Roth's novel, there is no ripping out the rug—if anything, the editorial revisions help secure it firmly beneath the audience's feet.

As such, we need to consider both the original manuscript and published version of *MORS* as inviting voyeuristic participation in Ira's sexual objectification of a pubescent girl. As we navigate the implications of Roth's depictions and the editorial revisions, we must also recognize how the cellar rape revises a celebrated cellar scene from *Call It Sleep*, which cast its young Jewish male protagonist's sexuality in sympathetic terms that Roth rejects in crafting the first-person accounts of rape in *MORS*.

Of Cellars and Consent

Positive reviews of *Call It Sleep* celebrated Roth's craft as well as the young, vulnerable protagonist, David Schearl. Understanding Roth's commitment to revealing Ira's depravity requires juxtaposition with David's sexual innocence. *MORS* revises an immensely popular image of Jewish male sexual innocence.

David Schearl never rapes a girl in a cellar, but he does have a famous prepubescent sexual initiation in the first section of *CIS*, titled "The Cellar." A girl named Annie initiates, convincing an unwitting David to play a game with her. Annie wants to "play bad," but she tells David that "Yuh must ask me" in order to displace her initiative of their play onto him (*CIS* 53). David cooperates, but when, "revolted," he attempts to stop the play, Annie unexpectedly insists on his continued participation: "Yuh must! . . . yuh ast me" (*CIS* 53). This scene inverts typical power and gender dynamics of rape. A boy withdraws consent he unwittingly provides prior to understanding the terms of play, but a girl asserts that a boy's consent, once provided, cannot be revoked. Annie's language ("*yuh* ast me"—my emphasis) also confuses who initiates the play.

David is at the mercy of a manipulative, confusing world, and his encounter with Annie reinforces that David is preyed upon, even by girls his own age. While Annie takes advantage of David in "The Cellar," Roth revisits this original famous scene in *MORS* when Ira rapes Stella in a cellar. The inverted gender and sexual power dynamics of the *CIS* scene invite revision; certainly, a boy's uncomfortable sexual initiation occurring via a girl's assertive sexual behavior is feasible, but the history of sexual power dynamics suggests that the earlier story enshrines male innocent vulnerability to an even more historically vulnerable class. Roth also knew from personal experience that the scene inverted more common sexual power dynamics.

In *MORS*, the power imbalance is clear: Ira is the sexual aggressor, moreover, the rapist. And while Ira does not explicitly threaten the use of force, Roth's language suggests the violence of the act, even as he also depicts Ira's projection of consent onto Stella:

> And standing tubby, standing in front of him, in front of Ira, burning now in predatory rut, in lecherous fury that he felt would kill him, if he didn't gratify it on her. "Why don'tcha sit down." He beckoned innocently at the twin seat at his back. "It's nice here. Quiet."
>
> And in vapid collusion she complied.
>
> Sitting opposite, his eyes fixed watchfully on the kitchen door, he tilted his head sideways, sought her mouth. She converged. She parted her lips for his tongue to delve—to plumb. Oh, yes, Jesus Christ, no doubt, discreet, ready, expectant. Where could he try? Boyoboy, his blazing passion could kill this little, oh, fat little heifer, supine, submissive, inviting murderous sacrifice. Jesus. But where? Where freedom for rut to erupt, where a minute of privacy, innocent seeming privacy? (2: 282–283)

Reading this scene's use of free indirect speech as revealing the mind-set of a rapist underscores the projective qualities of Roth's terminology. The characterizations of Stella, including Roth's usage of terms like "complied," "vapid collusion," and "discreet, ready, expectant," consistently portray Stella as passive. The notion that they suggest consent is undercut by the text's disinterest in Stella beyond as an object of lust and target of denigration, as well as the recurring violence of Ira's vocabulary. By foregrounding the scene's "predatory" character and referring to "murderous sacrifice" and a "passion" that "could kill" Stella, Roth clearly implicates sex with Stella as violence done unto her.

Ira then leads Stella to the cellar, where he continues to revise the content and symbolism of *CIS*'s "The Cellar." By revealing Ira's rape of Stella (and presumably Roth's rape of Sylvia) as what was truly concealed in the cellar, Roth revises an inversion of sexual power dynamics, divulges his own history of perpetrating sexual violence, and rewrites his own literary trajectory. "The Cellar" no longer merely represents the literal first pages—the advent—of Roth's iconic literary career. It signifies the recategorization of Roth's literary, ostensibly moral, artistic vision into the space of his moral failure, the space of his first rape.

While *MORS* complicates our reading of Roth's earlier novel's portrayal of sex and consent, the politics of Roth's depiction of rape remain quite patriarchal. Like Lyne, Roth draws his audience into Ira's subjective point of view in a way that indicts the male audience and male gaze. But Roth also incorporates dialogue that mobilizes common, insidious patriarchal rationales for rape:

> Already out with it, his charger ready, brute in the van, hauling creature after it, mind and body. "Ever do it before?"
>
> She hesitated a moment, reluctant to confess, and yet not to forgo, to miss by being remiss: "The painter."
>
> "The painter?" he approached. (2: 284)

In crafting this scene, Roth reveals himself as an architect of the type of sexist double standards that patriarchy utilizes to justify rape. The painter serves no other discernable plot point other than to establish that Stella has already been sexually active and thus exculpate Ira from responsibility for his own sexual assault. Catharine MacKinnon discusses how men often struggle to conceive of consent: "Virtuous women, like young girls, are unconsenting, virginal, rapable. Unvirtuous women, like wives and prostitutes, are consenting, whores, unrapable" (175). Depicting Stella as "reluctant to confess" is also enormously problematic: the characterization attempts an empathetic insight, but Roth reveals himself to be largely incapable of and disinterested in any meaningful empathetic understanding of Stella. Instead, characterizing Stella's "reluctance to confess" confirms Ira's belief that Stella bears responsibility for her prior sexual assault. Applying MacKinnon's theorizing to this scene indicates that Ira's patriarchal, flawed logic allows him to see Stella as unrapable because, paradoxically, she has already been raped.

As the scene continues, it becomes increasingly pornographic, and stylistically familiar:

> "After we moved in. The new rooms." Her shallow blue eyes glazed—Oh!—glazed, unblinking . . . at his penetration, unblinking, shallow blue eyes accomplice of his perpetration. Minnie closed her hazel eyes, but not Stella, shallow, blue stare, gone vacuous, gone void. It was working, working, it was working, working. Look at her eyes, shallow, blue, stupefied: stultified inanity fixed on him, his prey, accessory to his violation, Jesus Christ, intrinsic to his spraddling her. Destroy her, ah-h, straddling him—slump, mum, larva, squash her dumbstruck trance with guy-geyser brutish he—fucking her. Ai-i. Get out! Get away! Aoh, just when—
>
> It was over. (2: 284)

Roth, who gives ample attention to Ira's rejection of Joyce as literary forebear, provides a distinct Joycean rhythm to his depiction of sexual climax during rape.[6] Ira's visual engagement with Stella is almost entirely with her eyes. They are described as "glazed, unblinking . . . at his penetration," with the ellipses marking something that cannot find expression. Her eyes have "gone vacuous, gone void," and yet Ira narrates her "stultified inanity fixed on him." Ira's narration also characterizes her as "accomplice of his perpetration," and "accessory to his violation."

Ira's language casts Stella as a partner—"accomplice" and "accessory"—but these terms are more associated with criminal activity than consensual sex. Furthermore, the language reveals that Stella is not present other than in the physical sense. The emphasis on her eyes reminds us that she sees all of this too, but in depicting them as "gone vacuous, gone void," "stupefied," and as "dumbstruck trance," we might infer that Stella has "gone void" in order to manage an experience beyond her capacity to fully "see." Roth forces the reader to witness Stella's trauma within Ira's sexually graphic language. Given Ira's own victimization via sexual molestation, this scene may reveal Ira's simultaneous awareness of and sexual gratification at inflicting trauma upon Stella. But it is also important to think of eyes and seeing in terms of subjectivity. Roth's male rapist subjectivity is rendered here with explicit metaphoric cruelty: Roth insists the reader see, through his eyes, the fact that Stella herself, having "gone void," *cannot* see. Depicting Stella as unable to see what is happening to her amounts to something even more destructive than a silencing; Roth renders Stella as incapable of subjectively observing the assault Ira commits. Roth's language robs Stella of her very subjectivity.

This altogether disturbing rendering of rape finds further explication in an exchange with Ecclesias. When Ecclesias asks him why he did this, the elder Ira responds: "To alert the world to the menace of housepainters" (2: 285). Ira's attempt at humor seeks to minimize his confession/nonconfession to rape, and Ecclesias's response, "Dispense with the levity" (2: 285), may stand in for the reader's. But Roth gets to have it both ways here, as he does throughout the narrative, particularly with sex. The elderly Ira's question on the tenor of his narrative and the male gaze is revelatory: "Have I overstepped the boundary from the erotic into the pornographic?" (2: 285).

This is a stunning and revealing question. Having indulged in a lengthy free indirect depiction of rape tied to the rapist's point of view, Roth confirms his intent to depict sexual assault in an arousing fashion. The question's false presupposition involves Roth's unchallenged choice to overstep the boundary into the erotic. That the elderly Ira has chosen the space between erotic and pornographic as the meaningful boundary normalizes his decision to (at the very least) eroticize rape. There is no contrition or reflection. Ecclesias, ultimately a very limited superego, lets this question's implications go without challenge.

This question is posed in the same passage where Ira regards himself as "doubly liable to indictment for statutory rape" (2: 287). The elderly Ira contemplates his sex with Stella as erotic, as perhaps pornographic, *and* as statutory rape, simultaneously. The text self-consciously aligns rape and the erotic. For all the critical attention that stresses Ira's "confessional" voice, and the reading that presents Ira's journey as redemptive, the elderly Ira is not contrite. In fact, the manner in which the elderly Ira ponders the distinction between erotica and pornography almost serves as an aggression—the false presupposition so successfully normalizes sexual assault as erotic because of its indulgent depiction of Ira as seemingly reflective. We might think of this scene as a version of an apologia, a reworking of Max Pinkus's disturbing "some bury, some burn, I ate!" line (*Deconstructing Harry*). Ira, ostensibly calling himself to account for raping his cousin all those years ago, in fact only questions whether he made the rape titillating beyond the boundary of what high-minded literary critics will indulge. Like Max Pinkus, Ira mocks the very notion of thoughtful reflection and accountability.

Ecclesias, however, does challenge the elderly Ira on the presupposition that Ira has changed and is now contrite: "I do think that you wrote as explicitly as you did because you still are what you are. That the hold on you of what you were is, so to speak, still in force" (2: 286). Even Ecclesias concedes that it is impossible to square Ira's story, and the elderly Ira's eroticization of that story, with the notion that *MORS* is redemptive. But Roth's complex narrative structure cynically facilitates his having it both ways. Were we to look for moral structure, though, we would not find it in Roth's depiction of religiosity. If anything, Roth's depiction of Ira's (im)morality stems from his perspective on religious hypocrisy, especially as it involves Ira's relationship with his Orthodox grandfather.

Zaida's Unassimilable Lesson

Why did Roth, in the estimation of editor Robert Weil, have "no respect for" his cousin Sylvia (Gibbs, "Conversation" 157)? Scholarship that has considered Stella as primarily a double for Minnie reflects editorial decisions Gibbs discovered, regarding Weil overseeing edits that displaced sexual focus from Minnie onto Stella after Broder's legal challenge. However, this approach downplays Stella's stand-alone significance, and overlooks how sibling and cousin relationships are defined differently in familial, societal, religious, and secular contexts. Kellman makes numerous references to Ira committing "incest" with Stella (69, 97, 231), but first-cousin relationships were not commonly considered incestuous in the United States in the early twentieth century, nor were they in most contemporaneous iterations of Jewish religious traditions. For Ira, traditional Jewish acceptance of close endogamy and rejection of sibling incest functioned as a contradiction given his own understanding of family and boundaries. This fundamental tension may have contributed to his rejection of religion.

As with the different legal proscriptions against statutory rape in the 1920s versus the 1990s, views on first-cousin marriage have changed. Neither Torah nor Talmud prohibits cousin marriage. But cousin marriage and other forms of close endogamous marriage were neither especially taboo nor especially unusual in a range of ethnoracial groups through the early twentieth century.[7] Micah Fitzerman-Blue's research into uncle-niece marriage, legal for Jewish families in Rhode Island and endorsed by Talmudic commentary, mentions dowry as a device that incentivized close endogamous marriages (417). Chae-Ran Freeze uses historical records of the Jewish population of the Ukrainian town Korostyshev to uncover extensive consanguineous marriages, while also noting that as early as "the late nineteenth century, Jewish reformers castigated this consanguinity as detrimental to family health" (27). The biological geneticist David Goldstein contends that, "traditionally, Jewish groups have not regarded consanguineous marriages as taboo," but Freeze's research indicates that some level of Jewish ambivalence has surrounded consanguineous unions dating back at least to the Jewish enlightenment (103). And yet, as David Warren Sabean has demonstrated, cousin marriages were not historically uncommon among non-Jews either.

Freeze's observation that nineteenth-century Jewish reformers objected to consanguineous marriages for health reasons helps ground this conversation as one taking place alongside modernization. This also brings us back to Freud, and his "Aetiology" essay, which Alys Eve Weinbaum reveals to be assiduously preoccupied with the problem of how to discuss incest, child abuse, and consanguinity in the context of antisemitic associations of Jews with those terms. In sum, the history of Jewish cousin marriage, at least dating from the late nineteenth century and Haskalah (Jewish enlightenment), is also a history of Jewish ambivalence about the intersections of tradition, antisemitic pathologization, antisemitic medical discourse, secular marriage laws, and anxiety about genetic consequences of close endogamy.

Jewish American fiction, film, and memoir constitute a record for a range of representations of anxiety, fantasy, and ambivalence about cousin relations. Romantic or sexual engagement with first cousins appears in a variety of texts dealing with early twentieth-century Jewish families. In *Brighton Beach Memoirs*, for instance, Neil Simon mines the protagonist Eugene's attraction to his cousin Nora for humor.[8] While many Jewish American depictions of cousin relations (male-authored ones in particular) utilize humor, some texts depict cousin relations as points of tension, anxiety, and victimization. Kate Simon's memoir *Bronx Primitive* recounts her terror in the face of a cousin's secretive, but perhaps condoned, sexual advances. Simon depicts a childhood experience in which her older cousin snuck into bed with her and "pushed his big thing, pulsating like a machine, as near as he could to my opening but never went in" (123–124). Simon reports how following repeated molestations, her cousin pleaded for her not to report him to her mother: "He could be arrested and sent back to Poland if I said anything" (124). Significantly, Simon infers (and implies) that her father silently condones his nephew's behavior: "My father, like myself, slept lightly; he must have known what Yankel was doing and had done before" (172).

Ira's anxiety, unlike Kate Simon's, is that of the assailant. But Ira is particularly anxious about his Zaida (grandfather) discovering his behavior. Roth provides cues that this is because of his grandfather's religiosity, except the consequence Ira fears is very specific. It is not exile from the family that Ira fears but, rather, becoming further tied to his family: he dreads being forced to marry Stella. In a conversation between Ira and Stella's sister Hannah, Roth implies that Ira's cousins also consider their relationship in the context of marriage. When Hannah complains about their limited social opportunities, she remarks, "Only Jewish girls have to live, live—till a *khusin* comes along" (3: 315). Given Ira's relationship with Stella, and Roth's patterns switching from English to Yiddish, Roth puns on *khusin* (groom) and "cousin" here. Additional evidence points to the marriage prospect, including a specific conversation Ira has with his grandfather, just after a sexual encounter with Stella. The scene is distinct in that initially the elderly Ira recounts it (or attempts to):

> The old man did something he had never done before: he called Ira into his room again—just as Ira was leaving, walking down the hall toward the apartment door. And what had the old man done? Under pretext, Ira was sure, of reminiscing about his early boyhood, he had given Ira a lecture on how one obtained a wife, according to Judaism. Sitting at the keyboard of his word processor over sixty years later, Ira tried to remember his grandfather's version. It wasn't easy: how much sixty years had eroded! But it all seemed to add up to a hint on Zaida's part that he was on to something. It *seemed* a hint—until Minnie brought the tidings of Zaida's departure from Mamie's. Then it no longer seemed a hint; it *was* a hint, and a broad one, in fact, a disclosure of the old man's suspicions about the behavior of his two grandchildren. (4: 93)

Curiously, Roth's first allusion to the conversation draws attention to the elderly Ira's difficulty remembering the conversation. A few pages later, Roth revisits the conversation, here depicting the younger Ira's attempt to recall it: "But what the hell did the old man say when Ira was on the way out? Still with a Trojan on—did he or didn't he have it on? Disgraceful, downright sacrilegious, to sit down with a devout old man, with holy writ, a *siddur*, in front of him, and still be wearing a bag of sticky stuff: semen, Abraham's seed. . . . The more he ruminated on it, the daffier life was. Zaida communing with his third-generation offspring, with his fourth-generation seed caught in a condom (he hoped)" (4: 97). Roth dramatizes Ira's attempt to remember his grandfather's words, presenting us with the irony of Zaida's lecturing him about marriage directly after Ira and Stella had sex. The passage foreshadows the pregnancy scare that drives the fourth volume's plot, utilizing a crude metaphor for the regulation, and interruption, of male lineage. Roth again relies on humor to navigate discomfort as Ira attempts to recount Ira's grandfather's words: "But what the hell had the old guy said? Now think, think. 'When I was a child, I thought as a child—' No, no, no. That was Saint Paul" (4: 97). Roth, doubtless aware that he has presented his *frum* grandfather in clichéd terms throughout the novel, humorously deflects attention from the gravity of the conversation by again rendering him as cliché—except within the wrong liturgical tradition.

Eventually, Ira successfully recounts his grandfather's words, and they prescribe a religious resolution for Ira and Stella's situation. Zaida says that the Talmud reveals "three ways of getting a wife." After mentioning *kessef* (coin) and *shtar* (bond), he says, "And the third is by *biyah*."

> "By beer," Ira had chortled nervously.
>
> "By *biyah*. To have intercourse with her. You come upon her, and you have intercourse with her."
>
> "That's simple, Zaida." Ira had maintained his sangfroid with a show of facetiousness: "*Kessef, shtar,* and *biyah*. Anybody can remember those." Holy jumpin' Jesus! How much more did he need to be told? The old boy was driving the spike right through him. That was it, that was it.
>
> And the way he stared at Ira, out of hard, brown, uncompromising eyes. But then maybe it was just because of the cataracts he had in his eyes: "You say to her, 'By this act I have made you my wife.'" (Listening, Ira had forgotten his restiveness.) "What did I understand as a child of eleven: 'By this act'?" Old man with stained vest over paunch speaking, old man in a black yarmulka and with scraggly beard delivering his homily. "But you see how wise the Talmud was to prepare the immature mind for the time when the mature mind would understand?" (4: 98–99)

Zaida ends his lesson by stating that "before he knew desire, each child knew how God decreed desire should be satisfied: by taking a wife. And how wives were taken." Roth depicts Ira's anxiety immediately: "It's nothing, Ira assured himself. . . . It's nothing with nothing" (4: 99). Zaida's lecture leaves Ira shaken, but not merely because Zaida knew of his grandchildren's relations. Ira is disturbed because Zaida's proposed solution is for his grandchildren to marry; or rather, to suggest Ira had already made that decision by initiating sex with Stella.

Ira's cognitive dissonance comes from the intersection of Ira's conflicted, frayed sense of morality in a secular American context with his grandfather's distinct, unassimilable Jewish solution. Ira clearly knows that his relationship with Stella constitutes rape. Ira's disgust with Stella may, at some level, reflect his self-disgust at his behavior. Yet Zaida cites marriage as the only morally sound choice for a young man in Ira's position. Zaida attempts to teach his grandson that in the Jewish tradition, marriage—the sanctifying of Ira and Stella's relationship—is his only moral option. For Ira, this is unassimilable. Roth repeatedly draws attention to Ira's confusion about the speech. Not long after the scene, Ira again ponders the same question: "Still, why had the old man recited that business about getting a wife, especially that business about coming upon her and having sexual relations with her? Only a week ago, and so pointed in Ira's direction" (4: 106).

The answer to Ira's question is quite self-explanatory: Ira is morally obligated, according to his grandfather, to marry his cousin. But Ira continuously struggles to arrive at this conclusion and its implications. Ira fails to retain his grandfather's lecture because it speaks to the supposed abomination of his relations with his cousin as not actually being considered abomination in the light of familial or religious tradition. But Zaida's logic also implies that Ira has already made his sister into his wife as well. Josh Lambert has established that Ira's "frequent characterization of incest as 'sin' and 'abomination' reveals that he understands it in the context of Leviticus and, to some degree, his Jewish identity" (75). While Leviticus prohibits sibling relations, it does not prohibit cousin relations. Ira, however, understands both relations as being similarly forbidden. A passage that Lambert references in volume 3 mentions both Minnie as well as Stella, prior to Ira confessing that "he lusted for the prohibited, the proscribed" (120). Ira may combine prohibitive traditions here (seeing Stella as "prohibited" on account of statutory rape law), or he may be confused as to how traditional Jewish mores might allow for something he has internalized as forbidden.

Ira's alienation from Judaism may emerge from the trauma of Zaida's unassimilable lesson. Ira, psychologically unable to cease from sexually exploiting Stella, receives a Jewish lesson in (a)morality from his grandfather: a symbol of familial patriarchy and religious authority. Ira is not reprimanded; he is instead encouraged to marry his cousin. Learning that his behavior, and more specifically, his rape of Stella, can be assimilated into Jewish tradition might account for the ambivalence about religion Ira elsewhere pins on the "trauma" of growing up in a non-Jewish neighborhood.

Ironically, the very tension that complicates Ira's ability to distinguish his sibling incest from his cousin "incest"—the fact that one can be condoned by family and religion, while the other cannot be—replicates itself in scholarly focus on Roth that spotlights the sibling incest. But if sibling incest is indeed rare and rejected by laws of family, religion, and state, it may be, paradoxically, less taboo than cousin marriage. That is, sibling incest is universally condemned. Cousin relations were/are permitted and historically were not infrequent. *MORS*'s engagement with sibling incest presents an easily condemnable act that draws attention away from the more controversial act of first-cousin endogamy and Roth's depiction of rape. The scandal of sibling incest in *MORS* is not limited to the sibling incest itself. The scandal involves how sibling incest deflected attention from the artist's confession of rape, stymied conversation about the novel's ethics of representation regarding rape, and obscured Roth's depiction of patriarchal Jewish tradition's endorsement of marriage as a "solution" for rape in order to celebrate Roth's "redemptive" embrace of Israel and Jewish identity.

Roth's Africanism

Having examined *MORS* and its manuscripts' depictions of cousin relations, rape, and pedophilia, the text's preoccupation with racial others requires explication: what does *MORS* reveal about white Jewish racism? *MORS* manuscript revisions erased Ira's anti-Black racism, despite other characters' (Jewish and otherwise) anti-Black sentiments remaining. Two heavily edited but still extant scenes featuring hypersexual Black characters frame Ira's incest and close endogamy narrative. Even with the revisions, anti-Black racism structures the novel's engagement with Jewish sexual taboos. Still, the revisions reflect the broader whitewashing of the history of American Jewish racism as central to American Jewish white identity and protect Roth, Ira, and the readers identifying with both from being implicated as explicitly racist.[9]

Prior to close reading the specific scenes, we should consider American Jewish artists' popular representations of American Jewish masculinity in the mid- to late 1990s and early 2000s. Daniel Itzkovitz points out the increase in Jewish male protagonists in both films and television during this period, drawing special attention to movie stars like Adam Sandler, Ben Stiller, and Jason Biggs, each of whom performed versions of the schlemiel that indicated audience receptivity to Jewishly marked depictions of masculinity. Stiller's role in *Meet the Parents* (2000) and its sequels seems especially characteristic in intimating that Jewish men represent sexual and gender flexibility and difference (for example, the last name "Focker" and his job as a nurse), vulnerability to mild, veiled antisemitism (in the persona of Robert De Niro's skeptical character), yet desirability. The schlemiel's resilience in the face of (slight) marginalization involves something of the character's appeal. But this functions as decisively different from the sort of sexual transgressive threats that Sander Gilman hearkens to when he discusses antisemitic characterizations of Jack the Ripper in the nineteenth century (*Love + Marriage* 136). As Khalil Muhammad has observed, within American contexts, this did not happen by accident: "innovative racial demographers . . . explicitly sanitized and normalized the criminality of northern white working and immigrant classes. Consequently, the black southern migrant—the 'Negro, stranger in our midst'—was marked as an exceptionally dangerous newcomer" (6). Stereotypes associating Jews with incest or pedophilia did not vanish completely, but the extent to which these stereotypes registered as criminal receded, given prevailing trends to instead criminalize and condemn Blackness along these terms. Roth's novel, appearing in the midst of this new saturation of Jewish schlemiel protagonists, reveals how cultural productions could actively displace these stereotypes in consequential, harmful fashion.

The first pertinent scene occurs in volume 2, directly prior to the reveal of Ira's sister Minnie and their sexual relationship. This revelation aims to stun the reader—fully a volume and a half into the novel, the character shows up unaccounted for, asking her brother to "Fuck me, fuck me good!" (2: 140). Rather than attend to Roth's depiction of Minnie here, I want to investigate how Roth lays the groundwork for the reveal. The preceding scene finds Ira contemplating New York's African American community and America's history of slavery prior to visiting a Black prostitute. While working at Yankee Stadium, Ira flirts with a Black woman named Pearl Canby who eventually invites him to her home to pay for sex. Upon arrival, though, Ira meets a different woman, Theodora, whom he describes as "scrawny and homely and black-coffee brown" (2: 133). Ira loses his virginity: "He knew all along that was the way it was done, but he'd never done it" (2: 135). The subsequent scene, where Minnie appears for the first time and demands Ira have sex with her, thus requires suspension of disbelief. Ira has just learned how to have sex from Theodora. Ostensibly, we are to believe that Minnie greets her (to her knowledge) virgin brother with "fuck me good" despite their sexual engagement (per the logic of the sequence) never previously involving penetrative sex. Theodora "teaches" Ira about sex, but the language Roth crafts for Minnie indicates that she already knows. As with Stella's allusion to the plumber, Roth's depiction of Ira's initial sexual encounter with Minnie necessarily intimates that she is already sexually active (ostensibly, paradoxically, with Ira).

None of this makes much narrative sense. But it follows a racist, patriarchal logic. As Alan Gibbs, Lene Schott-Kristensen, and Steven Kellman have observed, Roth indicated to Robert Weil that Ira's encounter with Theodora was fabricated. In a video interview with Weil, Roth divulged this to help clarify that *MORS* was a novel, legally pertinent testimony given the fact that Broder had threatened a lawsuit. About Theodora, Roth disclosed: "It's completely made up! I never went there, I never had a black whore, and I was scared to death of that kind of woman anyway" (Roth Papers, box 22, folder 19a, interview transcription, p. 5).

The interview reveals that Roth incorporated the scene to move the plot. We can thereby infer that Roth needed his protagonist to receive initiation by a Black character in order to facilitate his narrative's arrival at the incest. Roth employs blatant fiction to arrive at his most personal autobiographical facts. Roth's use of fabricated interracial exogamy to tell his incest story exposes Roth's reliance on the same Africanist presence that Toni Morrison observes in canonical white authors like Poe, Melville, and others in *Playing in the Dark*. As Morrison remarks, "black people ignite critical moments of discovery or change or emphasis in literature not written by them" (viii): "Through significant and underscored omissions, startling contradictions, heavily nuanced conflicts, through the way writers peopled their work with the signs and bodies of this presence—one can see that a real or fabricated Africanist presence was crucial to their sense of Americanness" (6).

Reading *MORS* through Morrison's "American Africanism" lens highlights Roth's use of Black characters to structure his incest story and announce the "Americanness" of his protagonist and narrative. Hypersexualized Black characters narratively enable Ira's sex with Minnie and mark Ira's final published sexual encounter with Stella (which I address shortly). While these scenes remain, Roth's manuscripts show extensive revision and excision in areas involving Ira observing and commenting on Black people. The published version of *MORS* suggests to some readers that Roth was not especially concerned with or observant regarding Black people in New York. Kellman's biography notes that few Black characters appear in *MORS*: "the black population in Roth's fictional New York is extremely sparse" (100). The manuscripts, however, reveal more sustained, problematic engagements with Black people and Blackness.

In the manuscript version of the Yankee Stadium scene with Pearl Canby, Roth refers to "black mammies" (Roth Papers, box 27, folder 2, unedited, "Section I," vol. 2, 594). Roth also refers alternately to "niggertown" and "nigger Harlem" (Roth Papers, box 27, folder 2, unedited, "Section I," vol. 2, 594) in the manuscript, as opposed to "black Harlem" (2: 130). The manuscript employs the term *shvartzeh* and "darky" repeatedly. And after sex with Theodora, in the manuscripts, Ira immediately contemplates Black sexuality with the history of slavery:

> Dark 119th Street, ahead of him walking at a good clip toward the Cut, the trestle, the darker dark, the way she was on the bed—he smirked at

> himself—her twat licorice embedded in chocolate. So if you had slaves, the way they once did in the South, Jesus, all kinds of things you all of a sudden possessed: Darky wench, all right, darky wench. Then, you took her like an animal. If she had a child, darky he too, slave, not your cherished kid, but to sell, like, whew! Now wait a minute, before you cross Park Avenue, cross under the overpass, go by the pillars, oh! What he was thinking: This was worse, worse than with a slave. (Roth Collection, box 4, folder 27, edited version, vol. 2, p. 605)

Everything following "embedded in chocolate" is removed in the published text. In the margins, Weil writes, "Unfortunately we will be in big trouble if we leave this in. Things are controversial enough" (Roth Collection, box 4, folder 27, edited version, vol. 2, p. 605). Weil intimates that Roth has only a limited amount of audience goodwill; enough for incest, presumably, but not enough to depict Ira as racist.

The irony is twofold: the narrative depicts incest in graphic terms and concerns itself extensively with the societal injustice of even mild forms of antisemitism. Yet the excised passage reveals Ira's negotiation of his racial positioning vis-à-vis American history and makes clear that Ira processed his sexual encounter with a Black woman by contemplating American slavery, identifying with white slave owners, and imagining his own sexual ownership of Black women, as well as children born from such encounters. The passage is disturbing, but why is a passage suggesting that white Jewish immigrants identified with slave owners when contemplating race and slavery more disturbing than explicit depictions of sibling incest and cousin rape? Lene Schott-Kristensen has addressed the implications of some of these revisions, noting that "on request, Roth changed Ira's use of 'nigger' and '*schvartze*' to 'coloured,' a revision which seems wrong to me since it quite obviously misrepresents Ira and his culture" (205). Likely alluding to Weil's handwritten note, she observes that Weil "feared such passages would get Roth into trouble" (205). Revising fictional Ira also amounts to protecting the actual author. But while these revisions seemingly misrepresent Roth's culture, Weil does not put much effort into revising Roth's contemporaries' racist language. The published version finds Larry referring to "darkies" (3: 154). Stella calls three Black youths "niggers," language Ira uses only when quoting Stella (4: 207). The misrepresentation, then, has a particular logic: Jews *can* be racist, in *MORS*, but the antihero protagonist cannot be.

While sex with Theodora opens the door, structurally, to Ira's incestuous relations with his sister, the threat of rape from three Black teenagers facilitates Ira finally ending his relations with Stella. Kellman, in his biography of Roth, refers to these three characters once as "thugs" (100) and once as being "like avenging angels" (325) but states that they "harass" Ira and Stella, never mentioning their intent to rape. Gibbs writes, "Only after being interrupted by three youths in the movie theatre (when Stella's bravery is of considerable help in extricating them from a threatening situation) does Ira feel anything approaching admiration for her" (*Henry Roth's Semi-Autobiographical Tetralogy* 229). Gibbs omits the characters' racial categorization entirely, despite Stella's "bravery" involving her yelling "Rotten niggers!" as she "threw herself forward with flailing fist" (4: 207).

Manuscripts show that Weil has again removed multiple instances of Ira using the word "nigger" in this section. But Roth's original text also features a more complex narrative depiction of Ira's racism. To celebrate the end of a pregnancy scare, Ira takes Stella to the balcony of a movie house (he calls it "nigger heaven" in the drafts—a term referring to segregation in movie theaters), where she performs oral sex on Ira. When three Black teenagers notice, Ira and Stella abscond to a restroom. The teenagers follow, one produces a razor, and they demand sex with Stella before she leads her and Ira's escape.

The manuscript arrives at a different resolution. It proceeds in a similar fashion until Ecclesias interrupts the proceedings with the word "Wait." Ira responds, "I thought I had dispensed with you," alluding both to Ecclesias's diminished role in the manuscript and Ira's preference for Ecclesias's silence (Roth Papers, box 77, folder 4, "before editing," vol. 4, p. 1054). Ira, anticipating Ecclesias's critique, asks, "where have I failed?" Ecclesias's response is sharp and to the point: "You failed in representing your black or Afram youth as human beings, as varied human beings. You've depicted them, if not as thoroughgoing stereotypes, then as mere counters carrying out your will in effecting your larger design, in a word, your plot. They were merely serving your needs, not being the several and diverse individualities they are, giving no hint of their potential emergence as a distinct ethnic force. True or not?" (Roth Papers, box 77, folder 4, "before editing," vol. 4, pp. 1054–1055). This appraisal is accurate. Neither Ecclesias nor Ira discusses the scene in terms of its memoiristic fealty to history. Ecclesias instead implies the characters "serve" Ira's needs in a fashion suggesting that this scene, like the Theodora scene, was invented.

Ecclesias's observation also evokes Morrison's theory of American Africanism: "Just as entertainers, through or by association with blackface, could render permissible topics that otherwise would have been taboo, so American writers were able to employ an imagined Africanist persona to articulate and imaginatively act out the forbidden in American culture" (66). Ecclesias and Morrison both recognize the manner in which Black characters facilitate white authors negotiating taboos, and Ecclesias assesses this as an artistic failure; an inability to represent Black characters as human. But Ecclesias's observation, taken alongside Morrison's discussion of taboo, clarifies how Roth's ability to explore his own factual history of committing incest and rape are rendered "permissible topics" only through the incorporation of Black figures who may or may not have existed. If we zoom out, we see an unsettling set of bookends: Theodora initiates Ira into sex, "teaching" him so that he can then commence sexual activity with Minnie "the right way." Later, three Black would-be rapists essentially scare the white rapist straight. Encounters with hypersexual Black characters frame Ira's incest, rape, and predatory behavior; first facilitating it and then marking it as unacceptable.

The supposedly "redemptive" arc of Ira's journey requires the displacement of his sins and morally questionable characteristics onto a predictable scapegoat. In discussing how race, rape, and lynching intersect in turn-of-the-century novels, Sandra Gunning observes that "sexual and political agency became increasingly linked in the figure of the black rapist precisely because of the dependent definition of citizenship on definitions of (white) manhood" (7). Though Gunning's study (like Morrison's) does not consider white ethnic immigrant texts, her observations are quite relevant to *MORS*, which, though written in the 1990s, depicts the same approximate era she interrogates, one marked by "an unprecedented rise in the number of lynchings and white race riots directed specifically at African American communities" and "an outpouring of distinctive narratives concerned with white supremacy and alleged black degeneration in the wake of Reconstruction" (3). If Gunning, who focuses on Thomas Dixon, Kate Chopin, and Mark Twain, establishes the significance of the figure of the Black rapist for nonimmigrant white American authors, Roth's novel confirms that the figure was equally useful for ethnic white Americans attempting to integrate into white American society.[10]

In order to establish Ira's "(white) manhood," Roth contrasts Ira's masculinity with that of sexually threatening Black men. But Gunning's study is of fiction; what do we make of Roth's autobiographical fiction utilizing the same framework? Here too, the manuscript clarifies Roth's artistic choices and their barely concealed ideological ramifications. After Ecclesias's interjection, Ira interrupts Ecclesias midsentence and resumes narration, except instead of resuming *in medias res*, he reconceives the scene. Stella, who previously has run out yelling "poleese" is still trapped with Ira. This "second take" proceeds thusly:

> "What *you* here for?" the hulking black youth at the door—mute till now—demanded. He had a surprisingly soft, silky voice, not much above a whisper.
>
> "You know what I'm here for."
>
> "We here for the same thing." (Roth Papers, box 77, folder 4, "before editing," vol. 4, p. 1055)

In the published version, the demand for sex specifies the act: "She blow you, she blow us" (2: 206). But after Ecclesias's intervention, the manuscript finds

Roth emphasizing that young Ira and the youths are there "for the same thing." The distinction is not merely semantic; it aligns them. It complicates any notion of Ira as Stella's protector. Further, Ira's tone, conciliatory in the first version, becomes more assertive. He exclaims, "you're here to rape her!" and after Stella also protests, the second-take scene embarks on another narratively suspect turn:

> The hulking youth at the door ignored her. "Your people got plenty o' brown pussy whether they like it or not."
>
> "My people? My people had nothing to do with it!" Ira retorted outraged. ["]Slavery? Never! What're you talking about!"
>
> "Sure they did."
>
> "How? Tell me."
>
> "You never hear o' Judah Benjamin?"
>
> Taken aback Ira stared into the other[']s soft brown eyes, "Well, if you know that much, what the hell are you doing here?"
>
> "Same as you, I told you." (Roth Papers, box 77, folder 4, "before editing," vol. 4, pp. 1055–1056)

Just how taboo is white Jewish racism? So taboo that a scene ostensibly about attempted rape instantly, and bizarrely, shifts into one where Ira defiantly and defensively asserts that Jews "had nothing to do with" slavery. The "hulking black youth," who is named Chester, makes no explicit allusion to Ira being Jewish. Ira does not hear "your people" as indicating "white people" though; he interprets (correctly) the term to mean Jews and reacts with more indignation to this accusation than he does to the threat of rape.

In this reimagined version of the movie theater scene, Ira ends up debating whether white Jews function(ed) as white people in an American racial context. Stella's vulnerability to Chester and his associates' sexual threat becomes secondary, to Ira, to a defense of white Jewish innocence regarding the history of American slavery. When Chester names Judah Benjamin, the Jewish attorney general and secretary of state for the Confederacy, Ira is incredulous; but he clearly recognizes the name. That Chester should have such knowledge and still be a would-be rapist is something Ira cannot fathom; Chester's intelligence, Ira's question indicates, precludes this. But once again, upon being asked why he is there, Chester replies, "same as you." The irony of Ira's incredulity is apparent: intelligent, knowledgeable men of all backgrounds (including, of course, Ira's) can and do commit rape.

The scenes also undercut the sense of *MORS* as memoir or autobiography. How can this be a record of an event if the event happens twice and differently? We cannot know whether the Fox Theater scene was entirely fabricated, but

Ecclesias implies that it was ("they were merely serving your needs"). Moreover, it possesses self-consciously theatrical qualities: the scene is staged twice and with heightened stakes and drama. And it takes place in a movie theater.

The double scene reminds us that what we witness in movie theaters is often made-up. Valerie Smith, writing about the racist history of American cinema, observes that "despite their constructedness, media representations of members of historically disenfranchised communities reflect and, in turn, affect the lived circumstances of real people. But the relationship between media representations and 'real life' is nothing if not complex and discontinuous; to posit a one-to-one correspondence between the inescapability of certain images and the uneven distribution of resources within culture is to deny the elaborate ways in which power is maintained and deployed" (3). Smith reminds us that filmic representations of Black people have real effects, mentioning that D. W. Griffith's *The Birth of a Nation* set the tone for racist depictions of African Americans in film, while also having "direct impact on contemporaneous race relations" (1). The Fox Theater scene takes place in the early 1920s, just a few years after the release of *The Birth of a Nation* (1915), though Roth likely wrote it in the 1980s or 1990s. *The Birth of a Nation* casts Black men as sexual threats to white women, displacing a historical record in which white men raped Black women without Black women having access to legal recourse. Roth's movie theater scene casts Black men as a more dangerous sexual threat to Stella than Ira, despite the fact that Ira had been raping Stella from a young age, and any contemporaneous consent on Stella's part involves the impact of sexual abuse and grooming beginning when she was (in the drafts) eleven or twelve.

Smith also draws our attention to how "power is maintained and deployed." To that end, consider that what Roth reveals about white Jewish racism cannot be fully appreciated by merely looking at the edits, the language, and the staging of particular scenes. It requires pulling back and recognizing that Roth dedicates thousands of words in *MORS* to exposing the myriad ways antisemitism affected Ira's experience in New York City. Even as Ecclesias chides Ira for his racist choices in depicting Black characters, the overarching effect of the text confirms for readers the oppressive experience of growing up Jewish in a diasporic, antisemitic, non-Jewish New York City neighborhood, where non-Jews lurked as threats, and nonwhite non-Jews loomed most threatening of all. A brief mea culpa about the racist imagery from Ecclesias does not an anti-racist text make. In fact, the revisions suggest that stories highlighting American antisemitism may self-consciously remove Jewish racism to avoid complicating prevailing narratives of Jews as a comparatively disempowered and vulnerable class.

The tension in *MORS*'s depiction, revision, and omission of anti-Black racism reflects scholarly debates about the history of Black Jewish relations, or, as

Adam Zachary Newton calls them, "blackjewishrelations," indicating the extent to which the topic has become its own self-referential genre. Luther Adams observes that Black Jewish relations are "deeply implicated in the history of twentieth-century America" (902). In particular, Adams writes: "Jewish-black experiences stand at the center of urban history, our understanding of immigration and migration; assimilation and exclusion; the social construction of whiteness and blackness; the issue of power, access, and equality" (902). If one of the strengths of *MORS* is its seemingly encyclopedic depiction of New York City, one of its weaknesses is how the historical significance of Blackness to Ira has been scrubbed from its pages, and Ira's overwhelmingly condescending views on Black characters have been sanitized. In contrast, the manuscript details how the social construction of whiteness accommodated Jewishness and the role anti-Blackness played in that process.

Just as Weil removes so much of what Roth says about Black people, historians have made similar elisions in Jewish American scholarship. Regarding Harlem in particular, Joe W. Trotter notes how Jeffrey Gurock's *When Harlem Was Jewish* suggests that "Jews did not leave this particular community specifically because of their feeling any special aversion to, or fear of, living among Blacks" (203).[11] Yet Roth, in the manuscripts, published version, and his video-recorded interview with Weil, clearly reveals his fear and aversion to Black people, even emphasizing the fictionalized aspect of Ira's visit to Theodora by stressing he was "scared to death of that kind of woman anyway" (Roth Papers, box 22, folder 19a, interview transcription, p. 5).

Still, Weil's editorial attempts at erasing Roth's racism occasionally just made text into subtext. For example, when Ira complains about having to do manual labor at his job, in the manuscript, he thinks, "Lousy bastard manager, why didn't he let the nigger do it?" (Roth Collection, box 1, folder 3, original draft, vol. 1, p. 247). The revised version changes one word: "why didn't he let the porter do it?" (1: 184). The meaning of the sentence remains largely consistent: a thirteen-year-old Ira is indignant about being made to do work he considers beneath him yet appropriate for his adult Black colleague Harvey. But for some readers, the racism underscoring Ira's objection might go unnoticed with the elimination of the slur.

At other times, Roth's writing on race straddles the line between naive and disingenuous. For example, between the movie theater scenes, Ecclesias critiques Ira's narrative thusly:

> But more important, you failed to represent the changes that have taken place in your own attitude toward them, changes in the psyche of the writer: Where is the new element, the new ingredient impregnating your outlook, nay, your very approach, a new *natural* approach. An approach that was fashioned, among other things, by their decencies and sympathies and multitude of

> kindnesses shown you in your many illnesses, your sufferings, where the new comprehensions of their plight, their deprivations, the hideous cruelties they had to endure, but above all—to you—their infinite capabilities, as with all human beings: Their dynamic vigor, art, wit, not merely from the nurse who comes to the house, changes the dressing on your foot, chaffers [*sic*], counsels, or the physician who examines, prescribes, conscientious, thoughtful, colloquial, no, to the entire range of their massive ethnic force; unique, *eventually dominant*. Al [*sic*] these have changed your own nature, where have you acknowledged the change? (Roth Papers, box 77, folder 4, "before editing," vol. 4, p. 1055)

This claim that Ira overcomes his racism because of the kindness of his medical attendants is disingenuous. The allusion to Black people becoming "eventually dominant" reeks of the projection and racist paranoia white supremacists express in crying "white genocide." The invocation of "their massive ethnic force" indicates that Ira views his interests and Black interests as fundamentally opposed; if they are "eventually dominant," Ira (and whatever group Ira identifies with here) is eventually dominated, a characterization that echoes not just anti-Black but specifically white supremacist rhetoric.[12] Ecclesias chiding the elderly Ira for his racist prose actually provides an additional opportunity for Roth to saturate the text with antiblack suppositions.

Removing these multiple instances of anti-Black sentiment underscores just how taboo it would have been for Ira to read as racist. But if Jewish racism, Jewish pedophilia and rape, and Jewish incest are all taboo, what accounts for the different ways in which the revision process navigated each one? Certainly, Robert Weil played an important role in this decision-making, but Weil also acted in a predictable fashion, attempting to mold Roth's novel for a particular audience, inclined toward positively identifying with a type of Jewish male protagonist. Novels that depict rape and racism are common. Those that depict the male hero protagonist as a racist and rapist are less so. To make sense of why Ira could not be depicted as raping (or in Roth's disturbing words, "semiraping") an eleven- or twelve-year-old girl, any more than he could refer to (essentially all) Black characters with slurs, we might contemplate Roth and David Schearl as Jewish American icons.

Huck, David, and Jewish Narcissistic Mirroring

Although *Call It Sleep* garnered some positive reviews upon its release, only in the 1960s, thanks to the attention of scholars like Irving Howe and Alfred Kazin, did the novel become a best-selling phenomenon. At that time, Roth expressed ambivalence about the book's newfound success and distanced himself from it. In interviews, he suggested that he was no longer the same person who wrote the celebrated novel (Kellman 233). Wirth-Nesher reads *MORS* as reflecting Roth's desire "to set the record straight by shocking his readers into the realization that he was victimizer, not only victim, that the only child of *Call It Sleep* is an elegant evasion" (273).[13] Roth was eager for his audience to encounter the flawed protagonist of *MORS*. Prior to its release, Roth told a journal editor that "Volume two is scandalous," and, refusing to offer hints, offered, "You'll have to read it" (Kellman 301). Weil reports that Roth was impatient for him to arrive at the sibling incest passages in reading his drafts (Gibbs, "Conversation" 157). The novel's structure, which waits until volume 2 to present Ira as incestuous, pedophilic, or rapist, is also instructive. If we again consider Stockton's reading of Lyne's *Lolita*, in which the revelation of the child spoils the camera's erotic focus on the supposed woman, we might contemplate *MORS*'s focus on Ira: Roth attempts to spoil the male hero protagonist (in culturally specific terms, the schlemiel) by revealing the rapist.

Reviews of *MORS* regularly touched on the tension between Ira and David Schearl. Some reviewers were immediately sensitive to the differences in their character. Robert Cohen, reviewing volume 1 in *Tikkun*, referred to Roth's own childhood as "Schearlish" and observed that "if *Sleep's* David Schearl is portrayed as a kind of baffled innocent, Roth, these many painful years later, seems to have exhausted all sympathy for his earlier self." Others went so far as to essentially merge the two protagonists into a singular autobiographical protagonist in two different works. In *Newsweek*, Jack Kroll wrote, "'Call It Sleep' was an astonishing projection of the mind of a small boy, David Schearl, growing up in the slums of New York's Lower East Side. Roth picks up his autobiographical hero (now called Ira Stigman) in 1914 . . . and takes him to 1920 when he is 14 years old." Predictably, given Roth's authorship of such an iconic text, almost every review considered the new novel in light of the earlier one—often unfavorably and protective of *CIS*. Mary Gordon's review of volume 2 for the *New York Times* had an especially emphatic take on the earlier novel's superiority. In that review, Gordon quoted Roth's own allusion to Ira and David Schearl's relationship from a 1986 essay. Gordon wrote that Roth "says that the point of his project, the sequel to 'Call It Sleep,' is 'to take the ground from under the innocent victim' of 'Call It Sleep' and to show him as the 'victimizer, but more to the point, all of us as victims—in a degenerative society.'" Very aware of Roth's artistic intent, Gordon does not so much reject the premise as she does fault Roth's execution and Ira and Roth's lack of empathy for their sisters (fictional and real alike). Gordon concludes that "'Call It Sleep' remains a masterpiece; nothing is lost from it, or added to it, by reading its sequels."

So, while Roth clearly intended for *MORS* to issue a "corrective" to what he considered a dishonest portrayal of an autobiographical protagonist, not every reader accepted the denunciation of *CIS* or David Schearl. But Roth utilized the form of *MORS* as a form of bait and switch, to expose the protagonist as "victimizer" by withholding information from his audience and his editor, who had no knowledge of the second volume incest reveal until he came across it in drafts.[14] Thus, even while Roth articulated iconoclastic goals (toward himself and his character), he arrives at the iconoclastic moment having drawn the reader into identifying with what appears, at first, to be a familiar protagonist. The ambivalence Roth felt regarding Schearl extended to his audience; he felt Schearl was dishonest and punished his fans for their fealty to Schearl by creating a relatively similar protagonist, only to reveal the character's transgressions after having the reader bond with Ira for more than four hundred pages.

Weil's revision suggestions reveal his sense of the limits to what Roth's audience might have tolerated in a protagonist. Jonathan Arac, writing about white American emotional investment in Huckleberry Finn, may help contextualize readers' relationships—Arac uses the word "idolatry"—to David Schearl, Ira Stigman, and Roth: "Because the structure of the sublime joins reader, character, and author in interlinked identifications, it may lead to narcissistically fixed mirrorings rather than 'ecstatic' mobility. Readers may then tend to be highly protective of the characters and authors in which they are invested, and at the same time will feel themselves intimately threatened by anything that seems to criticize or diminish either Huck or Twain" (36). Arac writes about Huck and Twain as figures who, essentially, cannot be considered racist by white American readers because they represent white moral triumph over slavery and racism. A similar phenomenon may transpire with Roth and both Ira and David Schearl for Jewish American audiences: David Schearl's appeal involves an ambivalence about Jewishness, American identity, and assimilation, and a deep-seated guilt that Schearl carried as a result of an overdeveloped superego. Schearl's desire to purify himself does not emerge out of any act that most readers would identify as immoral; Schearl's appeal involves the guilt of an innocent. As such, Schearl invites mirroring because he reflects a narcissistic yearning by American Jews for an immigrant origin story that engages their own ambivalence about assimilation and Jewishness through a figure of innocence. Leslie Fiedler's observations on *CIS* as having Christological qualities, and Schearl as a Christ figure, reinforce a reading of Roth's novel as seductive origin story.[15] But showing Ira rape an eleven- or twelve-year-old girl and repeatedly refer to Black characters with racial slurs would have precluded narcissistic mirroring of the protagonist and the author.

Roth's goals and his publishers' goals were, in essence, at cross-purposes. Roth sought to make Ira Stigman abhorrent, thereby authoring a book that punished (or made complicit) his fans for their narcissistic mirroring of him and David Schearl. Weil's editorial task, meanwhile, involved blocking Roth from this objective, preventing Ira from becoming too fundamentally detestable a figure. Commercially and critically, keeping *MORS*'s protagonist "narcissistically mirrorable" made sense, given that Roth's commercial appeal stemmed from creating one of the most narcissistically mirrorable protagonists in American Jewish literature. *MORS* reveals that while compelling, interesting protagonists are always flawed, there may be particular, unexpected types of transgression that unexpectedly permit narcissistic mirroring by readers invested in a certain white male subjectivity. Arac theorizes that for readers engaging in narcissistic mirroring, some taboo element of self-identification with flawed hero protagonists is constitutive of the identification process. For Arac, white American identification with Huckleberry Finn involves celebrating Huck as an exemplar of anti-racism precisely because Huck's interactions with Jim actually establish him as a symbol of white supremacy. Narcissistic investment in Ira on account of his supposedly confessional, contrite rejection of his younger self's behavior actually facilitates celebrating Ira's graphic depictions of rape behind the disingenuous guise of celebrating Ira's moral transformation.

In conducting this analysis of Roth's work, my goal is to demonstrate the structural link between Roth's portrayal of close endogamy with his depiction of interracial exogamy. While the tension between fact and fiction regarding Roth's and Ira's relationship with their sister(s) has garnered scholarly and critical attention, less attention has been paid to the novel's engagement with rape and race. The attention heaped onto the "scandalous" sibling incest component, in effect, actually serves to deflect attention from the text's comparatively more demeaning sexual and racial politics. In this regard, even when an iconic and celebrated Jewish artist functionally confesses to incest, the imperative of Jewish community protective politics to defend white Jewish masculinity still operates. For Roth, Jewish community protective politics facilitated his publishing a novel "about" incest provided that said incest be presented as lateral and consensual, that the act of confession be celebrated as indicative of personal growth, and by ensuring that those components worse than incest—rape and racism—were disguised and revised accordingly.

I want to discuss one final editorial revision underscoring how Roth's text and its revisions, ostensibly about Jewish American identity, actively collapse the space between Jewishness and American whiteness and dehumanize nonwhites in service of that goal. The aforementioned attempted rape scene in the movie theater, in which Ira and Stella are confronted by Black youths, intersects directly with the Stella revisions. Stella, as we have seen, is made older than originally intended. For the Black youths that follow Ira and Stella into the bathroom, it is the opposite.

In the published version of *MORS*, Roth describes the characters as "elastic, brown striplings, fourteen years old, fifteen, who knew?" (4: 205). The manuscript reads: "Brown, alert striplings, seventeen years old, eighteen, who knew?" (Roth Papers, box 77, folder 4, "before editing," vol. 4, p. 1052). Even the sentence construction echoes Ira's inability to confidently assert Stella's age in volume 2—"How old was she? Fourteen? Was he crazy or was he right?" (282). Why make the Black characters three years younger? Aging Stella involved changing a number in order to make her read as less "innocent," more responsible for sexual activity, more capable of consent, even as her characterization remained the same. Making the Black youths younger does not accomplish the inverse; they do not read as more innocent. Instead, they read as more threatening.

In January of 1996, Hillary Clinton made her infamous "superpredator" comments. Conjuring a raced image of youth criminality, she said: "They are not just gangs of kids anymore. They are often the kinds of kids that are called 'superpredators.' No conscience, no empathy" (Byrnes). Clinton's two-decades-old comments received significant press attention during her 2016 presidential campaign, alongside consideration of the outcomes of the crime bill for which she advocated, the success of the Black Lives Matter movement in drawing sustained attention to Black vulnerability at the hands of America's police forces, and the consequences of racist rhetoric about Black male youth. Clinton's words reflect a broader history of race and racism's intersection with the concept of childhood, subjects analyzed by Stockton and Robin Bernstein, among others. Bernstein comments on the "underanalyzed exclusion of black youth from the category of childhood" (16) as a phenomenon dating back to the nineteenth century, and Stockton locates this rhetoric in late eighteenth-century literature (31).

While Lolita figures as a relevant literary comparison for Stella, the age revision of the Black youths in the movie theater invites contemplation alongside the way policemen and armed non-Black civilians described Black male teenagers like Tamir Rice, Michael Brown, and Trayvon Martin, prior to killing them. Timothy Loehmann, the officer who shot and killed the twelve-year-old Rice while he played with a pellet gun in a park, testified that he thought Rice was eighteen years old (Laughland and Swaine). This might initially seem like an inversion of the *MORS* revision, in which the characters are made three years younger, but the logic is consistent. To Ira and Stella (and the reader) the fourteen- or fifteen-year-old Black youths might appear more threatening, older, than their age would indicate, and the revision history confirms this: the characters were designed as seventeen- or eighteen-year-olds. Just as raising Stella's age preserves the notion of some innocent childhood that the text dare not disturb, lowering the Black teenagers' age underscores the premise that the sexually threatening qualities of young Black men exist regardless of the specifics of age or the concept of childhood.

The Intersections of *MORS*'s Racism, Sexism, and Homophobia

In closing, I want to touch briefly on immigrant pathologization before sketching out Roth's investments in white masculinity. Reading *MORS* as utilizing incest as a theme to evoke the close-knit reality of Jewish families upon their arrival in New York City and the "new world" requires minimizing numerous clues Roth provides about the cycle of sexual assault, while also disregarding the experience of women and girls who encountered the threat of sexual violence not just in their surrounding communities but in their own homes. Kellman, for instance, states that "incest is a dramatic manifestation of immigrant insecurity, the newcomers' inability to invest their emotions in anything beyond the reassuring confines of the clan" (70). This sort of reading overlooks the gendered power dynamics that facilitate women and girls being especially vulnerable to incestuous abuse. Such a reading also diminishes the significance of scenes in which Roth depicts sexual violence as a form of generationally replicated trauma, instructive passages regarding how *MORS* can be read as a literary examination of how victims of sexual abuse revisit their trauma upon others. Furthermore, framing the incestuous content as constitutive of immigrant experience or anxiety is profoundly othering, suggesting that the circumstances of immigration are such that certain groups no longer abide the incest taboo. Even though this specific example puts the onus of incestuous behavior on early twentieth-century Jewish immigrants, the (faulty) logic is too easily transferable to contemporary immigrant communities (and in that context, perhaps more easily recognized as demeaning and racist). If we consider Ira's sexual conduct with Stella and Minnie in the context of Ira's molestation at the hands of a stranger in Fort Tryon Park and later his Spanish teacher, we avoid pathologizing Ira as an immigrant and can instead interrogate Ira's inability to discuss his adult male abusers with anything other than homophobic vitriol, as well as how his abuse reproduces itself through his targeting of female family members societally, and domestically, more vulnerable than he.

Ira's homophobia, misogyny, and racism intersect in illuminating ways. A passage in volume 2 finds Ira in a euphoric state, expressing relief upon learning Minnie's pregnancy scare has ended:

> There was no brag, no parading, nothing but shame. Genie in a vase. Pandora's box. His sister's box! Can you imagine bragging about that? Jesus, it almost made him shut his eyes in the enormous twinge the very thought caused him. Hey, fellers, I thought I knocked up my sister! Was I scared. Boyoboy. Holy Jesus Christ, of all the things he had ever heard those guys say: pratt and blow and lap and go down on it, back scuttle, and every other goddamn thing he once believed was just make-believe, but even if it was true, nobody ever said

> I laid my sister. Yeah, the Italian kids said, aw, yer mudder's ass, yer sister's cunt—but what was that compared to: my sister's cunt? (2: 167)

Roth employs paraleipsis; he denies bragging about having sex with his sister only to set up extensive bragging about having had sex with his sister. His fantasized impulse to brag to "the Italian kids" requires consideration alongside his specific insecurities, though, and, in particular, his pronounced homophobia. Despite the revision of Ira's racial slurs, Ira refers to Mr. Lennard, the Spanish teacher who molests Ira, as a "fag" on multiple occasions (1: 148; 2: 155; 3: 119). Editing volume 1, Weil felt that Roth would "hint at things" and that Roth was "about to account for his homosexuality," as opposed to incest (Gibbs, "Conversation" 157). Where Weil senses misdirection, there is also meaningful linkage: Ira's misunderstanding and rejection of what he considers homosexuality is absolute. Not only does he conflate homosexuality with pedophilia, his bragging to the "Italian kids" involves emphasizing his heterosexual impulse, his strident inclination toward sex with women *or* girls. The premise of Ira's boast is that age or familial relation cannot stifle Ira's heterosexual urges. Warren Hoffman's *The Passing Game*, which engages with queer Jewish identity, asks, "To what extent do Jewish male narrators work to exhibit a virile heterosexual masculine identity that counteracts the stereotype of the effeminate Jew?" (15). Roth's novel indicates that the imperative for some narrators to express that virile heterosexual masculine identity can catapult them well past the bounds of an ostensibly unspeakable taboo.

MORS should not be read as a novel of redemption. Reading it in that fashion requires its audience to participate in the displacement of Ira's transgressions onto Black characters and cosign the misogyny with which Ira depicts Stella and Minnie. Ecclesias's ongoing conversations with the elderly Ira reveal that the protagonist evinces the same sexism, racism, and homophobia in his old age that impacted his behavior in his youth. As Ecclesias tells the octogenarian writer, "you still are what you are" (2: 286). One important facet of the manuscript's usability lies in its depiction of how racism, sexism, and homophobia intersect in Ira's attempt to craft his sense of self. This usability is diminished, but still extant, in the published novel.

In illustrating how an ideology of white supremacy involves the demarcation of a border, Ta-Nehisi Coates highlights the intersections of race, sexuality and gender: "The nigger, the fag, the bitch illuminate the border, illuminate what we ostensibly are not, illuminate the Dream of being white, of being a Man" (*Between the World* 60). Coates uses slurs to illustrate his point because the conception of whiteness requires demeaning categorization, even if polite society edits its language. That *MORS* required one slur be erased, while the others remained, speaks to a logic of how that border operates. But in suggesting Roth's second novel is redemptive, we misuse a disturbingly revealing text. I am uncertain as to whether we can use *MORS* in a responsible fashion without discussing the revisions that fundamentally altered the novel's presentation of race and rape. Certainly, in its present construction, the novel shares characteristics with other texts probing the limits, and logics, for the celebration of white patriarchal villainy, especially those presenting it in an ostensibly vulnerable masculine form. And Ira's myopic preoccupation with his Jewish vulnerability, which may facilitate his exploitation of those more vulnerable than he, compels analysis given the novel's engagement with power dynamics. But these revisions of rape and racism require attention because *MORS*, at heart, is a revision of *Call It Sleep*. And the editorial revisions facilitate *MORS* being read as an acceptable artistic expression of misogyny and racism, as opposed to an unacceptable one. That process, and the way that it implicates not just an author but an editorial process, a publishing house, and an audience, requires attention, meditation, and reflection.

Conclusion

This book demonstrates how Jewish community protective politics influence how stories about incest involving Jews are told and also how they are interpreted. Historical Jewish male vulnerability informs the cultural logics of how white privilege operates in stories of sexual assault and victimization implicating Jewish men. In order to protect the image of Jewish masculinity, embodied in these case studies by white Jewish men, Jewish community protective forces align to preclude white Jewish men from reading as incestuous or pedophilic, unless, as with Henry Roth, the incest is depicted deliberately in a way that draws attention away from other, more taboo presentations of white Jewish masculinity. The mechanisms of these community protective politics insist upon either white Jewish male innocence or secular excommunication. If a figure's innocence cannot be plausibly championed, he can still be functionally disinherited from his Jewishness. These political processes can be observed in how these stories are first told, via art and nonfiction, but also in the criticism, scholarship, and popular media coverage that arise surrounding stories involving Jews and incest.

Among my additional claims, I argue that the Jewish incest stereotype remains resilient, despite its relatively unacknowledged place in popular culture. Jewish artists, authors, and activists writing about incest indicate awareness of the stereotype, even when it is not explicitly stated. I also demonstrate how during the 1990s white Jewish men benefited from considerable white privilege in being treated sympathetically by mainstream media. And in my final chapters, I show how white Jewish male artists like Woody Allen and Henry Roth successfully marketed their incest narratives to audiences that would viscerally thrill to stories suggesting that white Jewish men could sexually transgress in ways that evoke Jewish incest and pedophilia stereotypes and live to tell the tale.

Most speculatively, I propose that Jewish community protective politics also serve white male interests more broadly. The narrative beats of these stories suggest that allegations that Jewish men might be sexual predators could be credibly fought with insistence that such insinuations were de facto antisemitic and libelous. Transitively, I contend that these stories can also be read as suggesting that allegations against white men (who happened to be Jewish) could be credibly fought with the insistence that these stories overlooked the history of white male vulnerability to false allegations. The rhetorical conditions of Jewish community protective politics, which subsume Jewishness into whiteness in order to benefit from its privileges and preclude explicit discussions of Jewish incest stereotype, facilitate white Jewish male vulnerability reading as a convenient and formidable expression of white male vulnerability.

To that end, attempts to deconstruct white privilege will necessarily require uncomfortable but unavoidable examinations of (and conversations about) how histories of vulnerability intersect with contemporary privilege and not merely in cases involving sexual transgression. Within this conclusion, then, my goal is to dig deeper into a few moments of "speaking out," not merely by victims or survivors, but by those adjacent to them, and how those moments can be productive, while also rhetorically risky. I am particularly mindful of how speaking out, for those adjacent to victims and survivors, invites risk in a similar fashion to what scholars and activists might encounter by openly discussing Jewish community protective politics. I also contend that especially amid the current crescendo of antisemitism and white nationalist accumulation of political power, Jewish community protective politics must be exposed, as they enable powerful and predatory white Jewish men, to the considerable detriment of other members of the Jewish (and non-Jewish) community.

This conclusion contemplates three different examples of "speaking out." First, I engage Dylan Farrow's brother (and Woody Allen's son) Ronan Farrow's discussion of his decision to dedicate himself to investigative reporting involving sexual assault. Second, I draw explicit attention to how speaking out about Jewishness and sexual transgression in public forums inevitably, even if unintentionally, invites the "approval" of white supremacist operatives, regardless of the nuance of the arguments, and how this disingenuous posturing by white supremacist activists cannot be allowed to dictate the terms of these conversations. And third, I return to the 1990s with a close reading of a non-Jewish-authored text, James McBride's *The Color of Water*. McBride's text reveals that even a memoir about how a white Jewish father's incestuous abuse plays a formative role in a daughter's wholesale rejection of Judaism can be read as showing how discussing that abuse facilitates a reconnection with Jewishness for that long-Judaism-estranged daughter and her non-Jewish son.

Ronan Farrow and the Limits of "All of It"

Ronan Farrow's role in the Me Too movement has been pronounced. Along with Jane Mayer, his reporting for the *New Yorker* on Harvey Weinstein helped draw public attention to the numerous allegations that Weinstein had sexually harassed and sexually assaulted women, while also providing intricate details regarding how Weinstein levied his influence with law enforcement to avoid being charged with crimes and used private investigation firms to intimidate victims inclined to speak out.[1]

While Ronan Farrow has been celebrated for his invaluable journalistic contributions to the movement, I want to draw attention to his articulation of his initial anxiety about "speaking out" in the context of his sister Dylan Farrow. The following is from an op-ed Ronan Farrow wrote about the "culture of acquiescence" surrounding Woody Allen, published more than a year prior to his string of articles on Weinstein:

> I had worked hard to distance myself from my painfully public family history and wanted my work to stand on its own. So I had avoided commenting on my sister's allegations for years and, when cornered, cultivated distance, limiting my response to the occasional line on Twitter. My sister's decision to step forward came shortly after I began work on a book and a television series. It was the last association I wanted. *Initially, I begged my sister not to go public again and to avoid speaking to reporters about it.* I'm ashamed of that, too. With sexual assault, anything's easier than facing it in full, saying all of it, facing all of the consequences. Even now, I hesitated before agreeing to *The Hollywood Reporter*'s invitation to write this piece, knowing it could trigger another round of character assassination against my sister, my mother or me. ("My Father, Woody Allen"; my emphasis)

I want to stress the enormity, but also the honesty, of what Ronan Farrow confesses to here: "Initially, I begged my sister not to go public again." Despite the reputation Ronan Farrow has achieved as a tireless advocate for survivors and victims, here he acknowledges making an attempt to silence his sister. He continues: "With sexual assault, anything's easier than facing it in full, saying all of it, facing all of the consequences." By avoiding pronouns in this sentence, Ronan Farrow speaks to how these dynamics operate not just for the direct victim, but for people like him, adjacent to victims. Presumably, Ronan Farrow alludes to Dylan Farrow in this statement, but also to himself, their mother, their siblings, and likely so many others whose lives touched or were a part of the Allen/Farrow family.

There is also something noteworthy about Ronan Farrow's subsequent phrasing: when he says "facing it in full, saying all of it, facing all of the consequences," he does not expand on the specifics of the "all" he invokes. And yet, his reporting for the *New Yorker* meticulously strives to say *all* of it; the level of detail in his work resulted in the publication of five lengthy articles on multiple angles of the Weinstein story, including so many of the consequences Weinstein's alleged victims faced, over the course of just two months of 2017.

The op-ed is remarkable, portending Ronan Farrow's journalistic attempts to say "all of it," but also transparently demystifying allyship. Ronan Farrow does not paint a picture of himself suggesting he emerged from his childhood home fully formed as an advocate or ally. Instead, he collapses the space between his role as a champion of victims and his role as one more voice arguing for silence. If even Ronan Farrow begged his sister to stay silent about Woody Allen, we get a terrifying glimpse of just how powerful the forces are that align to silence women and children victimized by powerful men.

My own thesis is that Jewish community protective politics function as one of many forces that align in these moments. But Ronan Farrow, despite his advocacy for the importance of "saying all of it," makes no mention of Jewishness in his comments on Allen. However, this is not surprising; I doubt Ronan Farrow *could* make any mention of Allen's Jewishness playing a role in how Allen avoided consequences even if he had considered them privately. Were he to make any comment along those lines, two things would likely happen: white nationalists would point to it as evidence of Jewish pathology, and some Jewish organizations and pundits would point to it as evidence of Ronan Farrow's antisemitism. Were Ronan Farrow to speak to this, the risk to his credibility would be enormous because of the function of Jewish community protective politics and because Farrow does not identify as Jewish. Yet given that Allen *did* insinuate to the public that antisemitism played a role in Mia Farrow's behavior and her supposed brainwashing of Dylan Farrow, it is not unlikely that Dylan and Ronan Farrow are aware of this dynamic, even as the cultural logics in play rhetorically prevent them from addressing it. The difficulty of "facing it in full, saying all of it, and facing all of the consequences" may encompass the fact that even now, they cannot speak to how Allen leveraged his Jewishness and their Catholicism, alongside a history of antisemitism, to make Allen's position sympathetic in so much media coverage. "Saying *all* of it" would risk, along with so much else, being labeled antisemitic.

To my knowledge, Ronan Farrow has made no direct mention of how his father's Jewishness operated in helping Allen frame storytelling about their family during (and since) the early 1990s. His reporting about Harvey Weinstein has similarly avoided engagement with Weinstein's Jewishness.[2] Jewish community protective politics play a role policing how Jewishness gets discussed—or stricken from the record—when prominent white Jewish figures are accused of sexual transgressions or crimes. The stakes are predictably higher for non-Jews making these connections, given their ostensibly greater vulnerability to being characterized as antisemitic. But reliably virulent antisemitism rears its head even when Jewish pundits or scholars attempt to engage phenomena involving Jews and hypersexuality, independent of ideology or efficacy.

Two examples help illustrate this point: the first, an article written by Mark Oppenheimer, for the Jewish web magazine *Tablet*, attempted to analyze Harvey Weinstein and his Jewishness in the context of the allegations made against him. The article was entitled "The Specifically Jewy Perviness of Harvey Weinstein." The piece had substantive argumentative flaws, as well as factual ones. Oppenheimer suggests that a "revenge-tinged fantasy" of exerting power over non-Jewish women is an essentialist Jewish attribute. It is not. Mistaking a misogynistic attribute for a Jewish attribute is certainly antisemitic, but the article's misogynistic qualities are equally insidious. Like so much misguided coverage of destructive white men, Oppenheimer expends a significant amount of energy inviting the reader to recognize Weinstein's humanity, as opposed to that of his victims. Various writers condemned the essay in essays and on social media.[3] But the white nationalist Richard Spencer tweeted a link to the essay, in which he wrote, "Tablet . . . or the Daily Stormer? Regardless, powerful easy [*sic*]" (Blumberg). White supremacist and former Ku Klux Klan leader David Duke followed suit with a tweet the following day.

Some might consider Spencer and Duke's tweeting of the article alone as indisputable evidence of its misguidedness. This logic intimates that white supremacists' promotion of an article necessarily taints the content of said article. But this is a slippery rhetorical slope and fails to account for the disingenuous way white supremacists engage Jewish writing. The second example helps clarify this danger. On his website, David Duke featured an article on Josh Lambert's book *Unclean Lips*, based on a podcast interview Lambert did for *Tablet*. The book deals with how American Jews, in various fields, engaged the topic of obscenity, inclusive of pornography, and how antisemitism informed how various Jewish authors, artists, publishers, and lawyers navigated these issues. But for Duke, featuring an article on Lambert's book had little to do with honest engagement with the ideas therein. Rather, the article is a thinly veiled attempt to further associate Jews with the very same antisemitic presuppositions that Lambert critically and intellectually interrogates. Duke's project is not to consider, in good faith, Lambert's critique of white Christian reactionary politics and how American Jews have combated that through fiction, lawsuits, and comedy. Duke's project is to disingenuously insinuate that because respectable Jewish scholars are studying Jews and pornography, some surreptitious link between Jews and pornography must actually exist and that even Jewish scholars admit it and celebrate it. This is a transparently cynical exercise, but a predictable one: find articles or persons with reputable titles, affiliations, or publications, intimate that their argument supports a white supremacist presupposition involving Jews and sex, and thereby "prove" that even respectable Jews and outlets concede that Jews are threats.

The effect of this disingenuous engagement is to chill discourse. Irrespective of the specific ideas being articulated, white supremacists equate any invocation of Jewish stereotype into a confirmation of Jewish stereotype. Furthermore, the very fact that they, as white supremacists, seemingly "promote" this work has the effect of exponentially increasing the taboo affiliated with the topic. If writing about certain subjects means an author is at risk for being tweeted or retweeted by David Duke, we can easily understand the appeal of avoiding that topic. To that effect, attempting to write about how Jewish community politics operate—or, for that matter, how any community protective politics operate—will likely serve as grist for white supremacist mills.

The problem with this particular risk is that there may be no way around it. However, the fact that avowed white supremacists will likely seize upon and distort these arguments must not stop scholars and activists from drawing attention to and analyzing phenomena that can illuminate how some powerful men exploit antisemitism anxiety to excuse inexcusable actions, and how the unspoken anxiety regarding sexual antisemitism impacts how people choose to tell stories about sexual transgression. Will open discussion on the subject of Jewish community protective politics yield disingenuous championing by white supremacists? Probably. But the goal is not to dialogue with white supremacists. The goal is to expose and thus combat the cultural logics that sexually predatory white Jewish men and their enablers exploit to get away with their behavior and that also serve to enable non-Jewish white men through the cultural logic's transitive implication that white masculinity is as inherently vulnerable to false accusations as white Jewish masculinity. Avoiding the unsettling aspects of these intersections is impossible, but it is necessary for a politics combating antisemitism, misogyny, racism, toxic masculinity, and rape culture to penetrate to the eye of this storm of discomfort.

On that note, I want to close this study with one final primary source, a memoir by James McBride. Unlike the other authors and artists I have analyzed, McBride is not Jewish. Yet McBride's memoir reveals something hopeful about how texts that do directly and openly engage with these taboos can depict Jewishness in positive ways even as they unflinchingly discuss incest in specifically Jewish contexts. *The Color of Water* understandably triggered Jewish community protective responses on multiple counts: it reproduces explicit accounts of white Jewish racism, depicts a Jewish father—and former rabbi—sexually molesting his daughter, and then chronicles that daughter's interracial intermarriage and conversion to Christianity as directly impacted by that abuse. This is the story of James McBride's mother, of how Rachel Shilsky became Ruth McBride Jordan.

McBride engages a veritable epicenter of Jewish communal anxiety. While that anxiety seems largely sublimated in most mainstream coverage of the memoir, some reviewers, like Leslie Cohen, writing for the *Jerusalem Post*, addressed it directly: "This book is bound to infuriate many people because of the portrayal of Rachel's upbringing. It makes one shudder at the so-called Orthodoxy that Rachel fled from. Furthermore, its strong Christian message may be experienced as a slap in the face—or worse—to Judaism." Cohen refers to McBride Jordan by the name she ultimately relinquishes while giving voice to specific anxieties the memoir might trigger within Jewish communities. These sentiments rarely found articulation in reviews. Still, some press coverage clearly indicated Jewish audience ambivalences. A reporter for a local Florida paper wrote, "Some Jewish institutions welcomed McBride, but a handful of others, including one in the Detroit area, asked him to come, then canceled, saying community members were disturbed by his portrayal of Jewish people. In detailing Ruth McBride [Jordan]'s background, her son doesn't gloss over the misdeeds of Ruth McBride [Jordan]'s father, a failed rabbi who molested his daughter and deserted his ailing wife" (Eversley). Another review—a brief blurb, also for the *Jerusalem Post*—describes McBride Jordan's father as "a rabbi father so cruel the Jewish reader feels shame just reading about him" ("Bookshelf"). Though positive about the book and its message, this review omits all reference to McBride Jordan's father's cruelty being sexually abusive in nature. This was relatively rare. Most reviews more directly addressed the abuse, as well as its sexual nature.[4]

As Leslie Cohen's review and Melanie Eversley's article indicate, Jewish community engagement with the text featured some ambivalence, and the conversion narrative certainly played a role alongside the sexual abuse, though they are clearly linked in James McBride's telling (and likely in the ambivalent and negative responses).[5] Still, independent of the sexually transgressive content, the text's portrayal of a departure from Jewishness undoubtedly led some individuals to conceive of it as hostile to Judaism. If Jewish community protective politics involve a presumed involvement with Jewish community, McBride's memoir likely triggered Jewish community protective responses that played out in evident ways (such as rescinded invitations) and less observable ones (invitations that were never considered, let alone proffered).

While we see some of these anxieties find expression in the reviews, a closer reading of *The Color of Water* actually refutes some of the anxiety-fueled presuppositions of Jewish community protective politics. What would it mean for a Jewish woman to tell her story of being molested by her father in her own words, without her Jewish father there to tell his side of the story? What would it mean for that Jewish woman to depict her Jewish family as, essentially, abandoning her after this sexual abuse and after she married a non-Jewish Black man? And what would it mean for the Jewish woman to intimate that her Jewish family's racism clearly played a role in this? And last, what if this Jewish woman intimated that her religious Jewish father's sexual abuse directly informed her decision to convert to Christianity? Presumably, these plot points would suggest a text with an unsympathetic representation of Jewishness, if not blatant antisemitism, as Leslie Cohen intimates.

But McBride's memoir, which skillfully combines his complex narrative journey with his mother's spoken accounts of her life, defies simple or reductive categorization. His frank depiction of his mother's parting with her Jewish heritage also reads as an autobiographical account of his desire to learn about it, write about it, and forge a meaningful connection to it. McBride lets his mother's words stand on their own, and she makes very clear just how centrally her experiences with incest connected viscerally to her own ethnoracial and religious identity. Considering just those portions of the text would permit reading *The Color of Water* only as a story about a Jewish woman converting to Christianity to escape her father's incestuous Jewish home. Except McBride's arc, where he discovers his own Jewish heritage, clearly indicates that his mother's personal reasons for journeying away from Judaism are not reflective of Jewishness as he encounters, understands, and experiences it. McBride Jordan's willingness to directly speak her truth and articulate the complexity of her grief also finds her recreating the Jewish home of her youth with nuance and detail, giving voice to various Jewish characters, which McBride does as well in his detective-like investigation into his mother's past.

How this all plays out in McBride Jordan's telling is at times remarkable. Consider the following passage, which discusses McBride Jordan's father's sexual abuse directly, but also touches on race, racism, and the Passover seder in provocative, moving ways:

> Of course I had something to run from. My father did things to me when I was a young girl that I couldn't tell anyone about. Such as getting in bed with me at night and doing things to me sexually that I could not tell anyone about. When we'd go to the beach in Portsmouth, he'd go into the water with me, supposedly to teach me how to swim, and hold me real close to his body near his sexual parts and he'd have an erection. When we'd get back to the beach, Mameh would ask, "Are you getting better at swimming?" and I'd say, "Yes, Mameh," and he'd be standing there, glaring at me. God, I was scared of him.
>
> Anytime he had a chance, he'd try to get close to me or crawl into bed with me and molest me. I was afraid of Tateh and had no love for him at all. I dreaded him and was relieved anytime he left the house. But it affected me in a lot of ways, what he did to me. I had very low self-esteem as a child,

> which I kept with me for many, many years; and even now I don't want to be around anyone who is domineering or pushing me around because it makes me nervous. I'm only telling you this because you're my son and I want you to know the truth and nothing less. I did have low self-esteem as a child. I felt low.
>
> *Folks will run with that, won't they?* They'll say, "Oh, she felt low, so she went on and married a nigger." Well, I don't care, your father changed my life. He taught me about a God who lifted me up and forgave me and made me new. I was lucky to meet him or I would've been a prostitute or dead. Who knows what would've happened to me. *I was reborn in Christ. Had to be, after what I went through.* Of course, it wasn't torment twenty-four hours a day being a Jew. We had good times, especially with my mother. Like on Passover, where you had to clean that house spic-and-span. Not a crumb or speck of leavened bread could be found anywhere. We loved getting ready for it. You had to use Passover dishes and we had a big seder, where the family sat down and the table was set with matzoh and parsley, boiled eggs and other traditional Jewish food. We set an empty chair for the coming of Elijah—see, Jews think the real Messiah hasn't got here yet. The Haggadah had to be read and Tateh would ask us children questions about why we celebrated the feast of Passover. Well, you can believe we knew the answer rather than get smacked across the face by him, but to be honest with you, I used to see the empty chair we left for Elijah at the table and wish I could be gone to wherever Elijah was, eating over somebody else's house where your father didn't crawl into bed with you at night, interrupting your dreams so you don't know if it's really him or just the same nightmare happening over and over again. (42–43; my emphasis)

This is a heartbreaking passage, but enormously rich in what it reveals about incest, the problem of speaking about incest, and how culture and religious custom provide the scaffolding for the vocabulary and metaphors people use to understand their predicaments. McBride Jordan twice refers to her father's acts as things she "couldn't tell anyone about," including explaining the first untellable acts with a repeat declaration of their untellability: "Such as getting in bed with me at night and doing things to me sexually that I could not tell anyone about" (42). Even as she shares the specific beach anecdote, the framing leaves open the very real possibility that McBride Jordan is still not, in Ronan Farrow's words, "saying all of it."

McBride Jordan follows the beach anecdote with reflective self-analysis. She talks about how the abuse resulted in low self-esteem. She acknowledges that articulating the effects of the trauma will result in judgment by her community. But she does not clarify with specificity from which community she anticipates the racist response she articulates. That is, when McBride Jordan says "Folks" and "They'll say," who are the "folks"? Who are the "they"? Does she mean her family? Or Jews? White Jews? Or white people? This may reveal a seemingly abrupt shift away from the Jewish familial context toward a broader white societal one, but it may suggest that for McBride Jordan, anti-Blackness linked public white supremacist societal norms with the Jewish familial space. While McBride Jordan recounts the antisemitism she and her family were subjected to by non-Jewish white southerners, she also communicates her father's anti-Black racism (often quite directly, as in: "Tateh hated black people" [61]).[6]

Directly after this self-analysis, and the subsequent consideration of how white people might respond to that analysis in the context of her intermarriage, McBride Jordan explicitly frames her conversion narrative as an escape. The phrasing of "I was reborn in Christ. Had to be, after what I went through" is explicitly determinative. But McBride provides McBride Jordan extensive and invaluable space to narrate her story, space that requires analysis and contemplation. Crucially: the notion that every Jewish girl abused by a Jewish father would need to disinherit her Jewishness is not what McBride Jordan suggests.[7] Rather, she asserts that for herself this was the case.

If we consider only the following framework for McBride Jordan's extemporaneous narration, we have a clear trajectory: she mentions her father's abuse, referring to him and her mother in Yiddish, self-analyzes regarding its impact on her self-esteem, considers how white people would denigrate her choice to marry a Black man based on that confession, and then stresses that McBride's father taught her about a Christian God "who lifted me up and forgave me and made me new" (43). Up until this point the text presents a clear, linear, and Christological conversion narrative.

Where McBride Jordan goes next, into the Passover tradition, (in microcosm) showcases the more layered components of her narrative. McBride Jordan's qualification of her words speaks to her awareness that her rhetoric might be interpreted as antisemitic, as well as her sense of humor: "Of course, it wasn't torment twenty-four hours a day being a Jew" (43). She then begins what seems like a heartening description of the tradition of cleaning the house for Passover. But when she arrives at the seder, Tateh returns to the scene, corrupting even that memory. The final sentence is at once deeply moving and a stunning example of how decades later, McBride Jordan processes her abuse in the cultural contexts of her Jewish upbringing. McBride Jordan (partially) explains to her son (and the reader) that Elijah heralds the coming of the Messiah. But for her, the emptiness of his chair signifies her potential, longed for absence/escape. "I used to see the empty chair we left for Elijah at the table and wish I could be gone to wherever Elijah was, eating over somebody else's house where your father didn't crawl into bed with you at night" (43). Considering again the difficulty survivors and those adjacent to them have in "saying all of it," note that it is through invoking Elijah's chair—through re-engaging the custom that she has left behind—that McBride Jordan arrives at her articulation of the torturous repetition of her father's incestuous abuse: "interrupting your dreams so you don't know if it's really him or just the same nightmare happening over and over again" (43). If processing trauma requires putting traumatic experiences into words, reacquainting herself with the language of Jewish tradition provides the tools for her to process and give voice to some of this trauma.

On the one hand, *The Color of Water* shows how telling the story of leaving Jewishness requires McBride Jordan to re-engage the Jewishness that she converted from. But the conversion narrative is inextricably bound up with the incest narrative. The process of addressing her trauma in culturally specific terms facilitates McBride Jordan passing along stories about her Jewish heritage to her son. While surface readings and surface anxieties might consider the subject matter of McBride Jordan's story's necessarily antisemitic, the actual words and storytelling process are far more complex and revelatory. By putting her story to words, McBride Jordan passes along not just the incest story that she hid away, but also the to-that-point-unshared culture of her Jewish childhood and the keys to her son re-establishing familial connections with descendants of those family members.

The Color of Water's treatment of McBride's grandfather mirrors aspects of *Roseanne*'s treatment of Al Harris. Like Roseanne Conner, McBride Jordan's subjective accounting of her experience is never questioned. And yet, it is difficult to know precisely how the memoir negotiated Jewish community protective politics. While the book sold remarkably well and garnered positive reviews, it was not a pop culture phenomenon on the level of the hit sitcom *Roseanne*. As Eversley's article indicates, some congregations and Jewish organizations embraced public discussion of the book, while others kept it at arm's length. And the presence of the conversion narrative, foregrounded or otherwise, makes *The Color of Water* an atypical text to put forward in Jewish communal spaces.

And yet, like *Roseanne*, *The Color of Water* is a meaningful text to consider in a Jewish studies context. It gives voice to a survivor's distinctive rendering of an abusive Jewish home, while also showing how putting those experiences into words provided McBride Jordan a means of asserting an ownership of her Jewish culture and history that she could then pass on to her son, complicating the linear conversion narrative. The text is also instructive for how both McBride and McBride Jordan negotiate Jewishness, whiteness, and Blackness from their own shifting subjectivities across decades of twentieth-century history, when the popular scholarly concept of (white) Jews "becoming" white sits against McBride Jordan's self-mythologization of "becoming" light-skinned.[8] The memoir penetrates to the very heart of taboos regarding Jewish American whiteness and sexuality: what would it mean if some white Jews, even rabbis, were ardently racist and some of their relatives complicitly so? What would it mean if some Jewish fathers, even rabbis, molested their children? But its oblique engagement with these taboo anxieties finds a clear implicit response: that it means, actually, absolutely nothing about Jewishness at all. Other than that Jews are human beings, and in a social structure in which they benefit from whiteness, their behavior *as* white people can be easily discerned if Black voices are allowed into the frame. And that because Jews are human beings, some Jews commit sexual assault, but even the Jews who respond to that trauma by leaving the faith pass something meaningful and positive along to their children about what Jewishness means and how it is a part of them even if they have been estranged from it for decades. Regarding its politics of Jewish representation, the memoir's simplified premise is far more easily dismissed as problematic than its rich and engaging prose prove to be.

To put it a bit differently, including *The Color of Water* in a discussion of Jewish community anxieties about Jewish sexual predators and incest (or even Christian conversion) shows that stories engaging these anxieties in specific iterations do not need to be reductive or in any fashion indulgent of antisemitism. Texts that engage these taboo themes can still be instructive and relevant to a body of literature dealing thoughtfully, meaningfully, and humanly with Jews and Jewishness. Directly addressing these taboo themes is also entirely necessary for McBride's overarching plot to make narrative sense: were McBride not to disclose what his mother shared with him about her father's incestuous abuse, the impetus for her escaping her Jewish home in Virginia could never fully come into focus. Without those unsettling details, McBride's depiction of his own journey to connect with his newly discovered Jewish heritage would be incomplete. In the afterword to the tenth anniversary edition, McBride mentions forging relationships with about "a dozen relatives" since the book was published, "many of them white and Jewish. I'm a better person, a fuller person, for knowing them" (291). Never saccharine, McBride also notes that not all of the newly relinked members of his extended family have shown interest in getting to know each other. That said, the memoir reveals how even the most taboo Jewish subject matter can be explored in a constructive fashion that functionally expands the confines and possibilities of Jewish community.

The text also serves as a blunt reminder that when Jewish daughters, non-Jewish daughters, or daughters who complicate that distinction speak out about their abusive Jewish fathers, we need to hear them. For Ruth McBride Jordan, this listening occurs very late in her life, but the text reveals that telling her story, being heard by her son, facilitated her own re-engagement with Jewishness and her Jewish childhood on her terms. Purposeful listening and reading creates space for survivors to speak out with the culturally specific terms they require to tell their stories; to say "all of it," or as much of it as they can or want to. Ultimately, the more successfully the patriarchal dynamics of Jewish community protective politics are exposed, the more effectively the Jewish community can advocate for its most vulnerable members, extending to or including those individuals who are not Jewish but are still vulnerable to the actions of those who abuse their power and weaponize the history of Jewish male vulnerability and sexual antisemitism.

Acknowledgments

This book emerged from a dissertation I wrote at the University of Massachusetts Amherst, and I am enormously fortunate that Randall Knoper, Laura Briggs, and Josh Lambert served on that committee. Their generosity, patience, insight, and labor were absolutely instrumental in helping me navigate the ideas in this book. I am also grateful to have learned from so many others at UMass and the neighboring colleges, including Mara Benjamin, Joe Black, Nick Bromell, Justin Cammy, Laura Furlan, Asha Nadkarni, Robert Rothstein, Rachel Rubinstein, TreaAndrea Russworm, Donald Weber, and Ron Welburn. Thank you to James Young for his steadfast support, and to Rachel Mordecai, David Fleming, and Adam Zucker for awarding me an English department summer dissertation fellowship. My English and American Studies cohort helped sustain me: Kate Marantz, Ashley Nadeau, Neelofer Qadir, and Lauren Silber provided support and instructive feedback on countless documents. Nirmala Iswari considered more writing and ideas than I responsibly ought to have sent her way. Outside of western Massachusetts, I am thankful to Samantha Baskind, Jonathan Freedman, Leah Garrett, Katya Gibel Mevorach, Jessica Kirzane, Jordan Kutzik, Jeffrey Melnick, Sharif Mowlabocus, Avinoam Patt, Eddy Portnoy, Rachel Rubin, Benjamin Schreier, Santiago Slabodsky, Valerie Smith, John Teehan, Amy Weiss, Sunny Yudkoff, and Saul Noam Zaritt for their support of my scholarship and teaching.

At conferences and symposia, I have had the privilege of presenting and workshopping this book's ideas with Zanita Fenton, Gillian Harkins, Lori Harrison-Kahan, Brett Kaplan, Helen Kim, Heather Love, Keren McGinity, Adam Meyer, Hayley Morgenstern, Cathy Schlund-Vials, Naomi Taub, and Stephen Whitfield; I appreciate their contributions to my in-progress thinking.

At the Futures of American Studies Institute, Ivy Schweitzer helped me organize material on *Roseanne* and put me in touch with Michael Bronski, whose feedback helped shape chapter 2. An earlier version of chapter 2 appears in *Shofar*, and I'm grateful to Eugene Avrutin, Zev Garber, Dianna Gilroy, Ranen Omer-Sherman, and *Shofar*'s editorial board for publishing the article and permission to use it here.

Thank you to Robin Judd and the Association for Jewish Studies First Book Subvention committee for their supportive grant. The Center for Jewish History, the Knapp Family Foundation, and the AJS provided financial support for travel to annual conferences where I presented material on Henry Roth.

Thank you to Hugh Roth and Felicia Steele of the Henry Roth Literary Trust for their permission to use the Henry Roth material and to Melanie Meyers and the staff at the CJH and the American Jewish Historical Society for facilitating that use.

Elisabeth Maselli's guidance and constructive feedback have been essential; I am so thankful that she saw potential in this project. Thank you also to her colleagues at Rutgers University Press for their work on the book.

I am indebted to those who have kept me physically and emotionally operational to conduct this work: Conor Delaney, Maria del Mar Farina, Stephen Gorfine, Martha Pierce, Bo Shen, and Thomas Ullman.

My family—Brombergs, Hoopers, Parkers, and Robinsons, among others—have been supportive throughout. Words are insufficient to express my gratitude and appreciation for all of your love, care, conversation, support, and presence. I do not take any of it for granted. To my parents, Sharon and Charney, thank you for investing so much love, patience, and encouragement, and for always indulging my all-too-often unformed ideas. To Tiffani, Zora, and Zinzi: I am inexplicably lucky and so thankful to have the three of you in my life.

Just prior to my beginning at UMass, my father-in-law, Rick Lewis z"l, passed away suddenly from an asthma attack and inadequate health insurance. I dedicate this book to him.

Notes

Introduction

1 Gilman's scholarship reveals how literature (in Europe as well as the United States) echoed the antisemitic pseudo-medical discourse's preoccupation with Jewish close endogamy as incest (*Love + Marriage* 138). Gilman also importantly links the lateral incest stereotype with sexual antisemitism that conjured the specter of the Jewish male sexual predator as threat to non-Jewish European children (as in representations of Jack the Ripper), which also played an oversize role in the non-Jewish European imaginary.

Alys Eve Weinbaum contends that by the time Sigmund Freud began publishing, the associations of Jews and incest were so prevalent as to influence Freud's very linguistic choices in authoring "The Aetiology of Hysteria." I discuss Weinbaum's analysis in more detail in chapter 1, but Weinbaum persuasively argues that we consider Freud's choices as a writer to be linked inexorably to a problem of signification: whether Freud explicitly wrote about Jewishness in his discussions of incest or not, his audiences would inevitably read Jews into his narrative. That was how strong the incest stereotype was at the time.

Last, Karl Abraham's 1913 essay "On Neurotic Exogamy" provides an important, early twentieth-century example of how this linkage of anxieties regarding incest and exogamy found continued expression within psychoanalytical texts. Abraham's essay explicitly situates the incest anxiety as tied to exogamous impulses, and though his argument is presented as universally applicable, he focuses extensively on Jewish male patients. This connection of incest anxiety and out-group partnering finds almost continuous expression in Jewish literature and films over the course of the twentieth century, most frequently in juxtapositions of the "shiksa" (non-Jewish, white, often blonde, Jewish male love interest) and the Oedipal complex.

2 While Michael Barbezat states it very directly ("The belief that Jews tortured Christian children, which has come to be known as the 'blood libel,' often featured a sexual component as well"), a significant amount of blood libel scholarship (including texts like Alan Dundes's collection *The Blood Libel Legend,* Hannah Johnson's *Blood Libel: The Ritual Murder Accusation at the Limit of*

Jewish History, and Darren O'Brien's *The Pinnacle of Hatred*) tends not to foreground any sexually predatory associations.

While the sexual component sometimes sits beneath the surface in blood libel scholarship, David Biale identifies the nineteenth century as a period where "blood libel served as a kind of bridge between medieval religious and modern secular forms of anti-Semitism" (137). In its modern incarnation, Biale observes, "rumors of sexual assault augmented the suspicion of ritual murder" (137–138). He identifies the sexual assault association as a "singularly modern aspect of the blood libel, since, to the best of [his] knowledge, no medieval case trafficked in sexual transgression" (138). But Biale also discusses the same infamous fifteenth-century woodcut that Barbezat alludes to in citing evidence for the sexual component of medieval antisemitism, purporting to depict the murder of Simon of Trent with "Jews extracting blood from the penis of a Christian child using implements that seem to resemble those of the *mohel*" (Biale 99). It is crucial to acknowledge the contemporary linkage of the blood libel to stereotypes of pedophilia, but historically, the blood libel may have always at least intimated that Jews posed a sexual threat to children.

3 A counterargument is that identifying Allen as Jewish would register almost as a redundancy, given how Allen has become culturally representative of a certain type of Jewish American masculinity. I discuss this phenomenon, which Diane Tobin calls "Woody Allen Syndrome," further in chapter 3.

4 Andre has discussed or in other ways referenced his Jewishness in interviews with Larry King and Conan O'Brien, and in various other televised or live performances (Klein).

5 Katya Gibel Mevorach, publishing under the name Katya Gibel Azoulay, in *Black, Jewish, and Interracial*, comments on the risks of associating "Jewishness" with "whiteness," not just in terms of allowing the term "Jewish" to more accurately represent various types of affiliation, but also the fact that Ashkenazi ethnoracial descent can and does also incorporate nonwhite ethnoracial descent. To that point, Andre, Allen, and Rogen are all of Ashkenazi descent, despite Andre not being white.

6 A version of these community protective politics can be observed in other marginalized group dynamics. R. Kelly, for instance, invites parallel consideration for how some of his defenders have enabled his repeated predation on young Black girls by emphasizing Black male vulnerability to racism and policing. The cultural critic and filmmaker dream hampton, whose six-part documentary series *Surviving R. Kelly* addresses many of these issues within the Black community, has also discussed these intracommunity politics and their misogynistic underpinnings in various interviews and features about the project, including an interview with Jelani Cobb for the *New Yorker* ("Dream Hampton on 'Surviving R. Kelly'").

R. Kelly's blatant flaunting of his transgressions via lyrics and visual aesthetics that allude to predatory behavior also echoes how some white Jewish male artists have flaunted their own sexually transgressive behavior. While R. Kelly benefits from patriarchy and society's devaluation of Black girls, though, he does not benefit directly from white privilege like Henry Roth and Woody Allen have, nor can he function as a stand-in for vulnerable white masculinity. Contemporary Black male vulnerability and white Jewish male vulnerability are certainly not perfectly analogous. Depending on the group, community protective politics weaponize the specter of vulnerability in importantly different ways and with different stipulations regarding whom these figures can get away with victimizing.

7 Racial formation, which Michael Omi and Howard Winant define as "the sociohistorical process by which racial categories are created, inhabited, transformed, and destroyed," serves as a crucial concept for considering how once prevalent, centuries-old stereotypes (such as those linking Jews and incest) can operate at a much more muted contemporary register (55).

8 Zanita Fenton's "An Essay on Slavery's Hidden Legacy: Social Hysteria and Structural Condonation of Incest" contends that legal circumstances provided white slave owners with the justification to consider their daughters' status as property to overrule their status as kin. Fenton makes the case that this facilitated incest with nonwhite daughters, while also inevitably weakening the incest taboo for their white daughters as well. Fenton's legal historical theorizing, which I explore further in chapter 3, provides an important model for thinking about incest in interracial families.

9 Alys Eve Weinbaum makes this important point in *Wayward Reproductions*, which I discuss in more detail in chapter 1.

10 Barbezat helpfully connects aspects of the "Pizzagate" conspiracy, which alleged that a pizzeria in Washington, D.C., served as a front for a child sex-trafficking operation that implicated Bill and Hillary Clinton (among other Democratic politicians and donors), with historical sexual antisemitism (including, importantly, the blood libel). The QAnon conspiracy theory builds on some of these connections in its suggestion that the "global banking elite" (read: Jews; often, specific figures like George Soros) are engaged in massive pedophilic sex-trafficking rings (Sommer).

11 This is meant not to dismiss the possibility of various pundits, publications, or networks that might still be considered "mainstream" occasionally expressing antisemitic sentiment but rather to stress that this occurred relatively infrequently compared to sympathetic coverage that treated white Jewish men essentially as white men in the context of allegations of sexual abuse.

12 There is a growing and invaluable body of scholarship for theoretical, anthropological, historical, sociological, and cultural studies approaches for Jews and racial formation. Michael Rogin's *Blackface, White Noise* serves as a sort of proto-text, especially as it involves the cultural studies aspects. Matthew Frye Jacobson's historical scholarship is vital, and *Roots Too* provides an important foundation for my engagement with the 1970s in chapter 1. Karen Brodkin's *How the Jews Became White Folks* takes a sociological approach, while Lori Harrison-Kahan's *The White Negress* and Jennifer Glaser's *Borrowed Voices* are superb cultural studies. And Melanie Kaye/Kantrowitz's *The Colors of Jews*, Helen Kiyong Kim and Noah Samuel Leavitt's *JewAsian*, and Katya Gibel Mevorach's scholarship, including *Black, Jewish, and Interracial*, also provide anthropological scholarship, theory, and testimonies regarding the often overlooked experiences of Jews of color.

Outside of Jewish studies, critical race theorists like Karen and Barbara Fields and Nell Irvin Painter observe, importantly, that white Americans in positions of power always stratified whiteness, including designating some newly arriving groups of immigrant whites as "inferior white races" (Fields and Fields 41). This sort of framework helps create space for thinking about vulnerable white identities, while also leaving room for nonwhiteness—or, more specifically, individuals of color who might or might not be Jewish—to operate on a separate vector.

The most common historical claim for the nonwhiteness of "white" Jews invokes the Holocaust. According to this logic, this genocidal history provides irrefutable evidence for Jews being racialized as nonwhite. Charles Mills, in *The Racial Contract*, suggests a provocative framework for reassessing what the Holocaust teaches us about Jewishness and race. Mills contemplates the notions of Jews as "off white" by considering the vast history of European Jewish persecution and oppression, before offering that the Holocaust might actually provide evidence for the whiteness of white Jews. Mills argues this point in two ways: first, he draws attention to the manner in which Hitler expressly conceived of acting upon European Jews in a fashion built upon the violence done via colonialism. The singularity of the Holocaust, in Mills's reading, is not the scale upon which Jews were racialized and dehumanized, but rather the innovation to racialize a group that was not, otherwise, a target of colonial and imperial violence. Mills is careful not to diminish violence done unto Jews in pogroms and by the state but broadens his lens in order to consider genocide committed upon Jews in the mid-twentieth century alongside, for instance, the genocide wrought in King Leopold's Congo. Mills's second point is that the assessment of the Holocaust into a "singular" atrocity—that is, *the* Holocaust as opposed to *a* holocaust—has been widely accepted not just in the Jewish community, but in the white non-Jewish community as well. This, in essence, obscures the fact of genocides of Black Africans like King Leopold's, and in so doing, rewrites the tragedy and singularity of the Holocaust not merely as one of genocidal violence and murder but one of genocidal violence and murder done by one group of white people against another group of white people.

Mills's theorization of white Jewish proximity to whiteness, then, helps reframe narratives of "becoming" white by instead shining a spotlight on Jews as, historically, being extremely vulnerable and victimized among European (i.e., "white") populations, and yet not subjected en masse to the horrors of imperialism and colonialization as nonwhite populations (i.e., Black, Asian, and Indigenous) in the modern era until the Holocaust (even as he acknowledges histories of pogroms in building to that moment).

13 A term like "white Jewish" might ring problematic to some historians, theorists, and activists. Zygmunt Bauman considers antisemitism as having various different bigoted (il)logical components. One of these is proteophobia, which identifies a salient aspect of antisemitism, while also illuminating why a term like "white Jewish" may carry such negative connotations.

Bauman's concept of proteophobia is helpful for considering how the entire scholarly and nonscholarly conversation about Jewishness and whiteness, and the inherent anxiety about that conversation, is part and parcel of an identifiable component of antisemitism. Proteophobia, in Bauman's words, is "the apprehension and vexation related not to something or someone disquieting through otherness and unfamiliarity, but to something or someone that does not fit the structure of the orderly world, does not fall easily into any of the established categories, emits therefore contradictory signals as to the proper conduct—and in the result blurs the borderlines which ought to be kept watertight and undermines the reassuringly monotonous, repetitive and predictable nature of the life-world." Bauman was not thinking specifically about twenty-first century discussions about white Jewish racial formation when he wrote these words. However, they help explain something of the charged nature of these discussions. White Jews' "whiteness" is contested not merely because of disagreement as to how antisemitism societally disadvantages them, and whether "white privilege" can apply to a group that only barely survived genocide. It is contested because the term seems to disregard, at a fundamental level, that the historical social racial construction of Jews has played on the notion of Jews as uncategorizable. That is, if racial construction otherwise plays upon ideas of recognizable notions of "difference" to categorize and structure racial hierarchy, for Jews, the immutable unrecognizability (their disquieting sameness) is foundational to their otherness.

14 We ought to consider this hypothetical expression of sexuality anxiety in the context of a history of sexual antisemitism, which, for centuries, rendered Jewish male sexuality and gender characteristics as outside of traditional Christian European norms. However, Daniel Boyarin contends that Jewish culture also, separately and positively, crafted a spectrum for expressions of Jewish masculinity in ways that actively rejected and challenged the confining norms of Christian European culture.

The notion of "castration complex" also bears some mention here, especially given Andre's invocation of it in his interview with Rogen. While Freud explored Jewish circumcision and culturally specific and universal forms of "castration complex," Jewish studies scholars (including Sander Gilman, in addition to Boyarin) have analyzed Freud's theorizing on the topic. For the purpose of this study, I am most interested in how Jewish anxiety regarding masculinity and sexuality intersected with the incest taboo, and so Judith Butler's theorization is particularly helpful. According to Butler's notion of the "heterosexual matrix," in most assessments (and certainly Freud's) of a "universal" incest taboo, the taboo reveals a prior proscription ruling out same-sex relations. Butler quotes Gayle Rubin as she builds this argument, calling attention to how Rubin connects the notion of taboos to the distinction between sex and gender: "A prohibition against *some* heterosexual unions assumes a taboo against *non*heterosexual unions. Gender is not only an identification with one sex; it also entails that sexual desire be directed toward the other sex" (J. Butler 99).

While Rubin (in Butler's analysis) is theorizing how sex, gender, and taboo sexuality operate (temporally) "before the law," I am interested in how this anxiety may function for Jewish artists who historically have had to contend with an incest stereotype as well as a discourse that, in casting circumcision as castration, challenged their gender identity and capacity for male heterosexuality. That is, what happens when one of these taboos can disprove the other? And further, what happens when one of these taboos disproves the other by asserting agency and power, which rules out the homophobically constructed "weakness" of the other taboo? Psychologically, can incest between a man or a boy and a woman or a girl, according to the homophobic logic of the heterosexual matrix, have the effect of "proving" masculinity *and* heterosexuality? Might the willingness to tell stories about transgressing the incest prohibition (as some artists do) permit that artist to reveal a supposed abundance, essentially, of heterosexual inclination? My close reading of Henry Roth's *Mercy of a Rude Stream* suggests that in Roth's novel heterosexual incest functioned as a badge of hyper-heterosexuality. This reading may speak to how Woody Allen has appealed to his audiences as well.

15 Sacco's observations echo Toni McNaron and Yarrow Morgan's theorization that the supposed taboo surrounding incest involves its discussion and not its existence. McNaron and Morgan cite the frequency with which women report incest as evidence that the taboo sits firmly on the side of the act's verbal expression (15). Florence Rush's *The Best Kept Secret*, which I discuss in detail in chapter 1, addresses child molestation broadly, though it also engages with incest specifically. Its title implies that the notion of child molestation as taboo is confused with the prohibition on its "telling."

16 Janice Doane and Devon Hodges comment on this phenomenon, noting that by the 1970s, incest found more frequent expression as a topic for analysis within white feminist literature and scholarship, and a topic for literary exploration in Black feminist novels and memoir. Looking back on this phenomenon in 2001, they write that "it may even seem that incest is now talked about too much" (1).

17 Michel Foucault's theory of the "repressive hypothesis" may have some relevance to incest discourse: if we discuss at length how we do not or should not talk about sex, we actually focus on it extensively. But incest cannot substitute for sex in Foucault's theorization.

18 For instance, W. Joseph Campbell argues in *1995: The Year the Future Began* that 1995 operated as a "watershed" year, in which specific events (including Bill Clinton's sexual encounters with Monica Lewinsky, and Clinton's battle with Newt Gingrich over "family values") presaged aspects of technological advancements, voluminous twenty-four-hour media coverage, and political extremism that distinguish our contemporary American era from prior historical moments.

While scholarly accounting of the decade, and whatever determinacies it had, will continue to take shape, a body of scholarship regarding sex and the 1990s has come into focus: Dagmar Herzog's work in *Sex in Crisis* situates the 1990s as an era in which the Christian Right's supposed "family values" crusade utilized rhetoric that "served not only to repulse but also to titillate its target audience" (61), while the erectile drug Viagra shifted conversations about sexual performance toward chemicals and away from sexual desire. Joshua Gamson's *Freaks Talk Back* considers the talk-show circuit of the 1990s, a genre often maligned for sensationalism, as providing platforms for LGBTQIA+ guests to frame their sexuality and identities in their own terms on broadcast television. James Kincaid's *Erotic Innocence*, despite being published in 1998, reveals a sustained contemporaneous focus on 1990s celebrity and media culture, as it argues that American society demands narratives and images that eroticize youth, a predilection that, for Kincaid, belies the moralizing tenor of conversations about "protecting" children. Kincaid makes compelling arguments, but historians and clinicians continue to compile considerable evidence that child sexual assault occurs, whatever the discursive hypocrisies of American media. And while Ross Cheit's *The Witch-Hunt Narrative* commences its examination of child sexual molestation cases in the 1980s, his meticulous examination of courtroom evidence broaches the 1990s as he argues that even cases contemporarily used as "proof" of the danger of witch hunts or false allegations (such as the McMartin preschool case) often reveal evidence of sexual transgression committed against children.

Chapter 1 A Victorian Freud

1 In "Aetiology," Freud indicates incest when he writes of "numerous cases in which some adult looking after the child—a nursery maid or governess or tutor, or, unhappily all too often, a close relative—has initiated the child into sexual intercourse" (276).

2 Freud is also enormously important to 1990s discussions and depictions of incest. Gillian Harkins addresses this at length in *Everybody's Family Romance*.

3 Abundant scholarship contemplates the significance of Freud's Jewishness to his own theorizing: John Murray Cuddihy contends that the oppression of the nineteenth century facilitated Freud conceiving of the "coarse, importunate id" from the "importunate Yid" (18). Estelle Roith argues that Freud's Jewishness had particular underexamined significance to how he conceived of "femininity." Freud biographer Peter Gay, in *A Godless Jew*, explores Freud's emphatic declarations of his atheism as critical to any understanding of his Jewish identity's relevance to his work. Sander Gilman's extensive scholarship has examined the link between European scientific racial and gendered formulations of "Jewish" and Freud's own ideas about race and gender, while warning against reducing Freud's scholarship to contemplation as merely a function of his Jewish identity (*Freud, Race* 5). More recently, Eliza Slavet's *Racial Fever* contemplates Freud's *Moses and Monotheism* for its serious contributions to contemporary conceptions of Jews, memory, and race. A lot has been written; Gilman's *Freud, Race, and Gender* features nearly four pages of endnotes on scholarship regarding Freud's Jewishness.

4 The contradiction in Freud's iconic status as a larger-than-life secular figure is perhaps best exemplified by the phrase "There is no God and Freud is his prophet," levied as a criticism of American society's oversecularization by Francis Cardinal George in a discussion of Pope Francis's election in 2013 (Brennan). Such a statement also features antisemitic undertones: Jewish secular influence fomenting a particular type of antireligiosity.

5 Edward Said argues that Freud's Jewishness possesses an unavoidable significance to his subjectivity and theorizing. For Said, Freud's writing as a whole reflects "a Eurocentric view of culture" (16), even while establishing Freud's Jewish identity as crucial to his intellectual endeavors, especially in his last major book, *Moses and Monotheism*.

6 Weinbaum discusses at length how Bertha Pappenheim is transformed into "Anna O.," but she persuasively accounts for how Freud's language contains hints regarding Jewish racial identifications for his subjects.

7 Notably, Stephanie Coontz has observed how Friedan's early drafts featured "parallels between the prejudices against women and those against African Americans and Jews" (104).

8 Fishman mentions a number of tensions between Jewish feminists and non-Jewish feminists. Israel emerges as a touchstone. Bernice Hausman's article "Anti-Semitism in Feminism: Rethinking Identity Politics," in which she writes, "I speak as a Jewish woman," provides a detailed assessment of how tensions regarding Israel and Palestine played out among Jewish feminists, nonwhite non-Jewish feminists, and non-Jewish white feminists, with regard to the UK feminist publication *Spare Rib* (83). Barbara Smith's "Between a Rock and a Hard Place" also addresses these tensions between Jewish white feminists and Third

World feminists, foregrounding the author's Black, Third World, lesbian subjectivity.

9 Brownmiller's 1999 memoir *In Our Time*, in contrast, pays comparatively thorough attention to the ethnoracial, religious, and regional backgrounds of almost every white feminist in her narrative.

10 Sandra Butler, who published the book-length incest study *Conspiracy of Silence* in 1978, also bears mention here; Herman wrote the foreword for the 1985 edition. Butler is Jewish, and while her text also merits scrutiny for its negotiation of Jewish versus other ethnoreligious identifiers in its discussion of incest, she omits Freud entirely.

11 Grace Paley's review, in *Ms.* magazine, thanked Rush for writing a book that provides "knowledge" that might "act to change childhood's delicate and fearful world" (40).

12 As indicated in the notes to the introduction, Sander Gilman roots these antisemitic stereotypes in the Christian failure to distinguish Jewish endogamy from incest (*Love + Marriage* 137). However, the root of the stereotype (traditional endogamy) does not preclude other evidence (scriptural record) that might align with an antisemitic reading from "confirming" a particular bias.

13 These Black feminist authors may have been in a similar double bind to Freud during the 1890s. That is, the pathologization of Black families was such that there may have been no viable "community protective" fashion in which they could have addressed incest in a manner that would not have immediately been considered a specific signifier for Black incest.

14 Originally published in *Chrysalis*, this excerpt of "Chain," copyright 1978, by Audre Lorde, from *The Collected Poems of Audre Lorde*, is used by permission of W. W. Norton.

15 The timing is worth mentioning here: Moody's *Coming of Age in Mississippi* was published in 1968; Angelou's autobiography in 1969; Morrison's *The Bluest Eye* in 1970; Jones's *Corregidora* in 1975. Herman might also have named Alice Walker's *The Color Purple*, which was published in 1982, and Audre Lorde. But several of these canonical Black feminist texts dealing with incest appeared at the close of the 1960s. For further reading on African American incest narratives, Hortense Spillers theorizes African American literary depictions of incest in "'The Permanent Obliquity of an In(pha)llibly Straight': In the Time of the Daughters and Fathers," marking Morrison's incorporation of incest in *The Bluest Eye* as a response to Ralph Ellison's Trueblood section in *Invisible Man*. Janice Doane and Devon Hodges's *Telling Incest* meditates on those two texts further, while also closely reading more contemporary "revisions" of Black incest narratives, such as Sapphire's *Push*. Gillian Harkins's *Everybody's Family Romance* considers race's role in the consumer appeal of these narratives and considers Carolivia Herron's *Thereafter Johnnie*. Herron's novel exposes the complexity of these distinctions: though her text fits within the Black incest genre, Herron was studying to convert to Judaism while writing it (Ghert-Zand).

16 An exception, Kate Simon's 1982 memoir *Bronx Primitive*, explicitly narrates molestation at the hands of a cousin and Jewish neighbor (along with non-Jewish acquaintances) and echoes the type of experience Florence Rush explores. Simon, born in 1912, also aligns generationally more closely with Rush (born in 1918) than most of the Jewish second-wave feminists who wrote more theoretical texts. While

I am certain there are additional exceptions, the trend might be generational, rather than chronological.

17 It is worth mentioning that Freud himself wrote about Jewishness and his Jewishness. That said, scholarly textual engagement with Freud's Jewishness was inconsistent. For instance, while Philip Reiff's *Freud: The Mind of the Moralist* made numerous references to his Jewishness, Lionel Trilling (in *Freud and the Crisis of Our Culture*) and Herbert Marcuse (in *Eros and Civilization*) make only passing reference to Freud's Jewishness; both Trilling and Marcuse were Jewish.

Chapter 2 Incest, Exogamy, and Jewishness on *Roseanne*

1 For more on Loftus and the "memory wars" (in brief, the battle over the political implications of the scientific credibility of "recovered memories" versus the frequency and scientific plausibility of instances of "false memory") and how they played out in popular culture during the 1990s, Gillian Harkins's *Everybody's Family Romance* provides a comprehensive account.

2 Barr's allegations of abuse extended to her mother, and some of these were also sexual; in *My Lives* she alludes to her mother having her "strike nude poses with her in various sexual positions" and "touching, but not of the kind of healthy, loving families" (178).

3 While the celebrity commonly known as "Roseanne" has gone by both Roseanne Arnold and Roseanne Barr, I refer to her throughout the rest of this chapter as Barr (her current surname) for clarity, and to distinguish her from the fictional Roseanne Conner (whom I subsequently refer to as "Roseanne").

4 The quickly canceled tenth season revival, and the Barr-less reboot as *The Conners* certainly merit critical attention for the show's content, Barr's decade-long embrace of vitriolic alt-right/white nationalist politics, and Donald Trump's symbiotic relationship with Barr surrounding the tenth season's ratings and reception. However, within this chapter, I consider just the initial nine-year run.

5 Season 8 features both actresses playing Becky at different points, with jokes playing on the viewers' awareness—for instance, Roseanne greets Lecy Goranson's Becky with "I'm so glad you're back this week" in the season premiere, a welcome the studio audience happily interprets as meant for Becky *and* original Becky actress, Goranson ("Shower the People You Love With Stuff").

6 Her routine about her father wearing a large turquoise Star of David belt buckle appears almost identically in her 1987 HBO special and her 2005 one.

7 Barr referred to Israel in 2009 as a "Nazi state," and in 2011, as a "brutal and undemocratic theocracy" (Zimmerman). Since 2015 or so, Barr's expressions of staunch Zionism have been accompanied by frequent Islamophobic and anti-Palestinian tweets and retweets (Zimmerman).

8 I do not refer to the Conner family as "part-Jewish" in this chapter (though I have in previous engagements with this material), as it poses several problems. The writers never have any family members self-identify as Jewish, in part or otherwise. By framing this in terms of heritage and inheritance, I mean to draw more specific attention to the way in which the show utilizes Yiddish, Russian, and the revelation that a prominent character was Jewish to suggest that Jewishness matters to the family (and show) in substantive ways, even though the show is undeniably vague in how it reveals (or hides) that substantive quality.

9 There is at least one version of the "Sweet Dreams" episode that, when shortened for syndication, had the "mensch" line edited out.

10 Antler also sees *Roseanne* as challenging the depiction of "benevolent" Jewish motherhood, such as on the 1950s sitcom *The Goldbergs*, an important precedent for televised, sitcom depictions of Jewish mothers.

11 Though Arnold plays the role of prototypical goy in Barr's stand-up routines, he converted to Judaism when he married Barr and was in fact born to a Jewish mother, though he was raised by his Christian father and stepmother after his mother abandoned him early in his life (Angel).

12 The very notion of "becoming white," when applied to American Jews, involves, essentially, an enhancement in social class. Karen Brodkin's *How the Jews Became White Folks* examines how the New Deal and other institutionally racist government and business policies that discriminated against African Americans and other nonwhite groups facilitated Jews "becoming" white. The fact that contemporaneous depictions of Jews in popular culture are so often middle class may speak to the inherent paradox of what working-class Jewishness represents about American race and class intersections. If the "whiteness" of contemporary American Jews can most easily be observed through class privilege, white Jews cannot be depicted as working class or "white trash" because the undergirding logic of ethnic whiteness involves a mythology of earning whiteness through overcoming hardship and "achieving" class mobility.

13 The show takes care in depicting different people responding to similar traumas in different ways. Jackie Harris also testifies to Al Harris's abuse, and while her character also deals with trauma in specific ways, an eating disorder is not one of them.

14 Jane Feuer writes about the market that developed for "Trauma Drama" in the 1980s. Joshua Gamson's work also engages these issues.

15 Noel Murray's close reading of "Wait Till Your Father Gets Home," which also touches on the parallels between Barr's personal life and the abusive figure of Al Harris, makes a very compelling case for the sheer quality of the show's aesthetic engagement with working-class households.

16 In this respect, *Roseanne* joins a long list of sitcoms from its era depicting families with nontraditional kinship relations (consider *Diff'rent Strokes* [1978–1986], *Who's the Boss?* [1984–1992] and *Full House* [1987–1995], among many others).

17 Sander Gilman cites Thomas Mann's "The Blood of the Walsungs" (1905) and Edgar Allan Poe's "The Fall of the House of Usher" (1839) as mobilizing less positively charged depictions of Jewish lateral sibling longing and its consequence (*Love + Marriage* 138–140).

Chapter 3 Woody, Wood Yi, and Communion Wafers

1 Colleen Glenn makes a similar observation, that "the private or offscreen Allen is virtually indistinguishable from the public/onscreen Allen—so much so that his audience generally perceives the two to be one and the same" (36).

2 Film critic Richard Dyer argues for the importance of reading celebrity figures through their relationships with particular social groups. Dyer's analytical framework helps for considering Allen's import to six decades of filmic depictions of whiteness, Jewishness, and masculinity.

3 Allen plays numerous individuals who fail to maintain successful relationships in his films, but these characters are always sexually active.

4 Mark Conard and Aeon Skoble's collection *Woody Allen and Philosophy* is representative of scholarship on Allen's artistic engagement with ethics and morality.

5 Ruth Wisse's *The Schlemiel as Modern Hero* sets up how the archetype emerged in Jewish literature in the context of the historic emasculation of oppressed Jewish men in antisemitic nineteenth-century Europe. Without alternative options to contend with the dehumanizing efforts of state sponsored antisemitism, wit and humor emerged as a way of undercutting the arbitrary humiliations of everyday life.

6 The "memory wars" are relevant to understanding Allen's comments here. Harkins frames this discourse beginning around 1992, a "struggle over the difference between 'true' recovered memories of child sexual abuse and 'false' memories implanted by therapy" (88). Of course, Dylan Farrow's *being* a child at the time made for one important distinction ("memory wars" more commonly involved contestations of adult memories of childhood abuse), while Allen's intimation that Mia Farrow implanted the memory made for another (more commonly, proponents of "false memory syndrome" implicated therapists as inclined to suggest memories to help account for symptoms). In addition to Harkins, Ross Cheit's *The Witch-Hunt Narrative* explores media coverage of high-profile child sexual abuse allegations, including the McMartin trial, demonstrating how at a macro level, media tended to suggest the frequency and plausibility of false allegations of child sexual abuse, obscuring the record of considerable convictions emerging out of child sexual abuse allegations during the 1980s and 1990s.

7 Kroft was very sympathetic to Allen in his interview. Allen later referred to Kroft as a "hero in this thing" and said, "While all the press was vilifying me, Steve Kroft and *60 Minutes* came to me and said, 'We want to help'" (McGrath 126). Allen later cast Kroft in *Small Time Crooks*. In an interview with Marion Meade, Kroft alluded to being "starstruck" by Allen. More troublingly, Kroft said that "some of the best material in the interview," which involved Allen's comments on Previn's revelation of "a total blind spot about the impropriety of his relationship with Soon-Yi," was "cut so as not to offend viewers" (Meade 241).

8 Allen's use of "bigoted" here may also signify the racist attacks on Previn, thus aligning with his strategy of presenting himself as her white (Jewish) liberal champion.

9 Significantly, while the press conference transcript in the appendix to Groteke's memoir features the phrase "and all that that implies," the *New York Times* article omits this loaded phrase.

10 MacCannell's description of the brothers as "changing roles whenever it suits" them may also resonate with my subsequent discussion of Allen, Previn, and Zygmunt Bauman's notion of proteophobia.

11 The circumstances of her childhood and adoption made Previn's exact age difficult to know. In her memoir *What Falls Away*, Mia Farrow wrote that in 1976, when she and André Previn began work on adopting Soon-Yi, her "precise age was not known, but estimated to be around five" (179). In April 1980, Allen and Farrow began dating each other, and in September 1980 Allen first met her children, including Soon-Yi, whom Mia Farrow describes as having been "seven going on

eight (her age was finally determined through the standard method of X-raying her wrists)" (191, 196).

12 Meade mentions Rob Schneider playing Previn in drag on *SNL*. *Mad TV* featured a sexualized Previn stand-in in a 1995 film trailer parody ("Crimes, Misdemeanors, and Payback") ("MADtv—S01E04"). In 2002, Martin Short's *Primetime Glick* featured a mock-Asian-accented Previn stating, "So good to make your acquaintance, honorable common-law stepdaddy" ("Woody Allen and the Family Affair").

13 This framing likely only works in Allen's almost exclusively white films. The racialized logic of the parody plays upon the contemporaneous absurdity of thinking of (nonthreatening) white Jews as monstrous. In contrast, nonwhite sexuality (and Black and Latinx sexuality in particular) continues to be cast as monstrous in pop culture and literature—I explore this in more detail in my chapter on Henry Roth.

Chapter 4 Blood Libel Humor and Incest Easter Eggs

1 *Deconstructing Harry* (1997), *Match Point* (2005), *Scoop* (2006), *Cassandra's Dream* (2007), and *Irrational Man* (2015) all feature plot points involving getting away with murder, specifically.

2 This is not an exhaustive list of films, or other works, in which Allen incorporates autobiographical elements involving the incest and molestation allegations. In *I Like to Watch*, Emily Nussbaum notes that in Allen's one-act play *Honeymoon Motel*, he features "a joke about the specific crime that Allen had been accused of by his daughter, which, to be graphic, was digital molestation" (109).

3 Marriage to an unmarried sibling-in-law is condoned, however, in the event of a spouse's death (known as Levirate marriage).

4 Knight's argument, that regret and guilt dominate late-era Allen films as he works through the sense of loss emerging from the events of 1992 is highly persuasive, but by ruling out the possibility that Allen might feel strong moral misgivings about a specific crime/behavior (the Dylan allegations), Knight diminishes the applicability of his own analysis and erases a vitally important aspect of the historical record. Any conversation about Allen's sense of guilt and remorse needs to engage a thorough consideration of what it is about which he might feel guilt, especially when there is copious material and testimony about a specific alleged transgression.

5 Shaina Hammerman alludes to Allen's "alleged sexual misdeeds" in "Reconstructing Woody" but does not mention Dylan Farrow by name (174).

6 Communications scholars James Lull and Stephen Hinerman touch on how "star scandals" also involve particular aspects of celebrity. They suggest that star scandals emerge "when the mass media reveal an instance of how the desires of famous people overrule social expectations, norms, and practices" (21).

7 I discuss David Biale's and Michael Barbezat's scholarly engagements with the sexual undertones of the blood libel in note 2 to the introduction.

8 The protagonist kills a neighbor (along with his pregnant ex-lover) in *Match Point* as well. That neighbors die when families are destroyed in Allen's films may suggest that collateral damage accompanies any targeted destruction.

9 *Deconstructing Harry*, *You Will Meet a Tall Dark Stranger* (2010), and *Celebrity* (1998) all feature variations on the husband informing an emotionally distraught partner of an affair with a younger woman.

10 As a child, Moses was critical of Allen during the custody case, though he's been supportive of Allen recently. He claimed in an interview that Mia "drummed it into me to hate my father for tearing apart the family" (Dennis). Dylan Farrow responded by labeling Moses's words "a betrayal to me and my whole family" (Dennis).

11 Allen wrote, "Not that I doubt Dylan hasn't come to believe she's been molested, but if from the age of 7 a vulnerable child is taught by a strong mother to hate her father because he is a monster who abused her, is it so inconceivable that after many years of indoctrination the image of me that Mia wanted to establish had taken root?" ("Woody Allen Speaks Out").

12 To expand slightly, we might consider this scene as another version of "apologia" (that is, a defense and not a true apology): even if he did it, Allen intimates, Mia Farrow should not have done what she did. Here, it is worth returning to a central piece of information that gets consistently lost in discussions of Dylan Farrow's allegations: Allen's problematic behavior with Dylan Farrow *prior* to her specific sexual molestation allegation was confirmed and well documented by Allen's therapists, one of whom he consented to see because he and Mia Farrow, then in a committed relationship, agreed that in order for Allen to be a better parent he needed to work through his issues with how to provide physical affection to his daughter (Meade 199). This too functions as a parallel with *Blue Jasmine*: Jasmine's failure to arrive at moral outrage regarding Hal's behavior prior to her learning of his affair proves her hypocrisy. Mia Farrow's failure to arrive at moral outrage regarding Allen's behavior with Dylan Farrow prior to her learning of the affair with Previn—despite the fact that her objection was significant enough for Allen to work with a therapist to "modify inappropriate behaviors" (Meade 199)—likewise seems consistent with Allen's casting her as hypocritical for reporting his actions to Dylan Farrow's doctor—even if he committed said actions.

13 Maureen Orth describes some of the issues with the Yale-New Haven report (some of which Wilk alludes to in his decision) in her 2013 article "Momma Mia!"

14 There is some irony in the fact that Allen's films appear to provide these female Mia surrogates with speech, despite the fact that Allen writes the lines. Hortense Spillers notes a similar phenomenon regarding male authorship of an incest narrative when she observes that "for all intents and purposes, the wife/mother Kate and the daughter/surrogate lover Matty Lou are deprived of speech, since what they say and did and when are reported/translated through the medium of Trueblood" (235).

15 Louise Mirrer considers the likelihood that these stereotypes overlapped meaningfully in medieval societies, as Jewish men were associated with homosexuality and effeminate characteristics, traits that overlap with the feminizing associations of the cuckold's horns (74). Richard Halpern also makes the connection in his close reading of *Ulysses* in *Shakespeare among the Moderns* (170).

16 That said, "June in January" was composed by a Jewish musician (Ralph Rainger), a pre-emptive (perhaps too-clever) rejoinder that any art form cannot be simplistically essentialized as "Black" (as Jonathan Freedman argues in *Klezmer America*).

Chapter 5 "Till a *Khusin* Comes Along"

1 Steven Kellman's biography of Roth features a fairly comprehensive examination of the interactions between Rose Broder and Roth after he told her he wrote about their sexual relationship in *MORS*. Broder was so hurt and angry about this revelation, one she contested until her death, that she threatened a lawsuit if Roth did not remove all subsequent depictions of Minnie and Ira having sex (Kellman 306, 311–312).

2 Josh Lambert's *Unclean Lips* notes how *CIS*'s obscenity, in the context of legal uncertainty regarding contemporaneous censorship laws, put the novel in a "literary-historical limbo" that may have affected the book's early sales (though reviews were favorable enough to secure Roth an advance for a second book) (88).

3 In New York, the age of consent was changed from ten to sixteen in 1890, and then raised to eighteen in 1920. It would only be lowered, to seventeen, in 1999 (Cocca 23).

4 Note that Stella is "only thirteen" in this manuscript passage, indicating that it occurs at a point where Ira had already been sexually active with her for some time.

5 Stella is not yet Stella, but instead Bella here. This constitutes a meaningful name choice vis-à-vis Roth's dismissal of James Joyce. He refers to Bella Cohen, the Jewish madame from *Ulysses* (along with the prostitute Zoe), in denigrating Joyce's representations of Jews: "Two whorehouse denizens have to be Jewish, and that's greeted by Jews as a pyrotechnic display of tolerance. With such a Judeophiliac who needs a pogrom?" (Roth Papers, box 28, folder 5, "Section III," vol. 2, pp. 706–707).

6 Roth's echo of Joyce's style invokes Leopold Bloom's masturbatory orgasm in *Ulysses*, which takes place as he ogles a girl (Gerty MacDowell) in a park. Ira's (and Roth's) rejection of Bloom (and Joyce) may ironically speak to anxiety regarding Joyce's depiction of Jewish male pedophilic sexuality.

7 David Warren Sabean's research into the German town of Neckarhausen explores kinship relations, focusing largely on non-Jews, but provides helpful contextual information regarding European traditions. While discussing a 1920s Wilhelm Reutlinger study concluding that Jews (based on a particular population enclave) were far more likely to engage in first-cousin marriage, Sabean suggests that this scholarship may have been flawed (categorizing even second- and third-cousin unions as first-cousin unions). Sabean also importantly contextualizes that non-Jewish groups also showed high rates of consanguineous marriage in studies from that time, due to economic circumstances (435). Sabean views economic circumstances as more determinative of the inclination toward cousin marriage across different groups. He notes, "The ecology of the enclave Jewish population . . . might well have supported an endogamy favoring first cousins" (435).

8 Other examples of cousin romance (or romanticization) include the Yiddish folk song "Di Grine Kuzine" (or "My Cousin the Greenhorn"), which tracks the disillusionment of a once beautiful, youthful female cousin who is worn down by life in America. Some versions meditate extensively on the physically attractive aspects of the cousin: "lipelech vi karshelekh a tsviling" (lips like a pair of cherries). More recently, the television show *Arrested Development* showcases a secular, but seemingly ethnically Jewish family, in which one first cousin, George Michael, pines for another (Maeby).

9 I focus on Roth's depiction of Black characters, but multiple inroads exist for considering Roth's thoughts on race and nation. Stella's mother has Puerto Rican boarders, often slurred as "Portorickies," and Minnie has a Latino boyfriend named Arturo. Rachel Rubinstein writes a compelling account of how Ira's conception of Native Americans informs his relationships with Edith, American identity, and Zionism in *Members of the Tribe*. The manuscripts also reveal offensive language regarding Arabs and Palestinians, which is excised in the published version.

10 Roth's novel also suggests a link between the racial politics of the late twentieth century and the nostalgic imagination for the early twentieth century.

11 Lila Corwin Berman's *Metropolitan Jews* addresses Jewish participation in white flight and suburbanization via an examination of Detroit's Jewish communities, with a more comprehensive historical engagement with race and racism in the post–civil rights era.

12 Other manuscript drafts confirm Ira's fear of a Black planet. A vignette depicting a dance at a Communist rally finds Ira reflecting upon being shoved by a Black man trying to stop a fight: "sent on my way by easy thrust, it seemed to me I glimpsed the power that would one day be theirs. How would I like that day, day of their mastery" (Roth Papers, box 26, folder 3, "Book II: 1928–1932 B," p. 331).

13 Roth's desire to shock his readers might be considered against his difficulty doing so with *CIS*. Consider Maxwell Geismar's take on the Oedipal overtones of *CIS*: David's relationship with his mother is "described so beautifully, so completely, that one realizes that the author, too, wrote this classic fable in all innocence of spirit" (Rubinstein 41). Even when Roth was writing about a boy's sexual yearning for his mother, it came across as so aesthetically compelling as to make the Oedipal complex itself adorable.

14 Weil confirmed in an interview with Gibbs that he did not know the content of volume 2 until after volume 1 was complete ("Conversation" 155).

15 Fiedler's influential essay "The Christian-ness of the Jewish-American Writer" expands on this and considers *CIS* as one of many similarly themed Jewish-authored texts.

Conclusion

1 Ronan Farrow's first article regarding Weinstein, "From Aggressive Overtures to Sexual Assault: Harvey Weinstein's Accusers Tell Their Stories" was published on October 10, 2017. By the end of November 2017 he had published four additional stories about Weinstein.

2 "Harvey Weinstein's Army of Spies" details Weinstein's work with Kroll and Black Cube, investigative outfits that employ ex-Mossad agents and former employees of other Israeli security agencies and appear to employ questionable legal practices. This material bears some mention here: Israel or Israeli organizations cannot and should not be read as synonymous with "Jewish"—and yet, they do signify, for arguably any reader, some element of Jewishness (and in many cases, understandably signify Jewish militarism and state power). Farrow does not delve into any deeper meaning here. However, the role that these organizations play in Weinstein's story requires further analysis in terms of how Israeli impact on American politics and popular culture plays out, and how "Israeli" and

"Jewish" are often (purposefully) conflated, across the political spectrum, in discussions of this phenomenon.

3 Antonia Blumberg wrote one such article, refuting Oppenheimer while also drawing attention to white supremacist engagement with his piece, in the *Huffington Post.*

4 The initial *New York Times* review is decisive in its summation of McBride Jordan's father: "Her father, rabbi turned storekeeper, was a cold, sexually abusive tyrant who kept his children in virtual servitude, exploited his black customers and ultimately abandoned his wife" (Geiger). A review in *The Nation* was even more explicit, revealing, "Her tyrannical father, an itinerant rabbi who became a shopkeeper in Suffolk, North Carolina, sexually molested her" (Budhos 32–33). *People*'s review described her father as "an authoritarian and abusive father who happens to be an Orthodox rabbi" and includes that she was "molested by her father" (Kalyn). Interestingly, *Jet* magazine's brief feature on the memoir notes that "McBride retraces his mother's life as the daughter of an Orthodox rabbi who fled her Virginia home," making no mention of her father's abusive nature, sexual or otherwise ("Black Journalist").

5 McBride Jordan's father being long dead at the time of the memoir's publication also played a role in its reception. Jewish community protective politics tend to emerge more predictably when a white Jewish male figure protests his innocence.

6 This comes up in a few places. Regarding the family store, McBride Jordan offers, "He'd sit my mother next to the door and say in Yiddish, 'Watch the *shvartses.*' He was robbing these folks blind, charging them a hundred percent markup on his cheap goods, and he was worried about them stealing from him!" (59). And elsewhere, "If there was one thing Tateh didn't like more than gentiles, it was black folks" (107).

7 There is also extensive discussion by McBride Jordan of her Jewish family's choice to sit shiva for her. McBride Jordan's framing her decision to convert as set in motion by forces beyond her control might reflect how McBride Jordan processed rejection from Jewish family members who were exceedingly judgmental regarding her choice to marry a non-Jewish Black man.

8 On the topic of McBride Jordan's self-identification as "light-skinned," scholars have engaged *The Color of Water* as a reverse-passing narrative. Reginald Watson reads McBride Jordan as a "tragic mulatto figure" and contemplates the significance of white/Jewish mother figures who "pass" as Black. Phillip Brian Harper suggests that McBride Jordan's "reverse racial pass" is unique on account of her "abiding silence about her undertaking," along with McBride's choice to reveal it (386).

Works Cited

Abraham, Karl. "On Neurotic Exogamy." *Clinical Papers and Essays on Psycho-Analysis*, Karnac Books, 1979, pp. 48–50.

Adams, Luther. "Expecting the Unexpected: Black-Jewish History in Twentieth-Century America." Review of *African Americans and Jews in the Twentieth Century*, edited by V. P. Franklin et al., and *Strangers in the Land*, by Eric J. Sundquist, *Journal of Urban History*, vol. 34, no. 5, 2008, pp. 901–914. *SAGE Journals*, doi: 10.1177/0096144208315574. Accessed 1 Oct. 2017.

Allen, Woody, director. *Anything Else*. DreamWorks, 2003.

———, director. *Blue Jasmine*. Sony Pictures Classic, 2013.

———, director. *Café Society*. Amazon, 2016.

———, director. *Cassandra's Dream*. Weinstein Company, 2007.

———, director. *Crimes and Misdemeanors*. Orion Pictures, 1989.

———, director. *Deconstructing Harry*. New Line Video, 1997.

———, director. *Hannah and Her Sisters*. Orion Pictures, 1986.

———, director. *Irrational Man*. Sony Pictures Classic, 2015.

———, director. *Manhattan*. United Artists, 1979.

———, director. *Match Point*. DreamWorks Pictures, 2005.

———, director. "Oedipus Wrecks." *New York Stories*, Buena Vista Pictures, 1989.

———, director. *Radio Days*. Orion Pictures, 1987.

———. "Retribution." *The Complete Prose of Woody Allen*, Wings Books, 1991, pp. 449–465.

———, director. *Scoop*. Focus Features, 2006.

———, director. *Shadows and Fog*. Orion Pictures, 1991.

———, director. *Stardust Memories*. United Artists, 1980.

———. "Woody Allen Speaks Out." *New York Times*, 7 Feb. 2014, www.nytimes.com/2014/02/09/opinion/sunday/woody-allen-speaks-out.html?_r=0, Accessed 18 Feb. 2017

———, director. *You Will Meet a Tall Dark Stranger*. Sony Pictures Classic, 2010.

Ang, Ien. *Watching Dallas: Soap Opera and the Melodramatic Imagination*. Translated by Della Couling, Methuen, 1985.

Angel, Ilana. "Tom Arnold Is a Mensch." *Jewish Journal*, 9 June 2010, jewishjournal .com/uncategorized/80210. Accessed 10 Feb. 2017.

"Another Mouth to Shut Up." *Roseanne: The Complete Series*, written by Janet Leahy, Richard Kaplan, and Eric Gilliland, directed by Mark K. Samuels, 1996, Mill Creek Entertainment, 2013.

Antler, Joyce. *You Never Call! You Never Write! A History of the Jewish Mother.* Oxford University Press, 2007.

Arac, Jonathan. *Huckleberry Finn as Idol and Target: The Functions of Criticism in Our Time.* University of Wisconsin Press, 1997.

Arnold, Roseanne (*see also* Barr, Roseanne). *My Lives.* Ballantine Books, 1994.

———. "A Star Cries Incest." *People*, 7 Oct. 1991, people.com/archive/cover-story-a -star-cries-incest-vol-36-no-13. Accessed 10 Feb. 2017.

Barbezat, Michael. "'Pizzagate' and the Nocturnal Ritual Fantasy: Imaginary Cults, Fake News, and Real Violence." *The Public Medievalist*, 4 May 2017. www .publicmedievalist.com/pizzagate-cults/. Accessed 9 Feb. 2019.

Barr, Roseanne (*see also* Arnold, Roseanne). *Roseanne: My Life as a Woman.* Harper & Row, 1989.

———. *Roseannearchy: Dispatches from the Nut Farm.* Gallery Books, 2011.

———. Video commentary on "Thanksgiving 1991." *Roseanne: The Complete Series*, written by Andrew D. Weyman, directed by Brad Isaacs, 1991, MCE, 2013.

Barron, James. "Striking Back, Woody Allen Denies Child Sex-Abuse Allegation." *New York Times*, 19 Aug. 1992, www.nytimes.com/1992/08/19/nyregion /striking-back-woody-allen-denies-child-sex-abuse-allegation.html. Accessed 2 May 2019.

Bauman, Zygmunt. "Allosemitism: Premodern, Modern, Postmodern." *Modernity, Culture and 'the Jew,'* edited by Bryan Cheyette and Laura Marcus, Stanford University Press, 1998, pp. 143–156.

Baxter, John. *Woody Allen: A Biography.* Carroll & Graf, 1998.

Berman, Lila Corwin. *Metropolitan Jews: Politics, Race, and Religion in Postwar Detroit.* University of Chicago Press, 2015.

Bernstein, Robin. *Racial Innocence: Performing American Childhood from Slavery to Civil Rights.* New York University Press, 2011.

Biale, David. *Blood and Belief: The Circulation of a Symbol between Jews and Christians.* University of California Press, 2007.

The Bible. The New Oxford Annotated Bible: New Revised Standard Version, Oxford University Press, 2010.

"Black Journalist Pays Tribute to White Mother in Novel, 'The Color of Water' (James McBride)." *Jet*, 1 Apr. 1996, pp. 62+. *Academic OneFile*, http://go.galegroup .com.silk. library.umass.edu/ps/i.do?p=AONE&u=mlin_w_umassamh&id =GALE|A18160062&v=2.1&it=r&sid=ebsco. Accessed 9 Feb. 2019.

Blumberg, Antonia. "No, There's Nothing 'Jewy' about Harvey Weinstein's Predatory Behavior." *Huffington Post*, 11 Oct. 2017, www.huffingtonpost.com/entry/harvey -weinstein-anti-semitism_us_59de57f7e4b00abf3645b90f. Accessed 20 Oct. 2017.

"BOO!" *Roseanne: The Complete Series*, written by Norma Safford Vela, directed by John Pasquin, 1989, MCE, 2013.

"Bookshelf." Review of *The Color of Water*, by James McBride. *Jerusalem Post*, 7 Mar. 1996. advance-lexis-com.proxy.mtholyoke.edu:2443/api/document?collection =news&id=urn:contentItem:3Y3G-78V0-00SV-F37J-00000-00&context=1516831. Accessed 14 Feb. 2019.

Boyarin, Daniel. *Unheroic Conduct: The Rise of Heterosexuality and the Invention of the Jewish Man.* University of California Press, 1997.

Bradberry, Grace. "I Wish I Hadn't Accused My Parents of Abuse." *The Times* (London), 1 Sept. 2000, *LexisNexis Academic*, www.lexisnexis.com/hottopics/lnacademic. Accessed 10 Feb. 2017.

Brennan, Patrick. "Cardinal George on Pope Francis: 'This Man Is a Pastor.'" *National Review*, 17 Mar. 2013, www.nationalreview.com/corner/343197/cardinal-george-pope-francis-man-pastor-patrick-brennan. Accessed 10 Feb. 2017.

Brighton Beach Memoirs. Directed by Gene Saks, written by Neil Simon, Universal Studios, 1986.

Brodkin, Karen. *How Jews Became White Folks and What That Says about Race in America.* Rutgers University Press, 1998.

Brook, Vincent. "The Gospel According to Woody: From *Annie Hall* through *To Rome with Love.*" *Woody on Rye: Jewishness in the Films and Plays of Woody Allen*, edited by Vincent Brook and Marat Grinberg, Brandeis University Press, 2014, pp. 3–33.

———. *Something Ain't Kosher Here: The Rise of the "Jewish" Sitcom.* Rutgers University Press, 2003.

———. "Woody's Revenge: The Farrow/Previn Scandal Lives! in *Blue Jasmine.*" *Mediascape*, 2 Apr. 2014, www.tft.ucla.edu/mediascape/blog/?p=2234. Accessed 21 Feb. 2017.

Brook, Vincent, and Marat Grinberg, editors. *Woody on Rye: Jewishness in the Films and Plays of Woody Allen.* Brandeis University Press, 2014.

Brownmiller, Susan. *Against Our Will: Men, Women, and Rape.* 1975. Bantam Books, 1990.

———. *In Our Time: Memoir of a Revolution.* Dial Press, 1999.

Budhos, Marina. "Black Man, Jewish Soul." Review of *The Color of Water*, by James McBride, *The Nation*, 22 Apr. 1996, pp. 32–34. *Academic Search Premier*, https://eds-a-ebscohost-com.proxy.mtholyoke.edu:2443/eds/pdfviewer/pdfviewer?vid=4&sid=63cb58bf-4f67-43cb-8761-1843b986210%40sdc-v-sessmgr04. Accessed 9 Feb. 2019.

Butler, Judith. *Gender Trouble: Feminism and the Subversion of Identity.* 1990. Routledge, 2011

Butler, Sandra. *Conspiracy of Silence: The Trauma of Incest.* 1978. Volcano Press, 1985.

Byrnes, Jesse. "Clinton Regrets Using Term "Superpredator' in 1996 Crime Speech." *The Hill*, 25 Feb. 2016, thehill.com/blogs/blog-briefing-room/news/270811-clinton-i-shouldnt-have-used-the-superpredator-remark. Accessed 12 Feb. 2017.

Campbell, W. Joseph. *1995: The Year the Future Began.* University of California Press, 2015.

Cheit, Ross. *The Witch-Hunt Narrative: Politics, Psychology, and the Sexual Abuse of Children.* Oxford University Press, 2014.

Chesler, Phyllis. *Women and Madness.* Doubleday, 1972.

CNJ. "Lanford Days Again." *Fanfiction.net*, 3 Nov. 2006, www.fanfiction.net/s/2648287/2/Lanford-Days-Again. Accessed 10 Feb. 2017.

Coates, Ta-Nehisi. *Between the World and Me.* Spiegel and Grau, 2015.

———. "The Black Family in the Age of Mass Incarceration." *The Atlantic*, Oct. 2015, www.theatlantic.com/projects/mass-incarceration. Accessed 10 Feb. 2017.

Cocca, Carolyn. *Jailbait: The Politics of Statutory Rape Laws in the United States.* State University of New York Press, 2004

"Coffee Talk: Barbra Streisand Stops By." *Saturday Night Live*, performances by Madonna, Mike Myers, and Roseanne Barr, season 17, episode 14, NBC, 22 Feb. 1992. www.nbc.com/saturday-night-live/video/coffee-talk/n10218?snl=1. Accessed 10 Feb. 2017.

Cohen, Leslie. "Transparency." Review of *The Color of Water*, by James McBride, *Jerusalem Post*, 4 July 1997, p. 23. *Nexis Uni*, advance-lexis-com.proxy.mtholyoke.edu:2443/api/document?collection=news&id=urn:contentItem:3SJC-CoMo-002T-31YP-00000-00&context=1516831. Accessed 14 Feb. 2019.

Cohen, Robert. Review of *Mercy of a Rude Stream*, by Henry Roth, *Tikkun*, vol. 9, July–Aug. 1994, pp. 65–67.

Conard, Mark T., and Aeon J. Skoble, editors. *Woody Allen and Philosophy: You Mean My Whole Fallacy Is Wrong?* Open Court, 2004.

Coontz, Stephanie. *A Strange Stirring: The Feminine Mystique and American Women at the Dawn of the 1960s*. Basic Books, 2011.

Cuddihy, John Murray. *The Ordeal of Civility: Freud, Marx, Lévi-Strauss, and the Jewish Struggle with Modernity*. Basic Books, 1974.

Davis, Angela. *Women, Race, and Class*. 1981. First Vintage Books, 1983.

"Dear Mom and Dad." *Roseanne: The Complete Series*, written by Danny Jacobson, directed by John Sgueglia, 1989, MCE, 2013.

Dennis, Alicia. "Dylan Farrow's Brother Moses Defends Woody Allen." *People*, 23 Sept. 2016, www.people.com/celebrity/dylan-farrows-brother-moses-defends-woody-allen/. Accessed 21 Feb. 2017.

Doane, Janice, and Devon Hodges. *Telling Incest: Narratives of Dangerous Remembering from Stein to Sapphire*. University of Michigan Press, 2001.

"Dream Hampton on 'Surviving R. Kelly,' Sexual Abuse, and Race." Interview conducted by Jelani Cobb, *The New Yorker*, 22 Jan. 2019, www.newyorker.com/news/the-new-yorker-interview/dream-hampton-on-surviving-r-kelly-and-necessary-conversations-about-sexual-abuse-and-race. Accessed 9 Feb. 2019.

Dresner, Samuel. "Woody Allen and the Jews." *Perspectives on Woody Allen*, edited by Renée Curry, G. K. Hall, 1996, pp. 188–198.

"The Driver's Seat." *Roseanne: The Complete Series*, written by James Berg and Stan Zimmerman, directed by Philip Charles MacKenzie, 1993, MCE, 2013.

Dundes, Alan, editor. *The Blood Libel Legend: A Casebook in Anti-Semitic Folklore*. University of Wisconsin Press, 1991.

Dyer, Richard. *Heavenly Bodies: Film Stars and Society*. 1986. Routledge, 2004.

Elkin, Michael. "ON THE SCENE: Tom's Terrific Role(s) as TV Star." *Jewish Exponent*, 5 Jan. 1993, p. 9X.

Ellison, Ralph. *Invisible Man*. 1947. Random House, 1994.

"An Elul for Woody." *Jewish Advocate*, 10 Sept. 1992, p. 10. *Ethnic NewsWatch*, search.proquest.com.silk.library.umass.edu/docview/205168344/A9AA71A8AA7F46BCPQ/1?accountid=14572. Accessed 18 Feb. 2017.

Eversley, Melanie. "Author Ponders His Roots; Biracial Son Writes about Jewish Mom." *Florida Time-Union (Jacksonville, FL)*, 7 Feb. 1997. *Nexis Uni*, advance-lexis-com.proxy.mtholyoke.edu:2443/api/document?collection=news&id=urn:contentItem:3SD5-J2J0-009G-N2RH-00000-00&context=1516831. Accessed 14 Feb. 2019.

Faludi, Susan. "Death of a Revolutionary." *The New Yorker*, 15 Apr. 2015, www.newyorker.com/magazine/2013/04/15/death-of-a-revolutionary. Accessed 10 Feb. 2017.

Farrow, Dylan. "An Open Letter from Dylan Farrow." *New York Times*, 1 Feb. 2014, kristof.blogs.nytimes.com/2014/02/01/an-open-letter-from-dylan-farrow. Accessed 18 Feb. 2017.

Farrow, Mia. *What Falls Away: A Memoir.* Random House, 1997.

Farrow, Ronan. "From Aggressive Overtures to Sexual Assault: Harvey Weinstein's Accusers Tell Their Stories." *The New Yorker*, 10 Oct. 2017, www.newyorker.com/news/news-desk/from-aggressive-overtures-to-sexual-assault-harvey-weinsteins-accusers-tell-their-stories. Accessed 20 Oct. 2017.

———. "Harvey Weinstein's Army of Spies." *The New Yorker*, 6 Nov. 2017, www.newyorker.com/news/news-desk/harvey-weinsteins-army-of-spies. Accessed 9 Feb. 2019.

———. "My Father, Woody Allen, and the Danger of Questions Unasked (Guest Column)." *The Hollywood Reporter*, 11 May 2016, www.hollywoodreporter.com/news/my-father-woody-allen-danger-892572.

Fenton, Zanita. "An Essay on Slavery's Hidden Legacy: Social Hysteria and Structural Condonation of Incest." *Howard Law Journal*, vol. 55, no. 2, 2012, pp. 319–338.

Feuer, Jane. *Seeing Through the Eighties: Television and Reaganism.* Duke University Press, 1995.

Feuer, Menachem. "Woody Allen's Schlemiel: From Humble Beginnings to an Abrupt End." *Woody on Rye: Jewishness in the Films and Plays of Woody Allen*, edited by Vincent Brook and Marat Grinberg, Brandeis University Press, 2014, pp. 79–99.

Fiedler, Leslie. "The Christian-ness of the Jewish-American Writer." *Fiedler on the Roof: Essays on Literature and Jewish Identity*, David R. Godine, 1992, pp. 59–71.

Fields, Karen, and Barbara Fields. *Racecraft: The Soul of Inequality in American Life.* Verso, 2012.

Firestone, Shulamith. *The Dialectic of Sex: The Case for Feminist Revolution.* 1970. Farrar, Straus and Giroux, 1993.

Fishman, Sylvia Barack. *A Breath of Life: Feminism in the American Jewish Community.* Free Press, 1993.

Fitzerman-Blue, Micah. "Consanguineous Marriage for Jews in Rhode Island: The Origins of a Statute." *Rhode Island Jewish Historical Notes*, vol. 14, no. 3, 2005, pp. 413–428.

Foucault, Michel. *The History of Sexuality: Volume 1: An Introduction.* 1978. Translated by Robert Hurley, Vintage Books, 1990.

Fragoso, Sam. "At 79, Woody Allen Says There's Still Time to Do His Best Work." *NPR*, 29 July 2015, www.npr.org/2015/07/29/426827865/at-79-woody-allen-says-theres-still-time-to-do-his-best-work. Accessed 1 Mar. 2017.

Frankfort, Ellen. *Vaginal Politics.* Quadrangle Books, 1972.

Freedman, Jonathan. *Klezmer America: Jewishness, Ethnicity, Modernity.* Columbia University Press, 2008.

Freeze, ChaeRan. *Jewish Marriage and Divorce in Imperial Russia.* Brandeis University Press, 2002.

Freud, Sigmund. "The Aetiology of Hysteria." 1896. Appendix B. Translated by James Strachey in *The Assault on Truth*, by Jeffrey Moussaieff Masson, Farrar, Straus and Giroux, 1984, pp. 259–290.

———. "The Interpretation of Dreams." 1900. Translated by A. A. Brill, MacMillan, 1913. https://psychclassics.yorku.ca/Freud/Dreams/dreams.pdf. Accessed 28 Mar. 2020.

———. *Totem and Taboo: Resemblances between the Psychic Lives of Savages and Neurotics.* 1913. Translated by A. A. Brill, Vintage Books, 1946.

Friedan, Betty. *The Feminine Mystique: Tenth Anniversary Edition.* 1963. W. W. Norton, 1974.

Gamson, Joshua. *Freaks Talk Back: Tabloid Talk Shows and Sexual Nonconformity.* University of Chicago Press, 1998.

Gay, Peter. *A Godless Jew: Freud, Atheism, and the Making of Psychoanalysis.* Yale University Press, 1987.

Geiger, H. Jack. "Rachel and Her Children." Review of *The Color of Water,* by James McBride, *New York Times,* 31 Mar. 1996, http://movies2.nytimes.com/books/97/03/09/bsp/ water.html. Accessed 9 Feb. 2019.

Genzlinger, Neil. "Sue Lyon, Star of 'Lolita,' Is Dead at 73." *New York Times,* 27 Dec. 2019, www.nytimes.com/2019/12/27/movies/sue-lyon-dead.html. Accessed 13 Apr. 2020.

Ghert-Zand, Renee. "Always a Jew, Always an Olivia." *Times of Israel,* 24 June 2012, www.timesofisrael.com/always-a-jew-always-an-olivia. Accessed 10 Feb. 2017.

Gibbs, Alan. "Conversation with Robert Weil, March 2002: Henry Roth's *Mercy of a Rude Stream.*" *The Emerging Landscape: Tradition and Innovation*, special issue of *Studies in American Jewish Literature (1981–),* vol. 22, 2003, pp. 154–162. *JSTOR,* www.jstor.org/stable/i40054082. Accessed 12 Feb. 2017.

———. *Henry Roth's Semi-Autobiographical Tetralogy Mercy of a Rude Stream (1994–1998): The Second Career of an American Novelist.* Edwin Mellen Press, 2008.

Gibel Azoulay [Mevorach], Katya. *Black, Jewish, and Interracial: It's Not the Color of Your Skin, but the Race of Your Kin, and Other Myths of Identity.* Duke University Press, 1997.

Gilman, Sander. *Freud, Race, and Gender.* Princeton University Press, 1993.

———. *Love + Marriage = Death: And Other Essays on Representing Difference.* Stanford University Press, 1998.

Girgus, Sam B. *The Films of Woody Allen.* Cambridge University Press, 2002.

Glaser, Jennifer. *Borrowed Voices: Writing & Racial Ventriloquism in the Jewish American Imagination.* Rutgers University Press, 2016.

Glenn, Colleen. "Which Woody Allen?" *A Companion to Woody Allen,* edited by Peter J. Bailey and Sam B. Girgus, Wiley Blackwell, 2013, pp. 35–52.

Goldstein, David. *Jacob's Legacy: A Genetic View of Jewish History.* Yale University Press, 2008.

Goodman, Walter. "TV VIEW; Roseanne Is No Cousin to Archie Bunker." *New York Times,* 1 Jan. 1989, www.nytimes.com/1989/01/01/arts/tv-view-roseanne-is-no-cousin-to-archie-bunker.html. Accessed 11 Feb. 2017.

Gordon, Mary. "Confession, Terminable and Interminable." *New York Times,* 26 Feb. 1995, www.nytimes.com/1995/02/26/books/confession-terminable-and-interminable.html. Accessed 20 Oct. 2017.

Gornick, Vivian. "Face It, Woody Allen, You're Not a Schlep Anymore." *Village Voice,* 5 Jan. 1975, pp. 9–11.

Grimes, William. "Farrow Tries to Avoid Role of a Woman Scorned." *New York Times,* 26 Mar. 2015, www.nytimes.com/1993/03/26/nyregion/farrow-tries-to-avoid-role-of-a-woman-scorned.html. Accessed 18 Feb. 2017.

Gross, Anisse. "Reelings #7: Blue Jasmine." *The Rumpus,* 25 Sept. 2013, therumpus.net/2013/09/reelings-7-blue-jasmine/. Accessed 21 Feb. 2017.

Groteke, Kristi. *Woody and Mia: The Nanny's Tale.* With Marjorie Rosen. Hodder & Stoughton, 1994.

Gunning, Sandra. *Race, Rape, and Lynching: The Red Record of American Literature, 1890–1912.* Oxford University Press, 1996.

Halpern, Richard. *Shakespeare among the Moderns.* Cornell University Press, 1997.

Hammerman, Shaina. "Reconstructing Woody: Representations of Religious Jewish Women in *Deconstructing Harry,*" edited by Vincent Brook and Marat Grinberg, Brandeis University Press, 2014, pp. 171–189

Harkins, Gillian. *Everybody's Family Romance: Reading Incest in Neoliberal America.* University of Minnesota Press, 2009.

Harper, Phillip Brian. "Passing for What? Racial Masquerade and the Demands of Upward Mobility." *Callaloo,* vol. 21, no. 2, 1998, pp. 381–397. *Project Muse,* doi:10.1353/cal.1998.0108.

Harrison-Kahan, Lori. *The White Negress: Literature, Minstrelsy, and the Black-Jewish Imaginary.* Rutgers University Press, 2011.

Hausman, Bernice. "Anti-Semitism in Feminism: Rethinking Identity Politics." *Iowa Journal of Literary Studies,* vol. 11, no. 1, 1991, pp. 83–96, ir.uiowa.edu/cgi/viewcontent.cgi?article=1361&context=ijls. Accessed 10 Feb. 2017.

Henneberger, Melinda. "Connecticut Prosecutor Won't File Charges against Woody Allen." *New York Times,* 25 Sept. 1993, www.nytimes.com/1993/09/25/nyregion/connecticut-prosecutor-won-t-file-charges-against-woody-allen.html. Accessed 19 Feb. 2017.

Herman, Judith Lewis. *Father-Daughter Incest.* With Lisa Hirschman. Harvard University Press, 1981.

———. *Trauma and Recovery: The Aftermath of Violence—from Domestic Abuse to Political Terror.* 1992. Basic Books, 1997.

Herron, Carolivia. *Thereafter Johnnie.* Random House, 1991.

Herzog, Dagmar. *Sex in Crisis: The New Sexual Revolution and the Future of American Politics.* Basic Books, 2008.

Hoffman, Warren. *The Passing Game: Queering Jewish American Culture.* Syracuse University Press, 2009.

Holpuch, Amanda, et al. "The Bill Cosby Sexual Abuse Claims—57 Women and the Dates They Went Public." *The Guardian,* 31 Dec. 2015, www.theguardian.com/world/2015/dec/31/bill-cosby-sexual-abuse-claims-57-women-dates-public-accusations. Accessed 21 Feb. 2017.

Horowitz, Daniel. *Betty Friedan and the Making of the Feminine Mystique: The American Left, the Cold War, and Modern Feminism.* University of Massachusetts Press, 1998.

"How Radical Jews Have Led the Making and Defense of Obscenity in America." *DavidDuke.com,* 2 Dec. 2013, davidduke.com/jews-led-making-defense-obscenity-america. Accessed 1 May 2019.

"Howard Stern: Wood Yi's First Appearance." *YouTube,* uploaded by Mendex187, 10 June 2012, www.youtube.com/watch?v=SKuMWCpxoj4.

Hyman, Paula. "Jewish Feminism Faces the American Women's Movement: Convergence and Divergence." *American Jewish Identity Politics,* edited by Deborah Dash Moore, University of Michigan Press, 2008, pp. 221–319.

"I Pray the Lord My Stove to Keep." *Roseanne: The Complete Series,* written by Kevin Abbott and Pat Bullard, directed by Charles MacKenzie, 1994, MCE, 2013.

"Inherit the Wind." *Roseanne: The Complete Series*, written by Allan Katz, directed by John Pasquin, 1989, MCE, 2013.

"Into That Good Night, Part 2." *Roseanne: The Complete Series*, written by Roseanne [Barr] and Allan Stephan Blasband, directed by Gary Halvorson, 1997, MCE, 2013.

Isaacson, Walter. "The Heart Wants What It Wants." Interview with Woody Allen, 24 June 2001, content.time.com/time/magazine/article/0,9171,160439,00.html. Accessed 19 Feb. 2017. Originally published *Time*, 31 Aug. 1992, pp. 59–61.

"It's a Boy!" *Roseanne: The Complete Series*, written by Rob Ulin, directed by Andrew D. Weyman, 1993, MCE, 2013.

Itzkovitz, Daniel. "They Are All Jews." *You Should See Yourself: Jewish Identity in Postmodern American Culture*, edited by Vincent Brook, Rutgers University Press, 2006, pp. 230–251.

Jacobson, Matthew Frye. *Roots Too: White Ethnic Revival in Post–Civil Rights America*. Harvard University Press, 2006.

———. *Whiteness of a Different Color: European Immigrants and the Alchemy of Race*. Harvard University Press, 1998.

Jhally, Sut, and Justin Lewis. *Enlightened Racism: The Cosby Show, Audiences, and the Myth of the American Dream*. Westview Press, 1992.

Johnson, Hannah. *Blood Libel: The Ritual Murder Accusation at the Limit of Jewish History*. University of Michigan Press, 2012.

Kalyn, Wayne. Review of *The Color of Water*, by James McBride. *People Weekly*, vol. 45, no. 13, 1 Apr. 1996, p. 38. *Academic OneFile*, edsgcl.18131283. Accessed 9 Feb. 2019.

Kantor, Jodi, and Megan Twohey. "Harvey Weinstein Paid Off Sexual Harassment Accusers for Decades." *New York Times*, 5 Oct. 2017, www.nytimes.com/2017/10/05/us/harvey-weinstein-harassment-allegations.html. Accessed 20 Oct. 2017.

Kaye/Kantrowitz, Melanie. *The Colors of Jews: Racial Politics and Radical Diasporism*. Indiana University Press, 2007.

Kellman, Steven. *Redemption: The Life of Henry Roth*. W. W. Norton, 2005.

Kieval, Hillel. "Blood Libels and Host Desecration Accusations." *YIVO Encyclopedia of Jews in Eastern Europe*, 22 Sept. 2016, yivoencyclopedia.org/article.aspx/Blood_Libels_and_Host_Desecration_Accusations. Accessed 2 May 2019.

Kim, Helen Kiyong, and Noah Samuel Leavitt. *JewAsian: Race, Religion, and Identity for America's Newest Jews*. University of Nebraska Press, 2016.

Kincaid, James. *Erotic Innocence: The Culture of Child Molesting*. Duke University Press, 1998.

Klein, Jessica. "Comedian Eric Andre's Most Iconic Jewish Moments." *Alma*, 2 Aug. 2018, www.heyalma.com/comedian-eric-andres-iconic-jewish-moments. Accessed 9 Feb. 2019.

Knight, Christopher. "Raging in the Dark": Late Style in Woody Allen's Films." *A Companion to Woody Allen*, edited by Peter J. Bailey and Sam B. Girgus, Wiley Blackwell, 2013, pp. 73–94.

Krieger, Rosalin. "'Does He Actually Say the Word Jewish?': Jewish Representations in *Seinfeld*." *Journal for Cultural Research*, vol. 7, no. 4, 2003, pp. 387–404.

Kroll, Jack. "A Long Literary Sleep." Review of *Mercy of a Rude Stream*, vol. 1, *A Star Shines Over Mt. Morris Park*, by Henry Roth, *Newsweek*, vol. 123, no. 5, 31 Jan. 1994, p. 59. *Academic Search Premier*, search.ebscohost.com/login.aspx?direct=true&db=aph&AN=9401267726&site=eds-live&scope=site. Accessed 15 Oct. 2017.

Lambert, Josh. *Unclean Lips: Obscenity, Jews, and American Culture*. New York University Press, 2013.

"The Last Date." *Roseanne: The Complete Series*, written by Gail Mancuso, directed by Eric Gilliland and Daniel Palladino, 1995, MCE, 2013.

Laughland, Oliver, and Jon Swaine. "Officer Who Killed Tamir Rice Says He Believed 12-Year-Old Was in Fact 18." *The Guardian*, 1 Dec. 2015, www.theguardian.com/us-news/2015/dec/01/tamir-rice-shooting-cleveland-police-timothy-loehmann-grand-jury. Accessed 12 Feb. 2017.

Lax, Eric. *Woody Allen: A Biography*. Alfred A. Knopf, 1991.

"Less Is More." *Roseanne: The Complete Series*, written by Maxine Lapiduss, Don Foster, and Amy Sherman, directed by Gail Mancuso Cordray, 1992, MCE, 2013.

Lorde, Audre. "Chain." *Chrysalis*, vol. 1, no. 1, 1977, pp. 46–48. Reprinted in *The Collected Poems of Audre Lorde*. W. W. Norton, 2000.

Loofbourow, Lili. "Brainwashing Woody." *www.lililoofbourow.com*, 8 Feb. 2014, www.lililoofbourow.com/?p=1140. Accessed 19 Feb. 2017.

Lull, James, and Stephen Hinerman. "The Search for Scandal." *Media Scandals*, edited by James Lull and Stephen Hinerman, Columbia University Press, 1997, pp. 1–33.

Lutkin, Aimée. "Malcolm-Jamal Warner Wants to Know Why Woody Allen and Roman Polanski's Films Are Still Aired." *Jezebel*, 5 Mar. 2016, jezebel.com/malcolm-jamal-warner-wants-to-know-why-woody-allen-and-1763055067. Accessed 21 Feb. 2017.

MacCannell, Juliet. *The Regime of the Brother: After the Patriarchy*. Routledge, 1991.

MacKinnon, Catharine. *Toward a Feminist Theory of the State*. Harvard University Press, 1989.

MacKinnon, Catharine, et al. "Summer Reading; Read and Run: A Cram Course for the Presidency." *New York Times*, 5 June 1988, www.nytimes.com/1988/06/05/books/summer-reading-read-and-run-a-cram-course-for-the-presidency.html. Accessed 10 Feb. 2017.

"MADtv—S01E04—Crimes, Misdemeanors, and Payback (Woody Allen's Die Hard Parody)." *YouTube*, uploaded by Noel Angelita, 22 Mar. 2015, www.youtube.com/watch?v=ktjhhlTLYak. Accessed 1 Nov. 2017.

Marc, David. "Roseanne." *Entertaining America: Jews, Movies, and Broadcasting*, edited by J. Hoberman and Jeffrey Shandler, Princeton University Press, 2003, pp. 199–200.

Marche, Stephen. "Re-Watching Woody Allen." *Esquire*, 4 Feb. 2014, updated 5 Feb. 2014, www.esquire.com/entertainment/movies/a27233/dylan-farrow-woody-allen-movies/. Accessed 21 Feb. 2017.

Marcuse, Herbert. *Eros and Civilization*. 1955. Beacon Press, 2015.

Marks, Peter. "Allen and Farrow Mute as Others Debate Their Judgment and Actions." *New York Times*, 31 Mar. 1993, www.nytimes.com/1993/03/31/nyregion/allen-and-farrow-mute-as-others-debate-their-judgment-and-actions.html. Accessed 19 Feb. 2017.

———. "Doctor Recounts Threats by Farrow against Allen." *New York Times*, 30 Mar. 1993, www.nytimes.com/1993/03/30/nyregion/doctor-recounts-threats-by-farrow-against-allen.html. Accessed 1 Nov. 2017.

Martin, Douglas. "Elliott Wilk, Judge and Dry Wit, Dies at 60." *New York Times*, 3 July 2002, www.nytimes.com/2002/07/03/nyregion/elliott-wilk-judge-and-dry-wit-dies-at-60.html. Accessed 1 Nov. 2017.

Martinez, Elizabeth. "History Makes Us, We Make History." *Feminist Memoir*

Project, edited by Rachel Blau DuPlessis and Ann Snitow, Rutgers University Press, 2007, pp. 115–123.

McBride, James. *The Color of Water: A Black Man's Tribute to His White Mother.* 1996. Riverhead Books, 2006.

McGrath, Douglas. "If You Knew Woody Like I Knew Woody." *Woody Allen: Interviews*, edited by Robert E. Kapsis and Kathie Coblentz, University Press of Mississippi, 2006, pp. 116–129.

McKee, Kimberly. "'Let's Not Get Hysterical': Was He Ever Her Father?" *Feminist Formations*, vol. 30, no. 2, 2018, pp. 147–174.

McNaron, Toni A. H., and Yarrow Morgan. "Introduction." *Voices in the Night: Women Speaking about Incest*, edited by Toni A. H. McNaron and Yarrow Morgan, Cleis Press, 1982, pp. 11–22.

Meade, Marion. *The Unruly Life of Woody Allen.* Scribner, 2000.

Melnick, Jeffrey. *A Right to Sing the Blues: African Americans, Jews, and American Popular Song.* Harvard University Press, 2001.

Michaels, Lloyd. "Woody Allen's Cinema of Regret." *Quarterly Review of Film and Video*, vol. 32, no. 5, 2015, pp. 469–481.

Mieher, Stuart. "Spike Lee's Gotta Have It." *New York Times*, 9 Aug. 1987, nytimes .com/library/film/080987lee-mag-profile.html. Accessed 21 Feb. 2017

Mills, Charles: *The Racial Contract.* Cornell University Press, 1997.

Mirrer, Louise. *Women, Jews, and Muslims in the Texts of Reconquest Castille.* University of Michigan Press, 1996.

Mitchell, Juliet. *Siblings: Sex and Violence.* Polity Press, 2003.

Morrison, Toni. *Playing in the Dark: Whiteness and Literary Imagination.* Vintage Books, 1992.

Muhammad, Khalil Gibran. *The Condemnation of Blackness: Race, Crime, and the Making of Modern Urban America.* Harvard University Press, 2010.

Murray, Noel. "A Personal *Roseanne* Episode Mirrors Its Star's Fluid Relationship with Her Past." *A.V. Club*, 15 Nov. 2012, www.avclub.com/article/a-personal-iroseannei -episode-mirrors-its-stars-fl-88765. Accessed 27 Feb. 2017.

Neustein, Amy, editor. *Tempest in the Temple.* Brandeis University Press, 2009.

Newton, Adam Zachary. *Facing Black and Jew: Literature as Public Space in Twentieth-Century America.* Cambridge University Press, 1999.

Nichols, Mary. *Reconstructing Woody: Art, Love, and Life in the Films of Woody Allen.* Rowman & Littlefield, 1998.

Nussbaum, Emily. *I Like to Watch.* Random House, 2019.

O'Brien, Darren. *The Pinnacle of Hatred: The Blood Libel and the Jews.* Hebrew University Magnes Press, 2011.

Omi, Michael, and Howard Winant. *Racial Formation in the United States: From the 1960s to the 1990s.* Routledge, 1994.

Oppenheimer, Mark. "The Specifically Jewy Perviness of Harvey Weinstein." *Tablet*, 9 Oct. 2017, www.tabletmag.com/scroll/246724/the-specifically-jewy-perviness-of -harvey-weinstein. Accessed 20 Oct. 2017.

Orth, Maureen. "Mia's Story." *Vanity Fair*, Nov. 1992, www.vanityfair.com/magazine /1992/11/farrow199211. Accessed 19 Feb. 2017.

———. "Momma Mia!" *Vanity Fair*, Nov. 2013, www.vanityfair.com/style/2013/11/mia -farrow-frank-sinatra-ronan-farrow. Accessed 21 Feb. 2017.

Painter, Nell Irvin. *The History of White People.* W. W. Norton, 2010.

Paley, Grace. Review of *The Best Kept Secret*, by Florence Rush, *Ms.*, Jan. 1981, p. 40.

Pogrebin, Letty Cottin. "Anti-Semitism in the Women's Movement." *Ms.*, June 1982, pp. 45–72. *Jewish Women's Archive*, jwa.org/media/anti-semitism-in-womens-movement-by-letty-cottin-pogrebin. Accessed 10 Feb. 2017.

Puig, Claudia. "Howard Stern Talks His Way to No. 1 Status." *Los Angeles Times*, 7 Oct. 1992, articles.latimes.com/1992-10-07/entertainment/ca-640_1_howard-stern. Accessed 19 Feb. 2017.

Randee, Dawn. "Mia Farrow: Son Ronan's Father Could 'Possibly' Be Frank Sinatra." *Today.com*, 2 Oct. 2013, www.today.com/popculture/mia-farrow-son-ronans-father-could-possibly-be-frank-sinatra-8C11319747. Accessed 9 Feb. 2019.

Reiff, Phillip. *Freud: The Mind of the Moralist.* 1959. University of Chicago Press, 1979.

Rogin, Michael. *Blackface, White Noise: Jewish Immigrants in the Hollywood Melting Pot.* University of California Press, 1996.

Roith, Estelle. *The Riddle of Freud: Jewish Influences on His Theory of Female Sexuality.* Tavistock, 1987.

"Roseanne Barr." *Jew or Not Jew*, 25 Nov. 2006, www.jewornotjew.com/profile.jsp?ID=66. Accessed 11 Feb. 2017.

The Roseanne Barr Show. Performance by Roseanne Barr, directed by Rocco Urbisci, 1987, Home Box Office Entertainment, 1990.

"Roseanne Reveals New Reality Show; Apologizes for 1991 'Incest' Claim." *Access Hollywood*, 15 Feb. 2011, www.accessonline.com/articles/roseanne-reveals-new-reality-show-apologizes-for-1991-incest-claim-97122. Accessed 16 Apr. 2020.

"Roseanne's Dad Dies with a Broken Heart." *National Enquirer*, 18 Apr. 2001, www.nationalenquirer.com/celebrity/roseannes-dad-dies-broken-heart. Accessed 11 Feb. 2017.

Rosewater, Mark. "A Roseanne by Any Other Name." *Wizards of the Coast*, 26 Dec. 2011, magic.wizards.com/en/articles/archive/roseanne-any-other-name-2011-12-26. Accessed 11 Feb. 2017.

Roth, Henry. *Call It Sleep.* 1934. Picador, 2005.

———. Collection. AJHS Archives P-694, American Jewish Historical Society, New York.

———. *Mercy of a Rude Stream.* Volumes 1–4. St. Martin's Press, 1994–1998.

———. Papers. AJHS Archives P-702, American Jewish Historical Society, New York.

———. *Shifting Landscape: Selected Essays and Short Stories.* St. Martin's Press, 1987.

Roth, Philip. *The Plot against America.* Houghton Mifflin, 2004.

Rowe, Kathleen. *The Unruly Woman: Gender and the Genres of Laughter.* University of Texas Press, 1995.

Rubin-Dorsky, Jeffrey. "Woody Allen after the Fall: Literary Gold from Amoral Alchemy." *Shofar: An Interdisciplinary Journal of Jewish Studies*, vol. 22, no. 1, 2003, pp. 5–24.

Rubinstein, Rachel. *Members of the Tribe: Native America in the Jewish Imagination.* Wayne State University Press, 2010.

Rush, Florence. *The Best Kept Secret: Sexual Abuse of Children.* 1980. McGraw-Hill, 1992.

———. "The Freudian Cover-Up: The Sexual Abuse of Children." *Chrysalis* vol. 1, no. 1, 1977, pp. 31–45.

Sabean, David Warren. *Kinship in Neckarhausen, 1700–1870.* Cambridge University Press, 1998.

Sacco, Lynn. *Unspeakable: Father-Daughter Incest in American History.* Johns Hopkins University Press, 2009.

Safer, Morley, correspondent. "Memories." Produced by Patti Hassler, *60 Minutes*, CBS, 17 Apr. 1994. Uploaded by Jvideos8, as "Child Abuse, False Memories Part One (of Two)," *YouTube*, www.youtube.com/watch?v=NhZjxkaCkzk. Accessed 11 Feb. 2017.

Said, Edward. "Freud and the Non-European." Verso, 2003.

"Santa Claus." *Roseanne: The Complete Series,* written by Chuck Lorre, Maxine Lapiduss, and Barry Vigon, directed by Andrew Weyman, 1991, MCE, 2013.

Schott-Kristensen, Lene. *The Leydn Jar: A Study of Henry Roth.* 2002. University of Copenhagen, PhD dissertation.

"Season 9: Breaking the Sitcom Mold." *Roseanne: The Complete Series,* interview with Roseanne Barr, 2007, MCE, 2013.

"Season 18: Episode 17." *Saturday Night Live*, hosted by Jason Alexander, NBC, 10 Apr. 1993, www.amazon.com/Saturday-Night-Live-Season-18/dp/B01EN8ZFD6. Accessed 19 Feb. 2017.

Senzani, Alessandra. "Class and Gender as a Laughing Matter? The Case of *Roseanne*." *Humor,* vol. 23, no. 2, 2010, pp. 229–253.

"Seth Rogen Part 2: The Eric Andre Show: Adult Swim." *The Eric Andre Show*, 20 Dec. 2014, www.youtube.com/watch?v=RY75KpDjCyw. Accessed 27 Feb. 2017.

"Shower the People You Love with Stuff." *Roseanne: The Complete Series,* written by Lawrence Broch, directed by Gail Mancuso, 1995, MCE, 2013.

Silberg, Joyanna, and Stephanie Dallam. "Out of the Jewish Closet." *Tempest in the Temple,* edited by Amy Neustein, Brandeis University Press, 2009, pp. 77–104.

Simon, Kate. *Bronx Primitive: Portraits in a Childhood.* 1982. Penguin Books, 1997.

Slavet, Eliza. *Racial Fever: Freud and the Jewish Question.* Fordham University Press, 2009.

Smith, Barbara. "Between a Rock and a Hard Place: Relationships between Black and Jewish Women." *The Truth That Never Hurts,* Rutgers University Press, 1998, pp. 132–153.

Smith, Valerie. "Introduction." *Representing Blackness: Issues in Film and Video,* edited by Valerie Smith, 1997, Rutgers University Press, 2003, pp. 1–11.

Sollors, Werner. *Neither White nor Black yet Both: Thematic Explorations of Interracial Literature.* Oxford University Press, 1997.

Sommer, Will. "What Is QAnon? The Craziest Theory of the Trump Era, Explained." *Daily Beast,* 6 July 2018, www.thedailybeast.com/what-is-qanon-the-craziest-theory-of-the-trump-era-explained. Accessed 9 Feb. 2019.

"Soon-Yi Speaks: 'Let's Not Get Hysterical.'" *Newsweek*, 30 Aug. 1992, www.newsweek.com/soon-yi-speaks-lets-not-get-hysterical-197958. Accessed 19 Feb. 2017.

Span, Paula. "Woody Allen and Mia Farrow, Lost in the Shadows and Fog." *Washington Post,* 1 Apr. 1993, p. D1. *LexisNexis Academic*, www.lexisnexis.com/hottopics/lnacademic. Accessed 19 Feb. 2017.

Spillers, Hortense. "The Permanent Obliquity of an In(pha)llibly Straight: In the Time of the Daughters and the Fathers." *Black, White, and in Color,* University of Chicago Press, 2003, pp. 230–250.

Stockton, Kathryn Bond. *The Queer Child, or Growing Sideways in the Twentieth Century.* Duke University Press, 2009.

"Sweet Dreams." *Roseanne: The Complete Series,* written by Rob Ulin, directed by John Pasquin, 1989, MCE, 2013.

Taylor, Kirstine. "Untimely Subjects: White Trash and the Making of Racial

Innocence in the Postwar South." *American Quarterly*, vol. 67, no. 1, Mar. 2015, pp. 55–79.
"Terms of Estrangement, Part 2." *Roseanne: The Complete Series*, written by Rob Ulin, directed by Andrew D. Weyman, 1992, MCE, 2013.
"This Old House." *Roseanne: The Complete Series*, written by Chuck Lorre, Jeff Abugov, and Michael Poryes, directed by Andrew D. Weyman, 1992, MCE, 2013.
Thomas, Kevin. "Flaws Aside, Kubrick's 'Lolita' Is Worth Look." *Los Angeles Times*, 12 Sept. 1996, www.latimes.com/archives/la-xpm-1996-09-12-ca-42787-story.html. Accessed 13 Apr. 2020.
Tobin, Diane. "Are All Jews White? The Woody Allen Syndrome." *Huffington Post*, 7 June 2012, www.huffingtonpost.com/diane-tobin/are-all-jews-white-the-woody-allen-syndrome_b_1577788.html, updated 7 Aug. 2012. Accessed 21 Feb. 2017.
Tornquist, Cynthia, correspondent. "Woody Allen Has Affair with Mia's 21-Year-Old Daughter." *Showbiz Today*, Laurin Sydney, anchor, CNN, 18 Aug. 1992, television transcript. *LexisNexis Academic*, www.lexisnexis.com/hottopics/lnacademic. Accessed 13 Apr. 2013.
"Transcript: Donald Trump's Taped Comments about Women." *New York Times*, 8 Oct. 2016, www.nytimes.com/2016/10/08/us/donald-trump-tape-transcript.html. Accessed 8 Feb. 2019.
Trilling, Lionel. *Freud and the Crisis of Our Culture.* Beacon Press, 1955.
Trotter, Joe W., Jr. "African Americans, Jews, and the City: Perspectives from the Industrial Era, 1900–1950." *African Americans and Jews in the Twentieth Century*, edited by V. P. Franklin et al., University of Missouri Press, 1998, pp. 193–207.
Ullman, Joan. "Woody, Again—Irrational Man." Uncharted Customs blog, *Psychology Today*, 13 Aug. 2015, www.psychologytoday.com/us/blog/uncharted-customs/201508/woody-again-irrational-man. Accessed 1 Nov. 2017.
"Wait Till Your Father Gets Home." *Roseanne: The Complete Series*, written by Amy Sherman, directed by Andrew D. Weyman, 1993, MCE, 2013.
Warwick, William. "Woody Allen Is Not a Monster. He Is a Person. Like My Father." *Gawker.com*, 7 Feb. 2014, gawker.com/woody-allen-is-not-a-monster-he-is-a-person-like-my-f-1518291644. Accessed 21 Feb. 2017.
Watson, Reginald. "The Changing Face of Biraciality: The White/Jewish Mother as Tragic Mulatto Figure in James McBride's 'The Color of Water' and Danzy Senna's 'Caucasia.'" *Obsidian III*, vol. 4, no. 1, 2002, pp. 101–113. *JSTOR*, www.jstor.org/stable/44511714. Accessed 9 Feb. 2019.
Weber, Bruce. "Public Disclosures from the Private Life of Woody Allen." *New York Times*, 18 Aug. 1992, www.nytimes.com/1992/08/18/nyregion/public-disclosures-from-the-private-life-of-woody-allen.html. Accessed 9 Feb. 2019.
Weinbaum, Alys Eve. *Wayward Reproductions: Genealogies of Race and Nation in Transatlantic Modern Thought.* Duke University Press, 2004.
"White Trash Christmas." *Roseanne: The Complete Series*, written by Lawrence Broch and William Lucas Walker, directed by Philip Charles MacKenzie, MCE, 2013.
Wild Man Blues. Directed by Barbara Kopple, New Line Video, 1998.
Williams, Melissa. "'Excuse the Mess, but We Live Here': Roseanne Barr's Stardom and the Politics of Class." *Film and Television Stardom*, edited by Kylo-Patrick Hart, Cambridge Scholars Publishing, 2008, pp. 180–204.
Willmore, Alison, and Kate Aurthur. "Woody Allen's New Movie Proves He Thinks He's Invincible." *BuzzFeed*, 14 July 2015, www.buzzfeed.com/alisonwillmore/woody-allens-new-movie-proves-he-thinks-hes-invincible. Accessed 1 Nov. 2017.

Wirth-Nesher, Hana. "Facing the Fictions: Henry Roth's and Philip Roth's Meta-Memoirs." *Jewish-American Autobiography, Part 2*, special issue of *Prooftexts*, vol. 18, no. 3, 1998, pp. 259–275, www.jstor.org/stable/20689522. Accessed 12 Feb. 2017.

Wisse, Ruth. *The Schlemiel as Modern Hero*. University of Chicago Press, 1971.

Witchel, Alex. "COUNTERINTELLIGENCE; What's So Funny About the 'Coffee Talk' Lady." *New York Times*, 14 Jan. 2001, www.nytimes.com/2001/01/14/style/counterintelligence-what-s-so-funny-about-the-coffee-talk-lady.html. Accessed 11 Feb. 2017.

"Woody Allen Affair with Soon-Yi: News Report August 1992." *YouTube*, uploaded by 20C History Project, originally aired on *Fox 5 NY*, 17 Aug. 1992, www.youtube.com/watch?v=cZxkoKDZLDc. Accessed 9 Feb. 2019.

"Woody Allen and the Family Affair." *Primetime Glick*, Comedy Central, 2 Mar. 2002, *Paley Center for Media*, digital recording.

"Woody Allen Defends Himself on 60 Minutes in '92." Interview by Steve Kroft, *60 Minutes*, CBS, 22 Nov. 1992. 60 Minutes Overtime, 5 Feb. 2014, www.cbsnews.com/news/ woody-allen-defends-himself-on-60-minutes-in-92/. Accessed 21 Feb. 2017.

"Woody Allen's Bride of Frankenstein." Performances by Ben Stiller and Andy Dick, *The Ben Stiller Show*, Warner Brothers, 1992.

Zimmerman, Amy. "How Roseanne Barr Abandoned All Reason and Embraced the Alt-Right." *Daily Beast*, 23 June 2017, www.thedailybeast.com/how-roseanne-barr-abandoned-all-reason-and-embraced-the-alt-right.html. Accessed 8 Feb. 2019.

Index

About the Author

Eli Bromberg completed his PhD in English and American Studies at the University of Massachusetts Amherst in 2017. He has taught at Fordham University, the University of Hartford, Hofstra University, Mount Holyoke College, and UMass. He has been published in *The Forward*, *In geveb*, *Shofar*, and *Studies in American Jewish Literature*.